Praise for Pico Iyer's

The Open Road

"Iyer has written one of the most thoughtful and eloquent books yet about the Dalai Lama. Considering his subject is one of the most analyzed and photographed men in the world, that's no small feat."
—*The Boston Globe*

"Allows us to imagine the Dalai Lama as something of an intellectual and spiritual adventurer, exploring fresh sources of individual identity and belonging in the newly united world."   —*The New Yorker*

"Intimate and insightful. . . . Succeeds as a work of biography, history and memoir."   —*Los Angeles Times*

"[Iyer has] an access and insight into the Dalai Lama that lifts his writing above the clichés that normally surround him. . . . Reveals more about its subject than any formal study."   —*The Economist*

"Lucid, probing and revealing, *The Open Road* is a meditation on the big responsibilities and big ideas—personal enlightenment, world peace, the meaning of freedom, Tibet's relationship with China and the wider world—one individual, plucked from a normal life in boyhood and named the Fourteenth Dalai Lama, has found himself having to wrestle with nearly all his life."   —*San Francisco Chronicle*

Pico Iyer

The Open Road

Pico Iyer is the author of seven works of nonfiction
and two novels. He has covered the Tibetan question
for *Time, The New Yorker, The New York Times, The New
York Review of Books,* and many other publications for
more than twenty years.

THE OPEN ROAD

THE OPEN ROAD

The Global Journey of the Fourteenth Dalai Lama

PICO IYER

Vintage Departures
Vintage Books
A division of Random House, Inc.
New York

 FIRST VINTAGE DEPARTURES EDITION, MARCH 2009

Copyright © 2008 by Pico Iyer

All rights reserved. Published in the United States by Vintage Books,
a division of Random House, Inc., New York, and in Canada by Random House of
Canada Limited, Toronto. Originally published in hardcover in the United States
by Alfred A. Knopf, a division of Random House, Inc., New York, in 2008.

Vintage is a registered trademark and Vintage Departures and colophon are
trademarks of Random House, Inc.

The author would like to thank the John Simon Guggenheim Memorial Foundation
for its very generous and gracious support in making the research and
writing of this book possible.

The Library of Congress has cataloged the Knopf edition as follows:
Iyer, Pico.
The open road : the global journey of the fourteenth
Dalai Lama / by Pico Iyer.
p. cm.
Includes bibliographical references.
1. Bstan-'dzin-rgya-mtsho, Dalai Lama XIV, 1935–   I. Title.
BQ7935.B777I94 2008
294.3'923092—dc22   [B]   2007043991

Vintage ISBN: 978-0-307-38755-4

Book design by Iris Weinstein

www.vintagebooks.com

Printed in the United States of America

So simplify the problem of life, distinguish the necessary and the real. Probe the earth to see where your main roots run. I would stand upon facts.

—HENRY DAVID THOREAU, March 27, 1848
(in his first letter to his new friend Harrison Blake)

CONTENTS

IN PUBLIC

ALL THIS IS A DREAM. Still, examine it by a few experiments. Nothing is too wonderful to be true, if it be consistent with the laws of nature.

—MICHAEL FARADAY, 1849

THE CONUNDRUM

The two young men had many things in common as they settled into the room under the snowcaps, bright Tibetan scrolls on the walls, pine-covered slopes all around. Both of them were travelers—exiles—who had left their homes behind and so were in a position to think about home in a new way, without the limitations of nationality or race. Both were philosophers, too, but philosophers with a keen interest in the real world and the ways in which politics and society could be transformed by being seen in a different light. Both were coming of age at a time when cultures could reach one another as never before, thanks to jet planes and television screens, and the first question before them, perhaps, was how to turn this global reality into a fresh opportunity.

The Fourteenth Dalai Lama was only twenty-four at the time, having come into India barely a year before, in March 1959, when Chinese troops had threatened to bring war to his capital of Lhasa and he had been forced to flee his native Tibet. Now, for the first time in his adult life, he was sharing a house with his mother and some siblings, relishing the chance to talk to strangers and come down from his throne as he could never have done in his old home. He loved to take walks in the high mountains in those early days, to picnic in meadows; he even started a garden as he had done in Lhasa. But every time he did, he later confessed, one of India's notorious monsoons would sweep through, reducing all his efforts to nothing, and a part of him would miss the high, dry plateaus of Tibet.

My father, when he came into the room, was moving in the opposite direction. He had been born five years before the Dalai Lama, to Hindu parents, and had grown up in a tiny apartment in Bombay, shared with six siblings, some cousins, even the occasional neighbor. He had been trained in British Catholic schools and had so mastered the Shakespeare and Augustine they had taught him that he had won a scholarship to Oxford and now (like my Hindu, Bombay-raised mother, too) was teaching political philosophy at the ancient university. He had a rare opportunity, he knew, to bring the great Western tradition of Plato and Plotinus and Kant together with the Hinduism and Buddhism he had absorbed as a boy.

At the time he sailed back to India and requested a meeting with the newly arrived Dalai Lama, my father was deep in research on Mohandas Gandhi. The Tibetan leader had himself been thinking intensely about Gandhi, of course, as he tried to see how he could lead a nonviolent struggle against a foreign occupation and summon political sophistication in a transpolitical cause; by chance, the house in which he was staying had been lent him by the same wealthy Indian family that had lent Gandhi his final home, in Delhi, and pictures of the Indian activist of just a generation before filled the building in which the young men met. The subtitle

Gandhi had chosen for his autobiography—*The Story of My Experiments with Truth*—might have applied to the Dalai Lama's story, too (he was a practical and lifelong lover of experiments), as he tried to construct a new, more durable Tibet outside Tibet and to see how he could protect the rights of his people without denying the legitimate rights of their "great neighbor," as he called it, Communist China.

Five years after that first meeting, my father brought out a book, *The Glass Curtain,* about the centuries of delusion and projection that had separated Asia from Europe. Its foreword was contributed by his new friend, the Dalai Lama, for whom cutting through differences to a deeper commonness was always a central goal. The book was dedicated—though it would take me decades to notice it—to a little boy called Pico and to "those of his generation for whom there will be no curtain."

Forty-three years after that propitious encounter, one of its beneficiaries woke up in his two-room apartment in suburban Japan on a brilliant autumn morning, at the dawn of a new millennium, to spend a day with the Dalai Lama. I'd been visiting him in his exile home for almost thirty years at that point, and had been following him on his global travels for almost as long. But still I was intrigued by the quiet revolution he was promulgating, challenging us to see politics, globalism, celebrity itself, in a larger and more spacious light, and I was interested to examine all the challenges and questions his experiments entailed.

He had been taking to the road more and more often in recent years, partly, as always, to speak for the six million Tibetans more or less imprisoned in Chinese-occupied Tibet, but also, increasingly, to speak on behalf of what he now called "global ethics," those basic principles of kindness and responsibility that anyone could implement in her life, whether or not she was committed to any religion. In my many years of traveling as a journalist, I couldn't remember any other Tibetan—or exile—I had met who spent no time mourning the past he had lost but concentrated his energies on how he could construct a more useful and inclusive future across the globe.

 Japan in November is a blaze of radiance and impermanence. The sky this day, as on most such days, dawned a startling blue, the temperature in the seventies, even as the leaves all around the town of Nara began to turn ocher, lemon-yellow, the russet of a Tibetan monk's robes. The very heart of Nara, the first Buddhist capital of Japan, thirteen centuries before, is a deer park that brings to mind the park in which the Buddha delivered his first discourse, in India. Everything changes, falls away, dies, the leaves in the Japanese autumn say, and yet everything comes back again, and change itself is a kind of constancy. Life, as some Buddhists have it, is a "joyful participation in a world of sorrows."

We got up early, my longtime companion Hiroko and myself, the morning light throwing pools of gold across our ceiling, and traveled by bus and train out to the musty Nara Hotel, a ninety-year-old hunting lodge of a place that sits at one corner of the deer park like a keepsake that has fallen out of some absentminded visitor's pocket. Just before nine a.m., we were ushered into a small conference room, where ten local academics and monks—all men, most of them in formal black—were seated around a table, trying to stifle their yawns, and sitting upright and a little stiffly in the Japanese way. We took up folding chairs against the wall, observers, and I thought of how the Dalai Lama himself had already been up for more than five hours, awakening, as he always does, at three-thirty a.m., to spend his first four hours of the day

meditating on the roots of compassion and what he can do for his
people, the "Chinese brothers and sisters" who are holding his
people hostage, and the rest of us, while also preparing himself for
his death.

When he came into the room, accompanied by a group of aides
and hosts, his stooped figure pressing forward—"He looks like a
middle linebacker," his old friend and admirer Abe Rosenthal,
longtime managing editor of the *New York Times,* had once said to
me—there was a sense of sharpened attention in our midst. He
was looking around him as ever, picking out familiar faces, making
eye contact with strangers, taking his new surroundings in (when I
went to see him in Dharamsala, eighteen months later, many of the
examples he would use would come from this brief trip to Japan).
His hands were joined before him, in a gesture of respect, and his
bearing, the opposite of remote, was aimed, I thought, to try to dissolve all borders and get formality out of the way. We're all in this
together, his body might have been saying; let's see if we can use
this session for some good.

Taking his seat at one end of the table, he looked around the
room with frank, unembarrassed curiosity, and at the translator
chosen for this meeting—a local American hippie, by the looks of
him, with a thick gray ponytail and a Gypsy vest. (The Dalai Lama
can rarely catch sight of a beard or a male ponytail without wanting
to tug at it.) As the Tibetan offered a few words of introduction, I
noticed, as I had not quite seen before, that he was coming into the
room, essentially, as a spokesman for "potential," to use one of his
favorite words. A team of scientists in Wisconsin, complemented
by researchers at Princeton and Berkeley, he said, in his measured,
deliberate way, passing in and out of English and Tibetan, had been
conducting a series of experiments on monks and practiced meditators to measure the effect such training can have upon the mind.

So far they had found that those who had meditated for years could lower their heartbeats by three or four beats a minute (even, in a few exceptional cases, more), could alter their brain scans, could even boost their entire immune systems. Conclusive results had yet to be firmed up, but the research suggested that just as so many of us these days had taken to training and strengthening our bodies, perhaps we could do the same with our minds?

And if we could control our heartbeats, our theta waves, even the heat of our bodies, perhaps we could also do more to control our thought patterns, our anger, our perceptions? Certainly, the new neurological idea of "brain plasticity" suggested that we had much more potential for change than had previously been imagined. The mind was something we had the potential to transform. So, too, therefore, was the world that the mind created.

Siddhartha Gautama, the Buddha, was, first and foremost, an empiricist, a scientist of self; what he learned he learned by conducting experiments on the closest specimen to hand, himself. First he walked out of his gilded palace at the age of twenty-nine, in order to see firsthand the realities his father had tried to screen from him, the abiding truths of old age and suffering and death. Then he traveled and traveled, consulting teachers, practicing austerities, and, finally, sitting down under a pipal tree and vowing not to get up again until he'd come to some understanding of the nature of suffering and, further, of how we could come to a liberation from suffering. Then he traveled for the rest of his life, extending and sharing the understandings he'd gained.

He always took pains to tell people he was no more than an experimenter, doing nothing that the rest of us could not do; his aim was simply that of a doctor at a sickbed, eager to find an immediate solution to the problem at hand, without claiming his was the only or even the best solution. By speaking, as he often did, of a "path," he was saying, in effect, that we could always go further, that everything was in a constant state of flux and that all he was doing was showing the way so that others could take it in new directions.

The Fourteenth Dalai Lama had been pushing along the same road for several decades now, turning around corners to meet a world in which almost every culture could access every other, and a single image had the power to reach the entire planet; he had traveled out of the mud-and-stone village in which he was born to the center of a kingdom that had no roads linking it to the outside world even in the 1950s, and then right into the heart of the twenty-first-century whirlwind. But he always stressed that, like the "scientist of mind" who was his root teacher, he had no wish to claim final authority.

"Our master gave us liberty to investigate even his own word," I would hear him say two years later in Zurich, of the Buddha, "so I take this liberty fully!" As a boy he early showed a fascination with all things scientific, fixing the old generator in the Potala Palace in Lhasa, using a telescope left to him by the Thirteenth Dalai Lama and seeing that—contrary to Tibetan teaching—the moon did not generate its own light; delighting (as the Thirteenth Dalai Lama did) in taking watches apart and then trying to put them together again. Even now he kept a plastic model of the brain with labeled, detachable parts on his desk at home and loved to meet scientists who could improve his understanding of the world and mind, in part by disproving his assumptions about them.

Science, he said to the Japanese intellectuals, "mainly deals with matter; faith mainly deals with the observer itself." Both, however, tell us "there is no independent objectivity." And both, he said, are concerned with "reducing the gap between reality and perception." Recent research, he might have added, soon to be featured on the cover of *Time* magazine, suggested that those who score high on tests for happiness live longer than others, in part because happiness is a function not so much of our circumstances as of our perceptions. People who win the lottery often profess themselves no better off than before—they don't know who their friends are, they feel uncomfortable in their posh new neighborhoods, they spend all their time with lawyers; yet others, who are suddenly rendered paraplegic, after roughly a year of adjustment confess themselves really no worse off than before. The mind, as Milton puts it at the beginning of *Paradise Lost*, "can make a Heav'n of Hell, a Hell of Heav'n."

The idea, I think, is to explore the world closely, so as to make out its laws, and then to see what can and cannot be done within those laws; the Dalai Lama's favorite words, I notice more and more this morning, are "investigate" and "analyze" and "research." He does not mention Buddhism, if only because the people assembled around the table are here as scholars and, besides, some of them (like myself) may not even be Buddhists. The more important part is what anyone can do, whether she is a Christian or a Marxist or even an enemy to Buddhism. A scientist's religious views are beside the point; what matters is what his experiments have disclosed, and that he be aware, as when doing nuclear research, of the real-world consequences of what his mind is discovering.

As the session goes on, I—and perhaps not just I—feel that at times the visitor sounds too optimistic, too ready to bring realism and confidence together. The recent demonstrations against the American invasion of Iraq, he says (referring to the military action begun eight months before), are something positive, "encouraging," even though there has been no sign of a nongovernmental alternative to implement that longing for peace. Many others, I suspect, might suggest that the fact that so many people are out on the streets today could mean only that too many people have something to complain about. Yet still the principle remains: if we believe that beauty is in the eye of the beholder, then maybe strength and possibility and neighborliness are, too?

The other banner under which he clearly walks is reason, and a refusal, as the Buddha said, to take anything on blind faith or because we want it to be true. "At that time," he says, of the outbreak of the war, and speaking with his characteristic matter-of-factness, "some people asked me, 'Go to Baghdad!' But then I thought: that's senseless. That's unrealistic. I have no friends in Baghdad. I am Buddhist monk—even I may not find the road!"

On the walls of the temple next to his home in India, I recall, there are only two quotations from the Buddha. One of them reads, "As one assays gold by rubbing, cutting, and melting, so examine well my words and accept them, but not because you respect me."

"At that point," the Dalai Lama goes on, "I strongly felt that some individual, like President Havel, whom the world knows, and some Nobel laureate, like Jimmy Carter or Archbishop Tutu, some individual like that should go there, talk with Saddam Hussein and talk with his advisers." That anything would come of it, he concedes, is "a remote possibility." But there would be nothing lost in trying. "Because usually even representatives of the United Nations, people not much trust. Always suspicion."

As the local translator renders the words into Japanese, the Tibetan visitor looks around the room with the interest of a newcomer. He pulls out a silver pen from within his capacious robes at one point, and makes a note. He sits in front of the scientists as unself-consciously as if sitting alone in his room at home. People always talk about his smile and his almost palpable charm; but if his ideas are really going to have some effect, I think, they must arise from acuity and alertness.

"The great home of the Soul," D. H. Lawrence once wrote, in a typically pinwheeling account of Walt Whitman, "is the open road. Not heaven, not paradise. Not 'above.' " The soul, in Lawrence's vision, is "a wayfarer down the open road," and "true democracy" flowers in that place "where soul meets soul, in the open road." In that sense, the road also seems the natural home of someone who is visibly pressing along a path, to talk to anyone he meets along the way and to see how foreigners, specialists, fellow travelers can instruct him.

As soon as the Dalai Lama has finished speaking, the experts around the table, one after another, offer responses, generally in the form of dry and somewhat formal readings of prepared statements. Then, however, one man—the youngest in attendance, perhaps in his late thirties—suddenly addresses the Dalai Lama directly. "I am a realist," he says. "All this talk of *ahimsa* and nonviolence, it's all well and good, but how has it really helped the world?" People are dying in Iraq, in Afghanistan, all over, he hardly needs to add. Instantly, the Dalai Lama comes to life, as in one of the debates that his school of Tibetan Buddhism cherishes as a way to sharpen the mind and cut through fixed assumptions. Governments are slow to catch up with the possibilities that individuals discern, he says; and in any case, it takes time to change and slough off the habits of old. The answer comes with such assurance that I begin to wonder if this, too, isn't one of the many questions the Dalai Lama asks himself every day.

A religious teacher who is telling people not to get confused or distracted by religion; a Tibetan who is suggesting that Tibet does not have all the answers; a Buddhist who, more and more, is urging foreigners not to take up Buddhism but to study within their own traditions, where their roots are deepest: at the very least, something quite radical is being advanced, it seems. The world at the beginning of the new century is more divided than I have ever seen it, and its strongest power is fractured by loud disputes; in the middle of this, the head of Tibetan Buddhism is urging people not to listen to doctrine, which can so often be a source of divisions of its own, but to push behind it to something human, in which ideas of "clashing civilizations" can seem remote.

As the burly Tibetan walks out into the broad sunlight—people are holding up signs saying FREE TIBET along his path and waving the Tibetan flag, now banned in Tibet—I realize there's something incongruous about this skeptical journalist and nonbelonger (myself) devoting so much of my time to trying to figure out what this man is saying.

But the Dalai Lama impresses, or disarms, me by doing away with many of the categories with which we imprison ourselves. The only truths that can possibly make sense to us, he suggests, apply to all human beings, as much as Pythagoras's theorem or the laws of thermodynamics do; if they pertain only to a specific tradition or culture, they're not human truths at all. And the only thing that an Easterner—or Westerner—can offer is a window on these truths that allows the rest of us to see them more clearly than we have done before. To someone like me, who's grown up in many cultures but refused to believe that lacking a physical home means lacking an inner center, this is all as encouraging to hear as the idea that we don't have to define ourselves by differences.

I follow along as he moves down the white-gravel paths of central Nara and notice, as people reach toward him to try to get a blessing or a handshake, how he is switching, as always, at lightning speed from monk to head of state to philosopher-scientist to regular man. But what is more striking, I realize, is that he's pushing all these roles together, as if they were all intertwined, to see how one might throw light on the others. I don't know many monks who are so keen to affirm only what stands up to scientific testing. And there are even fewer politicians who try to speak from the collected stillness and attention of a monk. Pope John Paul II, the Dalai Lama's good friend, is also traveling more and more in the global order, using planes and cars to take him everywhere; but when he travels, he tends to visit fellow Catholics, to proclaim his faith and to offer doctrinal guidance. The Dalai Lama, by comparison, seems to exult in meeting people from different traditions than his own—Catholics, neuroscientists, even Maoists—and seeing what they have in common beneath their designations.

I can't help but think this is an interesting response to an age in which some kill others in the name of Allah, some in the name of the Christian God. But just as I am thinking all this, I see the tanks that surrounded me in Ethiopia not long ago, the armed soldiers I met in Arabia who were scrambling after pennies. I remember the guerrillas who came into the room where I was sitting in El Salvador, during its civil war, the shacks I saw in Soweto where philosophical ideas seemed unlikely to bring any food to the table. I can't say, after twenty years of covering wars and revolutions as a journalist, that any one man is likely to have all the answers (and the Dalai Lama, I know, would not say that either); it's the questions he puts into play that invigorate.

After a quick lunch break at the Nara Hotel, his home for the day, the Dalai Lama comes out again into the bright afternoon, for what will surely be the high point of his visit: a trip to Todaiji, in the deer park, the great temple that is often described as the largest wooden building in the world. It was from here that the Japanese monk later known as Kobo Daishi traveled to China twelve centuries before, and brought back a form of Buddhism—Shingon—that might be a rough translation of the Tibetan kind; and for more than a millennium, a great Buddha, more than fifty feet tall, has sat at the heart of the prayer hall.

The place is always crowded with sightseers from around the globe, trying to catch the giant Buddha on their cell-phone cameras or posing for pictures within its enormous courtyard, but on this day I realize that for a Buddhist its meaning may be something deeper. Two times the great structure has burned to the ground, and two times it has come up again. The Buddha's hands date from the sixteenth century, its head from a later period, and other parts of the body have been here ever since the first construction. In that way, it's not so different from the Dalai Lama: the vehicle, the physical vessel, is clearly very perishable. But the message it speaks for goes on and on.

When the Dalai Lama gets out of his car at the outermost gateway to the compound—usually closed but thrown open today— Hiroko and I follow him up the short flight of stone steps that lead to the formal entrance, and for a moment I am involuntarily silenced. Everywhere across the great expanse of the courtyard there are people. Mothers holding up their toddlers so they can catch a glimpse of the famous visitor. Tibetans from across Japan extending ceremonial white silk scarves. Foreigners in tribal hippie gear and high-heeled girls with Vuitton bags asked to postpone their visits for a few minutes. I come here often as a resident of Nara, but never have I seen it turned, as today, into a global throne room in the sun.

The Dalai Lama moves along the path, stopping often to ask a question of some Westerners, to bless a baby, to chat with local kids; as someone who individually blessed seventy thousand people when he arrived in Lhasa at the age of four, he's never felt out of place in crowds. After going into the temple and sitting quietly before the Buddha, then peppering his hosts (through a translator) with questions, he comes out again and offers a few words of thanks and greeting to the assembled, in an English as reassuringly ragged as their own.

Then he is bustled toward the next stop on his itinerary, a meeting with the abbot of Todaiji at a subtemple around the corner, and he begins to move away, surrounded by forty or so bodyguards and secretaries and anxious hosts and hangers-on, such as Hiroko and myself. As he is heading away from the public space, suddenly, he sees something and veers off. The rest of us struggle to keep up. Alone at the far end of an empty colonnade, two Japanese women are standing above a girl of ten or so with a mop of black hair and thick glasses; her legs, in bright, striped socks, barely reach the ground from the wheelchair in which she is sitting.

Within seconds, the Dalai Lama is by the girl's side and leaning down to talk to her.

"What is her problem?" he asks the women—a mother and a friend, I assume—and is told that her eyes are fine, but that the use of her legs is gone.

For a long, long moment he looks into the little girl's eyes. Then he leans forward and places his head against her cheek. Then, looking at her again, he says something else and tweaks her affectionately, before heading back toward his schedule.

The mother of the girl, as he turns around, is dabbing at her cheeks with a tissue, saying, "Thank you. I'm so sorry. Thank you." The woman beside her looks as if her face is about to crumple. The little girl is swinging her legs back and forth as if the day is just beginning.

The Fourteenth Dalai Lama, when he is asked who he is, usually says (in exactly the same words deployed by the Thirteenth Dalai Lama) that he's a "simple Buddhist monk." This does not do justice to the fact that he's the temporal leader of the Tibetans, organizing fifty exile communities around the world, dealing almost every day with the two great powers of the day, Beijing and Washington, while living in the third, India, making statements and decisions every hour, as every head of state must do. It does not really take in his practical obligations as head of one of the major schools of Buddhism, scholar and administrator and teacher, who has to deliver lectures, write books, and organize a highly complex hierarchy, now scattered around the globe. It does not even take into account the everyday person he is, worried constantly about his people, angry (he confesses to interviewers) if his time is not well used, moved to tears, he's told me, when he hears the stories his people bring to him.

And yet the answer is, as far as it goes, as precise as most of the other things he says. He really does live simply, decorating his bedroom when he travels with just a few pictures of his teachers and his family and a portable radio. He really is a full-time, lifelong student of the Buddha, who taught him that nearly everything is illusory and passing, not least that being who declares that nearly everything is illusory and passing. And he really does aspire, as every monk does, to a simplicity that lies not before complexity but on the far side of it, having not dodged experience but subsumed it. Even the name by which he goes—Tenzin Gyatso—is not his own.

This Dalai Lama has, in only a few years, and unexpectedly, become one of the most visible figures on the planet. And yet, I sometimes think, that very visibility often gets in the way of the ideas he's speaking for or the people on whose behalf he's talking. His very warmth and charisma are so strong that those who listen to him sometimes don't see behind them to what is really lasting and has little to do with his particular being. In that sense, he may be one of the least-seen figures on the planet.

The Buddha, whenever his followers tried to create a religion or a doctrine around him—a cult of personality, even, around a figure who was speaking for the flimsiness of personality—always stressed that he was just a human being, doing what any one of us could do if we resolved to sit still and see through the delusions of the mind. He was nothing special in himself, he always said; he was just a signpost, akin to what Zen monks call a finger pointing at the moon. The most prominent Buddhist in the world today, I think, would likely say that this is even truer in his case: he is just a finger pointing at a finger pointing at the moon.

As night begins to fall over the deer park and the first pinch of winter comes to the day, the Dalai Lama heads to his last engagement of this visit, in a modern theater not so far from Todaiji, and for most of the people in the city, this general address is what he will ultimately leave behind him. He gives such talks at almost every place he visits nowadays, usually on some general principle of how our lives are intertwined and what that means in terms of possibility and transformation. By now he has given them so often that he can deliver them even when unwell and in his improving English, the way a politician might deliver a campaign speech (though this is a campaign less for self-advancement than its opposite).

"We are not talking about God," he explains to the two thousand people who've poured into the place (a group of Raelians, meanwhile, stands up with a sign reminding us that our hope lies in outer space). "We are not talking about Nirvana. We are only talking about how to become a more compassionate human being." His gift in such contexts, I think again, is to leave much of what is so technical, or foreign, about Tibet and Buddhism and monasticism behind, and just speak as a human being, as a doctor tries to do.

"I am sixty-eight years old," he goes on, "and yet I am striving, day after day." (The Buddhists in attendance no doubt notice how close this is to the Buddha's final words before he died: "Work out your own salvation with diligence.") I remember how Tibetans generally draw a distinction between suffering and unhappiness: suffering is the state of the world, they say, but unhappiness is just the position we choose (or can not choose) to bring to it.

His energy is discernibly lower as the day nears its end, and the Dalai Lama often talks about sleep as one of the most important activities of the day, even calling on old texts to suggest how sleep can in fact be positively used, as almost anything can, for the clarification of the mind. It appeals to him, I think, because it is one activity that every member of humanity has in common, and the nature of our sleep plays a large part in how clearly we see the world. Yet the minute a chic woman steps onto the stage, stands at a podium on one side, and offers to read questions collected from the audience, the Dalai Lama comes to life. "This is my chance to learn from you," he says, with evident sincerity (through a Japanese woman from Dharamsala whom he's using to translate for this public address). "Please don't be shy. Ask anything. Don't hold back or be too formal. We're all just human beings."

To my surprise, the Japanese, though generally hesitant or reserved, don't seem shy at all. They don't hold back, and do seem ready to ask anything. Most of the questions come from women, identified only by age and gender, and with each one the Dalai Lama seems to enter another mood or voice. (Paul Ekman, the world's leading scientist of the emotions, has said that the Fourteenth Dalai Lama uses his facial muscles more vigorously and with greater precision than anyone he has studied in forty years; every feeling—mirth, sharpness, solicitude, reflectiveness—is fully inhabited for a moment, and then gone.)

Someone asks a question about Tibet, and the man onstage, seated cross-legged in a chair under a large golden banner, turns solemn, even grave. Someone asks him about how she can get on better with her boss, and he breaks into hearty laughter— "Maybe you can join with others in your company and form a circle. Or if that doesn't work, just go on strike!"

Someone asks about Buddhism in Japan, and he becomes a diplomat. Someone asks about daily Buddhist practice, and he turns into a practical instructor, counting off points on his fingers, breaking down every point into clear and logical steps, moving his sturdy, elegant hands up and down as he outlines certain effective techniques. His voice, famously, goes up and down, from the depths of a basso profundo, ideal for muttering Tibetan chants at dawn, to a young boy's high-pitched squeal of incredulity or delight. He speaks largely with his body, leaning into things, moving with all of himself, rocking back and forth on his raised chair, eye clearly alert to pick out salient details.

The question period after the forty-five-minute talk is scheduled to last only fifteen minutes, but the Dalai Lama goes on and on, as if this is his chance to impart something useful. Every time the mistress of ceremonies looks to him, seeing if he is ready to call a halt, he says, in English, "Next question! Next!" (She, in turn, answers with a formal, almost military *"Hai! Arigato gozaimashita!"*—meaning "Yes, sir. Thank you very much!"—and at one point, mischievous, he briefly mimics the *"Hai!"*) For almost an hour he continues, using the moments when his answers are translated into Japanese to look up and take in the banner above him, to pick out a friend in the audience and offer a cheerful wave, to sit alone, eyes closed, for all the world as if he were meditating in his room at dawn. At times he pulls out a piece of tissue from his shoulder bag and polishes his glasses—which might, I realize, be a metaphor for what he's encouraging all of us to do.

At another point, clearly curious himself, he asks for a show of hands of those under twenty-five, and then of those under thirty (they are the ones who will make the future, he is evidently thinking). He even asks who in the audience doesn't have a religion (quite a few hands pop up) and who doesn't drink. At the beginning of the talk, as at every such event, he has taken off his watch, with its sturdy stainless-steel band, and the *mala* beads he wears around his wrist. Know exactly how much time you have, he might be saying to himself, and use that time for some good.

As the Dalai Lama moves off toward the next stop on his global itinerary—getting up while it is still dark to complete his four hours of meditation—people around me say, as they often seem to do after such a visit, that it feels as if a light has come on in the city. For a brief moment, friends and neighbors seem a little more hopeful, as if given heart by a wandering uncle. Yet I, ever the journalist, am keen to see how much of what he's said and done remains, and what effect it would have, if any, on someone who'd never seen him. The overall impression I come away with from the visit is one of energy and speed, the way a doctor on call in a hospital will not let a second go wasted (especially, perhaps, if he is also here to talk about others in desperate need far away).

When Hiroko and I step into the dusty old room in the Nara Hotel he's been given to receive visitors, we find him standing at the window, looking out at the deer. The Fourteenth Dalai Lama, known in Beijing as a "wolf in monk's clothing," is famous for his love of animals.

"You're lucky to be in a place where the deer are effectively the bosses," I say. "They've been ruling Nara, in their way, for thirteen hundred years."

"Perhaps you will be a deer in your next life," he says, breaking into laughter. "A deer who writes!

"How do you say?" he goes on, turning to a private secretary. "With hoof! A deer who writes with his hoof!"

"No," says Hiroko, always quick with her perceptions. "With his head." She mimics a deer writing on the ground with its antlers, and the Dalai Lama, now sitting down, claps his hands with delight and falls about laughing.

"You see," he explains, "some people tell me that because I like animals I will come back in my next life as an animal." He has a German shepherd at home, he says, and she is so compassionate, she has even adopted a rabbit from his garden. ("Even the rabbit is trying to suck at the dog's teats. Of course, a little disturbing for the dog!") Whereas the dog of his other private secretary, now minding the store in Dharamsala—"famous for his fierce nature!"

This is not, I'll realize later, just idle chitchat. In his public address, he stresses the phrase "social animals," if only to remind us that nurturing is as much an instinct with us as being predatory. And when he talks about how the Nara deer, lacking sharp claws, were clearly meant by nature to be vegetarians, I will see—though only much later—that he's making a point about humans, too, likewise lacking sharp claws.

Yet the main thing he's keen to talk about, as always, is what he's learned from his current tour, and particularly from his meetings with physicists in Tokyo. In old Tibet, he says, mandalas showed the sun and moon as being of equal size, as if equidistant from the earth. That is wrong, he declares, with the vigor that he increasingly often calls upon; nothing can be maintained once disproved by science. "The Four Noble Truths, *shunyata*"—the doctrine of emptiness, or interdependence—"those we Buddhists need." Everything else, goes the implication, is autumn leaves.

I remember how he had lit up when challenged by the young Japanese philosopher around the conference table; Buddhism itself, he now says, can only gain from being debated, just as Hinduism did before it. Whole kingdoms used to be at stake, he declares, with evident excitement, when Buddhism debated its positions against Hinduism, and people watched the clash of ideas as later they watched the struggle of armed men.

And whole kingdoms are at stake now, I think, as I remember all the Tibetans who are urging the Dalai Lama to be more decisive in his opposition to Chinese oppression, to accept no compromise, to speak for action and full independence and not just the religious principles of forbearance and looking for points in common.

This is, in fact, the most agonizing and mounting of all the conundrums he travels with. For even as he has charmed this small corner of Japan and begun to pass on some confidence, the country that he was born to rule is slipping ever closer to extinction. In the course of his life, and thanks in part to him, Tibet and Tibetan Buddhism have become a living and liberating part of the global neighborhood; and yet at the same time, on his watch, his own people have lost most of their contact with their leaders, their loved ones, and their culture, and one of the great centers of Buddhism, five times as large as Britain, has been all but taken over. The leader of the Tibetans finds himself carrying an entire culture on his shoulders; and even as he's trying to support six million people he hasn't seen in half a century, he is obliged to create a new Tibet among those who have seldom or never seen Tibet.

One evening in Dharamsala, I notice clouds beginning to gather above the Kangra Valley below. The little town in northern India where the Dalai Lama and his government have made their home for more than forty years now is a bedraggled and makeshift place, but if you catch it at the right angle, as in the little guesthouse where I stay, it can give off something of the light of fairy tale. From the garden where I sit, all I can hear are the sounds of chants and gongs from the temple across the way, set next to the Dalai Lama's home; if I sit on the sunlit terrace outside my room, all I can see are young monks racing along the whitewashed terraces of a monastery, their red robes laid out under the snowcaps to dry.

This little corner of the hill station is a perfect symbol of how Tibet is being rebuilt, in compact, more conscious form, outside the borders of Tibet. On this day, however, as I watch a storm building in the valley, it begins to rain furiously, and the wind starts to shake the solid three stories of the building, the trees outside beginning to shiver and crack. Then there is a crash from somewhere down below, and electricity across the settlement is gone.

Looking outside, I see nothing but dark. Shouts rise up from the road down below, and I can hear the people who live along the road scrambling for shelter. It seems madness to go out into the elements, but if Hiroko and I do not honor tonight's engagement, I'm not sure when, or whether, it will come again.

We struggle out together into the rain, our umbrella tearing as we slip and slither down an unpaved slope, every attempt at respectability suitably mocked, and, after many minutes, find a minivan that is not taken. As it wends its way down the precipitous mountain road, we see occasional figures sheltering under trees, beggars huddled together under stoops.

When, finally, we arrive at our destination, our host comes up to us with a typically urbane, unflustered "Come. Are you sure you're okay?" and we step into the shelter of Ngari Rinpoche's home. The younger brother of the Dalai Lama—more than a decade

younger—Ngari Rinpoche was discovered to be a *rinpoche,* or high
incarnate lama, when he was a boy and trained as a monk, in
charge of large numbers of other monks in the Indian areas of
Zanskar and Ladakh. Early on, however, he shed his robes and
recast himself as something of the loyal opposition to institutional
Tibet. Of course I was declared to be a rinpoche, he more or less
said; I was the younger brother of the Dalai Lama. (In fact, their
eldest brother had also been taken to be a high lama even before
the Dalai Lama was born, but still the point remained: Tibet's system of incarnations has always left room for manipulation.)

In the years that followed, the Dalai Lama's youngest sibling
became a paratrooper in the Indian army; he smoked and de-
voured steaks; to this day he loves to shock those he meets
with his equal-opportunity irreverence: say something positive
about Tibet, and he's likely to reply, "You're just a susceptible
Westerner, a groupie." More and more, as the years go on, he asks
me, when we meet, if I'm preparing to become a monk by losing all
my hair.

He leads us now into his spare, elegant living room, which looks
out over the huge valley below. Lightning breaks across the
expanse, and the electricity flickers on again, then dies. On one
table I see the new English translation of a three-volume Tibetan
text from the fifteenth century that Ngari Rinpoche is studying in
his evenings (his written English is in places more confident than
his Tibetan, since he left Tibet when he was barely thirteen).

I have not seen Ngari Rinpoche—who now prefers to go by the
secular name Tendzin Choegyal—for seven years, and the change
in him is remarkable. He has always seemed to be the uncensored
private side, the alter ego, of the Dalai Lama, having lived beside
him in Dharamsala for more than forty years, working with him as
translator, filter, even private secretary (their eldest brother moved

to Bloomington, Indiana, to teach, in 1968; their second-eldest brother lives in Hong Kong and works as a businessman, going to and from Beijing as a kind of unofficial emissary; their sister oversees the Tibetan Children's Village in Dharamsala; and their third-eldest brother, who had lived simply in New Jersey as a janitor called "Sam" until his cover was blown by the *New York Times,* died in his early fifties).

Tonight, however, I notice how much Ngari Rinpoche is coming to resemble his most celebrated sibling. The voice, low and deep, could be the Dalai Lama's, especially on a night like this when the room is almost dark. The laugh, sudden and wildly accelerating— all conversation stops with it—is identical. And of course what he's saying is often word for word what his brother would say, in part because they are brothers, but even more because they are both lifelong students of the same philosophy, and Ngari Rinpoche has spent his life studying under and talking to the Dalai Lama. When Hiroko begins telling a story of imagining she saw her estranged brother in a temple in Tibet, our host leans forward in the thin light, a single candle picking up his high cheekbones, his attentive eyes, the look of a doctor listening for symptoms, and it's impossible not to think we're up the hill in the Dalai Lama's house, though unofficially.

"You should tell His Holiness when you see him next week," he says to Hiroko, and a part of me bridles at the romanticism of imputing too much to this disrobed monk—Tibet lends itself much too easily to such ideas—while another part of me notices that she is in fact looking a lot better.

We go to sit at the dinner table—lightning breaking across the valley again, and every syllable intimate in the near dark—and I remember how, the last time I had seen him, the unorthodox lama had told me about what he called the "Shangri-La syndrome," whereby foreigners were much too ready to ascribe all kinds of wisdom to every Tibetan they met, and Tibetans much too ready to take advantage of that. Fluent in Chinese and English as well as Tibetan, having grown up for a year in Beijing and then in northern India as well as Lhasa, Ngari Rinpoche speaks for the part of Tibet that is both modern and global.

We retire, after dinner, to the living room for tea, and suddenly, with his characteristic directness, our host turns to me in the near dark.

"Do you think I've done anything for Tibet?"

"Of course," I say, stumbling a little, because taken aback. "You've been an intermediary between Tibetans and the Western world."

"You're saying I'm just a Westerner."

"No." Less trained than he at ritual debating, I fumble for a second. "But you can take information to His Holiness that he wouldn't hear otherwise."

"He has other people who can do that. Take my word for it."

I shuffle uneasily in my chair, hoping he'll change direction.

"You're being polite," he goes on (and again I think of his brother's impatience with mere formality). "Mine is a serious question. Do you think I've done anything to make Tibetan lives any better?"

"You have, by knowing the world outside Tibet."

He laughs dismissively, as if I've hit an easy serve ten feet over the line. We go on talking for a while, and then Hiroko and I make our way back to our little room in the guesthouse up the hill. As we get there, I recall how I had heard almost exactly the same sentence fourteen years before, from the Dalai Lama, the day after his Nobel Prize had been announced. "I really wonder if my efforts are enough," he had said, at the very moment when he was being most feted by the world. All we can do, he had told me, is try, even though it sometimes seems to be in vain.

At the end of the evening, I pick up my pen. Of all the many books and films that have brought the Fourteenth Dalai Lama and his people to the world, I'm not sure any of them has addressed that most central of questions.

I and my four cameramen were rendered speechless by the emptiness of the landscape, the invisible wind that swept across the barren land, the high boundless sky, and the utter silence. My heart and soul felt clean and empty. I lost any sense of where I was or of the need to talk.

—THE BEIJING JOURNALIST XINRAN XUE,
describing Tibet in her book *Sky Burial*

THE FAIRY TALE

Ｗhen I was a little boy, barely old enough to know what the "news" meant (small children live in a different sense of time), my father began telling me a story every night before I went to sleep. The stories he told me were often of angels and demons and many-headed gods, drawn from the ancient myths of the India where he grew up, or spiked with the Shakespeare and Dickens of the England where we were living. Down the road, a five-minute walk away, C. S. Lewis and J. R. R. Tolkien were gathering regularly at the Eagle and Child pub, and stories of magical wardrobes and hidden hollows, of minglings both evil and good, were developing. The story that my father told that especially transfixed me, though, was of a little boy born in a simple rural cowshed far from anywhere, and very high up, who was seen by some passing monks one day and declared to be a king.

The little boy, not much older than the wide-eyed kid listening to his father in Oxford, was taken to a faraway capital, after a long passage on horseback, and installed in a palace with a thousand rooms. He was instructed in all the philosophies and sciences of his ancient culture, by two strict tutors in red robes, while his family was sent to live in a summer palace, bright with flowers and animals and lakes. Only one elder brother kept him company in the cold, dark palace overlooking the city.

One day, the story went on, the boy, while still a teenager, was asked to be the full-fledged leader of many millions of people, as well as its ruling monk, and traveled in a caravan again and a yak-skin coracle to a far-off city of the Emperor, who intimated that he would overrun the little boy's country—"liberate it," in his terms— unless the boy could persuade him otherwise. He refused to do what the Emperor said, so the Emperor attacked. One night, with his mother, his younger brother, and a few trusted friends, just after he had finished his final exams, the boy stole out of his palace, dressed as a soldier, and undertook a long, hazardous journey across the highest mountains on earth.

At this point the story picked up. Our little transistor radio would crackle in the evenings, and when it was turned off, my father would turn to me, in the last days before television, and fill me in on the day's events. The young king was fleeing, across cold, high mountains, and his pursuers were very close behind him. Sometimes the watch fires of the enemy could be seen at night, the tents of the soldiers only a few hundred yards away. The small group had disappeared into the mountains. A mysterious plane— friend or foe?—was circling overhead. Tonight the fugitive party was said to be a little closer to freedom at the border.

It was a story not so different from the ones I heard in class, at St. Philip and St. James school. It spoke of other flights, other precious jewels hustled across the border to safety before the enemy could get to them. What little boy could resist?

Would the boy and his little brother make it to safety? Would right win a terrific victory? The two-year-old in Oxford, in the simplicities of his excitement, spoke of "good Tibetans, bad Chinese." At last one day—the Tibetans had risen up against the Chinese the very day the little boy's father had turned twenty-nine—the news came through that the team had arrived, half-broken, and sick, in freedom. The site of that freedom, happily for the little boy, was his own hardly seen homeland, India (which meant the boy-king, as in a fairy tale, was returning to his master's home). Right had not exactly won, but it had at least managed to keep one step ahead of wrong.

The only trouble was, it wasn't a fairy tale, except in the eyes of a two-year-old. It was a story, painfully real, that soon got complicated, with eighty thousand other Tibetans leaving the country in the following months, and hundreds of thousands more staying behind and fighting and losing their lives, and the CIA coming to whisk off some of the freedom fighters to an isolated area where they could learn guerrilla warfare (from those who were losing a guerrilla war at the time), while young Chinese boys were being sent by the battalion to their death or at least discomfort on the high plateau. The problem for Tibet, as for so many of its people throughout its history, has been that it has seemed to wear the contours of fairy tale. It feels—or we need to make it feel—more like Shangri-La than a place that could have a seat at the United Nations. We have plenty of exile leaders and men with exotic causes; we don't need another. It's transparent wise men with ready smiles and a boyish sense of humor that our myth calls for.

The Fourteenth Dalai Lama, in fact—this perhaps the most fairy-tale-like element of all—had come into the world at almost the very moment, in 1935, when the notion of Shangri-La was filtering into the Western imagination, James Hilton's novel *Lost*

Horizon and then the Frank Capra movie of the book, telling us not just that there was a place where lamas lived for centuries and people could enter a magical world of gardens and Platonic learning but that there had to be such a place inside us whether there existed one on earth or not. The natural setting to locate it was the place we would never see (as of 1950, Tibet had been visited by fewer than two thousand Westerners, one thousand of whom had come in a single British military expedition in 1904).

My father, who had grown up on stories of Tibet told by H. P. Blavatsky, Nicholas Roerich, and other wandering mystics, traveled all the way back to India to meet the Dalai Lama, months after our nightly broadcasts, because he was aware, as not so many people were then, that a great treasure had come out into the world for the first time, really, in history. (The Thirteenth Dalai Lama had been forced to flee Lhasa twice, as outside forces moved in, but he was never truly available to the world the way his successor would become in 1959, when, in a disquieting augury of what was to come, he appeared on the cover of *Time* magazine beside the legend "The Escape That Rocked the Reds.") Full of a young man's indignation, my father complained to the Dalai Lama that the Indian press concentrated only on the material treasure that was said to have come out with the Tibetans into exile; the young Dalai Lama, as he would now, counseled my father to be patient and said that understanding would come in time.

His only child, my father went on—a three-year-old boy in England—had followed the story of the Tibetans' flight with unusual intensity. The Dalai Lama, in response, sent a picture of himself, as a small boy on the Lion Throne in Lhasa, to me in faraway Oxford, and wherever I went in the years that followed, I kept it on my desk, like a talisman from fairy tale. It accompanied me to California when we moved there, and if ever I felt out of place or

burdened, I could look at this photo of a four-year-old, taken from
his home and family and set upon the throne of his country, and
put things into perspective. Then a forest fire swept down from the
hills nearby, and the photo, like everything I owned, was gone.

One spring in Dharamsala I got in the habit of waking early, just
before the sun showed over the mountains, and going to the central compound, from which gongs sounded every morning. It was
always a magical walk. Street people hadn't appeared yet on the
slope outside my guesthouse garden, and the cars hadn't begun to
congregate at the intersection. There would be the smell of early
cooking fires from some of the houses nearby, a monk walking
alone up one of the steep roads, or a woman gathering a pail of
water on the rooftop of her house. Dogs barked constantly—packs
of them ran wild along the gulleys and dusty mountain paths of
Dharamsala—and the lights had not yet been put out in the
houses across the valley below.

At the central temple, even at this early hour, were scores of
Tibetans, walking and walking, telling their beads, pushing large
bronze prayer wheels to make them spin, muttering chants or
praying for the long life of their leader. Many were very, very old—
women with healthy skin and pigtails and traditional *chuba* aprons
around their waists, old men in cowboy hats, men with bowed legs
or faces that suggested their minds were not quite right. Young
local kids, too, who had never seen Tibet but upheld their Tibetan
traditions even in sunglasses and lipstick, above San Francisco
49ers T-shirts. A great parade of them, while a monk or two swept
the area clean, and in a little chamber next to the temple, lights
were set in a sea of butter lamps to make a field of tiny candles.

Every day, as the sun came up over the far-off ridge, turning the snowcaps pink, then gold, both of the temple's prayer halls were filled with rows of monks reciting their chants. One in particular caught my eye. He had a flamboyant mustache, unusual in Tibet, and it gave him some of the special charisma of the Thirteenth Dalai Lama. He was the leader of the second prayer hall, offering two weeks of special prayers for world peace (Washington had attacked Iraq two weeks before), and when a dog came in one day and sat on one of the meditation cushions, the head monk broke into a big smile. The dog threw back his head and bayed as the monks chanted, and when two of them tried to carry him out, he scrambled right back and sat on the cushion again, baying in time with their chants. In Tibet it is said that dogs stay around temples not just because of the food and the kindly (it is hoped) company but because they were weak monks in their past lives and now are hoping to win their way back into their rightful homes.

The Tibetans crowded past, walking and walking around the temple. Below us, unseen through the trees, many dozens more were making a larger circumambulation, around the whole hill on which the temple, an adjoining monastery, and the Dalai Lama's house across from them stand. In the midst of their chants, their collected hopes, I kept my eye on the praying monks, and especially this one charismatic character.

On this particular day, after two weeks or so of prayer, when I went to the temple at dawn I happened to see the monk I had been taken by, his weeks of chanting finished, standing outside the hall among the visitors. He was surprisingly ready to talk; his eyes lit up when he saw me and he gave me his business card, featuring his address in an affluent part of California, and made an urgent appeal for me to visit him and become his student. When he saw my glamorous Japanese companion, his eyes lit up even more. He gave her a business card, too, and then another, in case she lost

one. He caught her eye and held it and told her how happy he
would be if she visited him.

"We watched you every day," I said, to try to take the conversation back to the temple around us, the prayers.

"I've been to New York many times," he said.

He had some power, no doubt of it—a real magnetism, com-
pounded by mystery and the glamour of his robes, his origins.
Another young Japanese girl showed up, and he came close to her
and pressed a business card (or two) on her. He'd been so much
more appealing when I knew nothing at all about him and was free
to project all my hopes, my accumulated fairy tales upon him.

A trivial incident, but less and less an untypical one. Here is
the Tibetan conundrum in miniature, as Ngari Rinpoche always
stressed. In the cafés of Dharamsala, young Tibetan boys with hair
down to their waists and strong cheekbones—their smiles a glow
of white, their eyes mysterious and soulful, able to tell palpitating
stories of crossing the Himalayas to be near their leader, breaking
into old nomad songs from Amdo when not making conversation
in broken English—roam around like the packs of wild dogs, and
few visitors are able to resist them. Many of the foreigners one sees
in Dharamsala are, for whatever reason, female, and young, and
unattached (drawn to the calm and graciousness of Tibetan culture
after the grabby swarm of India, perhaps); these boys look like the
exotic movie stars of their dreams, and have tragic stories to boot.
The Indian shopkeepers stand amid their pyramids of biscuits and
look on with envy, ill-disguised frustration, as Lhamo or Sangye
takes a girl's arm and draws a Tibetan mandala on her palm, or
pulls out from his inside pocket a picture of the village he left
behind him, in the Dalai Lama's province.

This is one of the problems that weighs on the Dalai Lama and
those around him, though it will fit no part of the Western story

about him; in some ways, it is the second most urgent story in his life, after the story of the Tibetans in Tibet itself. These boys and thousands more who, like people in poor countries everywhere, long to come to the West, and will call upon all their wits and charm in order to make it happen, will use Tibet whenever it suits them, even if they are not Tibetan in knowledge (how could they be? The very use of the Tibetan language in schools is fading in Tibet). They have little motivation to hold on to the culture and history that made them, though every motivation to turn it to global advantage. They know how to play the fairy tale, over and over.

In this respect, as in so many others, Tibet seems to speak for more and more places across the globe, as if it were a setting for a parable; as fast as globalism has answered some needs, it has complicated thousands of others. We now have access, increasingly, to more and more cultures across the globe, and the result is that restlessness has gone global, and hopefulness, and the sense of an answer to be found somewhere else. "When they were in Tibet, they dreamed of Dharamsala," a high Tibetan philosopher said to me one day over dinner as he considered the Tibetan boys prowling the streets around us. "Now that they are in Dharamsala, they dream of the West. What will they dream of when they get to California?"

Buddhism, more than any philosophy I am aware of, has no interest in "dreamlands," or in the places in our head that stand in the way of our engagement with what is happening right now; the Buddha, after all, took his very name and meaning from the sense of being wide-awake in the middle of confusion and ignorance. The philosophy that arose out of his teaching affirms no absolute paradise of the kind hymned in Christian or in Islamic texts; for those in the Dalai Lama's tradition, Nirvana itself is just a way station, a state of mind, really, that the true *bodhisattva* sees not as an endpoint but a viewpoint, to carry back with him into the clamor of the world.

Yet one curious aspect of the global order is that the Other is everywhere nowadays, and it's ever easier to assume that he has the answers that we do not. The Dalai Lama thus finds himself, almost poignantly, in the midst of conflicting dreams. We look to him for his monasticism, even his remoteness; and yet in order to fulfill his monastic duties and to protect his community, he is obliged to travel constantly, away from his home, and come out into our very different world.

In the process, those Chinese officials who feel threatened by him can say that he's merely a politician, advancing his cause while hiding out in monk's robes, and those foreigners who've never seen or heard him can imagine that he's just a flavor of the media moment, the plaything of movie stars and millionaires. For decades now, the Dalai Lama has stressed that one of the virtues of exile is that it has brought him and his people "closer to reality," as he puts it, and, as he stressed to me twenty years ago, "there's no point now in pretending." Yet those who are most anxious to listen to him ask him to be not just another figure from the real world but an emissary from some other world that doesn't exist.

In the Age of the Image, when screens are so much our rulers, anyone who wishes to grab our attention—and to hold it—does so by converting himself into a "human-interest story," translating his life into a kind of fable. The boy from Hope, the barefoot peanut farmer from Plains—the names themselves enforce the air of allegory; in India, as in the United States, it's commonplace for movie stars to step onto the political stage, simply carrying their larger-than-life appearance and association with happy endings from one auditorium to another. Those who long to be entrusted with real consequences in our lives acquire that power increasingly by presenting themselves as fairy tales.

The Dalai Lama, by nature and training, is in the odd position of trying to do the opposite: he comes to us to tell us that he is real, as real as his country, bleeding and oppressed, and that he lives in a world far more complex than a two-year-old's cries of "Good Tibetans, bad Chinese" (the Dalai Lama would more likely say, "Potentially good Tibetans, potentially good Chinese"). As a longtime student of real life, ruler of his people before the age of five, he listens every morning to the Voice of America, to the BBC East Asian broadcast, to the BBC World Service—even while meditating—and devours *Time* and *Newsweek* and many other news sources (I think of how the Buddha is often depicted with one hand touching the earth, in what Buddhists call the "witnessing the earth" gesture). His own father—according to some members of their own family—was poisoned to death at a picnic, and his father's father died in the same way. When the current Dalai Lama was a small boy, the regent who was overseeing him went away on an extended retreat, and power was handed over, temporarily as it seemed, to an older man. When the regent, Reting Rinpoche, returned (as the Dalai Lama's mother has it), the other man declined to relinquish power. In response (though there are as many different accounts of what followed as there are Tibetans), the deposed man's supporters sent a package to the rival that, when opened, exploded and killed one of the rival's men. Civil war broke out, and the monks of Sera, one of Lhasa's great monasteries, ran amok, killing more than two hundred of their fellows, including an abbot. Reting Rinpoche was found dead in prison, the victim, some assumed, of the son of a man whose eyes he'd had gouged out. When the plotters were brought to trial and sentenced to be flogged, one of them committed suicide before full justice could be served.

The eleven-year-old Dalai Lama witnessed all this, seeing his former regent in a prison inside the very Potala Palace where he lived; the young ruler was even, by one account, said to be a false Dalai Lama and taken to the central Jokhang Temple to be tested ← against a rival (three times the ceremonial lots were drawn, and three times the current Dalai Lama's name came up). A little after this monastic coup attempt, he heard that his eldest brother had been urged by the Chinese to try to kill him. The Thirteenth Dalai Lama, soon after he came to office, had also had an attempt made on his life, by a rival who placed the outline of a human figure in a new pair of shoes belonging to the young leader, in a kind of Tibetan voodoo.

In all the years I've listened to him, I cannot remember the Dalai Lama ever using the words "fairy tale" or "romance" or even "wishfulness," least of all as something good. His domain is the present, and the word he always stresses (as his Christian friends stress "Creation") is "Reality." In some ways, his power as a political and global thinker derives from the fact that he is a hyperrealist who bursts into fits of contagious laughter when he thinks of such unrealistic gestures as fellow Tibetans hanging on to their heavy brocade in the heat of southern India or activists hoping they can reverse centuries of history and go back to the fifteenth century. Where the Christian believes in the transcendence of everyday life, through finding a higher life in God, the Buddhist generally believes in the transformation of it, by finding the better life in the here and now.

And yet for many of us—like myself as a little boy—the power of the Fourteenth Dalai Lama's story comes from the fact that he was found at the age of two by a search party of monks, led to him after rainbows arced across the northeastern skies of Lhasa, a star-shaped fungus appeared on a pillar of the Potala Palace, and the head of the corpse of the Thirteenth Dalai Lama repeatedly moved in a northeasterly direction. He lives in exile with four state oracles and a lama specializing in the art of bringing rain. The robes in which he speaks of examining reality are sometimes capped by what looks like a conical wizard's hat, studded with stars, and he sits in front of *thangka*s, or scrolls, that swarm with grinning skulls and lascivious deities whose meanings the rational mind can't grasp.

More profoundly, all of us still choose to call the never-never land where we dream of putting the world behind us and rising to a higher place in ourselves "Tibet" (the elevated kingdom hidden behind the world's highest mountains). In Tibet, as the British historian Peter Hopkirk writes in describing the visits of early explorers who tried to steal into the sequestered land, "one can suffer from frostbite and sunburn simultaneously." The sky is so clear in places that you can see figures ten miles away; other gorges are so deep that the light catches them for less than an hour each day. You can plunge your hand into boiling water in Tibet and not retract it (since water boils at a lower temperature at fourteen thousand feet, the average altitude of the Tibetan plateau); you can walk for eighty-one straight days in parts, a Western traveler has reported, without seeing another soul.

I remember the first time I visited Tibet, in 1985, as a hard-headed writer on world affairs for *Time* magazine determined not to repeat all the usual clichés (the stuff, I thought, of comic books like *Tintin in Tibet*). I flew into Lhasa from the Chinese city of Chengdu and, after the two-hour drive in from the airport, walked along the city's main road with my suitcase, decidedly untransported. The only two guesthouses on offer had rooms that were lightless boxes gathered around a small, central hole in the ground, with a single water pump in a courtyard; the Holiday Inn on the other side of town was an abandoned ghost town with oxygen tanks beside every empty bed. Traveling through Beijing and Guangzhou, and on the railway between them, had trained me in a strikingly unglamorous life in which creature comforts were still some years away.

And then I settled down in a little bare room and began to walk up to the Potala Palace, and out to the edges of town where the old monasteries stood (once the largest in the world, now largely in ruins). And very soon I was in another world, one that hardly touched the one I knew. Monks came out into the sunlit courtyards to play with my camera; dogs sat in the lanes around the shrines, completely silent. In little rooms thick with the smell of melted yak butter the light came in from the high sun, falling in shafts on dusty monks who sat in the corners, reciting prayers. I went to the great, heartrending ruins of Ganden Monastery, outside Lhasa; I saw fistfights and butchers slicing up human bodies in the traditional Tibetan way to feed to predatory birds; I wandered out of town before sunrise, past the occasional lights of yak-skin nomads' tents, and realized that whatever I saw and thought hardly belonged to the life I knew, as had not, and has not, happened to me in a lifetime of traveling.

In *Sky Burial,* a story by the longtime Beijing journalist Xinran Xue of a Chinese woman she met who went missing in Tibet in search of her husband, the Chinese radio broadcaster writes of her subject, "She was coming to understand that the whole of Tibet was one great monastery. Everyone was infused with the same religious spirit, whether they wore religious robes or not." The author begins her account by speaking of the "legendary cruelty" of Tibetans and ends it by reminding us that "the Tibetans' savagery was legendary." But in between, she refers to kindness and devotion and a magical innocence that begin to transform the visitor from China who has always looked down on the Tibetans as savages. (The book reads, in fact, a lot like the captivity reports of early American settlers abducted by natives who come to see that there is a strength and power to the Indian way that they don't know in their own.)

Perhaps it's in part the altitude and the thin air that work this transformative effect (though I have never felt the same thing on three trips to La Paz, Bolivia, which sits a little higher than Lhasa); perhaps it's the unworldliness of the location, intensified by culture shock and jet lag. Perhaps it's also the years of stories of Tibet that move us to see the magical place we've always heard of. Those who've never visited Tibet wish for it to be transporting, and those who have seen it want their stories to be spellbinding.

The net result, though, is that when China attacked eastern Tibet in 1949—at the time, there was not a single airstrip in the entire country and there were all of five foreigners in residence— the government appealed to the U.N. and never received an answer; its allies in London and Washington and New Delhi were able to pretend that Tibet hardly existed as a real place at all (though six years earlier F.D.R. had sent a letter and two Office of Strategic Services emissaries to the seven-year-old Dalai Lama, asking for help in the transportation of American supplies through Tibet during World War II). When the young Dalai Lama made his first foreign friend, the Austrian traveler Heinrich Harrer, he asked him to help him set up a projector so that (as it were) he could get a real, unprojected sense of the wider world, and he religiously watched newsreels that told him what was going on outside his isolated kingdom; yet for Harrer, as for too many of us, before and after, the lure of Tibet and its leader lay in their distance from the real world as we know it.

I've noticed, whenever I follow the Dalai Lama around, that people's faces don't light up much when he says, "Dream—nothing!" in stressing to a questioner that for a resolution of her situation, "the main responsibility lies on your own shoulders," or when he says, "We expect peace, compassion to come from the sky. Nonsense! Someone must start it," in reminding us of the virtue of real action instead of daydreaming. Over and over, he counsels a practical realism and a refusal to get caught up in the lures and distraction of mindless optimism, least of all the kind that comes from indiscriminate faith. This emphasis on how much we can do ourselves lies at the heart of his own optimism and infectious confidence; yet it's not always the part that most of us want to hear.

The Harrer story is a poignant reminder of this. An Olympic skier from Nazi Austria—the metaphors come ready-made—manages, somehow, to steal out of a prisoner-of-war camp in British India in 1944 and stumbles into what is then known as the "Forbidden Kingdom," Tibet. He walks for two years across the highest plateau on earth, picks up Tibetan, is even mistaken for a Tibetan by unworldly locals who have never seen a foreign face before. Finally he makes his way to the capital, where the teenage Dalai Lama, hearing of the curious blond-haired wanderer, asks to see him, and the two become fast friends.

The European constantly feels that he's entered a magical world of flower-ringed cottages and garden parties and sturdy outdoors people like himself, who treat him as an honored guest; he feels that he's slipped out of real life and into a golden fairy tale. But very soon, and inevitably, reality appears again, as Chinese troops cross into eastern Tibet in 1949 and the wayfarer is forced to abandon his idyll and return to a broken Europe.

In the years that followed, while Harrer was writing of his sojourn in a never-never land, Amdo, the province in eastern Tibet where the current Dalai Lama was born, was turned into the largest gulag in the world, set up to accommodate as many as ten million prisoners. One in every five Tibetans—more than a million in all—died of starvation or in direct encounters with the Chinese, according to Tibetan estimates. One in ten found himself in jail, while all but thirteen of the more than six thousand monasteries in Tibet were laid waste and centuries-old scriptures were incinerated. Parents were forced to applaud as their children were shot to death.

In recent years, more details of what the International Commission of Jurists described at the time as a "genocide" have come to light, as have the stories of many of those who escaped at last from incarceration. (One monk, questioned by the Dalai Lama when finally he made it to freedom in exile in India, said that he had been truly afraid while in prison—afraid that one day he might lose his sympathy for his Chinese captors.) Yet what we tend to notice, too often, are the larger-than-life contours of the story, and not the brutal realities that we can do something to transform.

In 1932, one year before his death, the Thirteenth Dalai Lama issued what is known as his "Last Testament," in which he predicted what would come to pass if Tibetans failed to open up to the world, refused to adapt to modern developments, and continued squabbling among themselves. "It will not be long," he wrote, as one translation has it, "before we face the red onslaught at our own front door. It is only a matter of time . . . and when it happens, we must be ready to defend ourselves. Otherwise, our spiritual and cultural teachings will be completely eradicated. . . . Monasteries will be looted and destroyed, and the monks and nuns killed or chased away. . . . We will become like slaves to our conquerors, and will be made to wander helplessly like beggars. Everyone will be forced to live in misery, and the days and nights will pass slowly and with great suffering and terror."

The Thirteenth Dalai Lama worked hard to try to defend Tibet against his fears, setting up the first mint and postal system in his country's history, bringing telephones and passports to Lhasa, even sending four Tibetan boys to be educated at Rugby School in England (one of the boys returned and helped bring electricity to Lhasa). Yet what suits our fairy tales most is the remarkable prescience, as it seems, of his vision—and not, in fact, all that it entailed. Fully eleven centuries before, Padmasambhava, the great Indian reformer of Tibetan Buddhism, whom the Tibetans revere as Guru Rinpoche, had, by some accounts, declared, "When the iron bird flies and horses run on wheels, the Tibetan people will be scattered like ants across the face of the earth, and the Dharma will fetch a good price in the land of the red man." And in 1956, when the current Dalai Lama was assessing his options, his state oracle, Nechung, who offers counsel in a trance, had said, "The real light will shine from the West" (he was referring, as it happened, to India, which is west of most of Tibet, and yet it was a radical prophecy given that only one Dalai Lama in all of history had ever been outside Tibet).

These hard-to-explain networks of cause and effect make us marvel at the secret powers of Tibet and overlook the fact that when Mao Zedong's troops invaded, the Tibetan army numbered all of 8,500 men, protected by fifty pieces of artillery and a few ancient guns, and that Tibetans in the aftermath of their miscalculations were tortured and subjected to electroshock treatment, forced sterilization, and rape. The Dalai Lama has seen more than 300,000 foreign troops stationed in his homeland, and nearly a hundred nuclear missiles.

As I watched the Dalai Lama over the years and thought about what his mission was, this commitment of his to "Reality," as if it were the swarm of energies he was investigating to see how it all worked, began to seem more and more compelling. Many of the problems Tibet had suffered, he always stressed, were at some level the result of mistakes the culture itself had made, in not becoming informed enough of the truths of the outside world, in not studying itself honestly enough to consider reform; and circumstances had now given him and his people an ideal chance to learn from their mistakes and to create something more solid. Tibet could at last become part of a global family.

For a journalist like me, this was all as refreshing, even as liberating, as running into a man carrying a stethoscope instead of a white paper around the world. Most of the politicians I'd met in my twenty-five years of covering the news rooted themselves firmly in the future and the promises they made, or in the past and the grievances they promised to redress. But the scientist of self lived entirely in the present and had no more interest in the projections of romanticism than in the delusions of cynicism. A Buddhist talks not so much about good and evil as about ignorance and awakening; in that sense, he brings all responsibility inward, so as not to waste time blaming people outside himself, but to see how he can better understand (and therefore solve) the problem within.

The one time when I saw the Dalai Lama most vehement in the more than thirty years I'd been talking to him came, in fact, when I asked him one autumn day about Buddhism's ability to adapt to the modern world and to circumstances the Buddha himself could not have imagined. He responded, as I knew he would, by saying that Buddhism outlines a set of principles that, at their core, apply to all humans at any time; the surface details may change, but the basic laws of the value of compassion and the value of training our minds so as to see past our suffering to the path to freedom have nothing, really, to do with the modern or the ancient world exclusively.

Then, suddenly, he veered off in another direction. "With this incarnation," he said (referring, as he often does, to the role of the Dalai Lama as if it were just a robe he happened to be wearing), "there are some translations, especially of the Chinese, that say, 'Living Buddha.' That is totally wrong!"

He looked at me almost fiercely, to make sure I understood. "The Chinese word means 'Living Buddha.' In Tibetan the word 'lama' is a direct translation of 'guru.' That is, someone who is respected because of his wisdom, or because of the indebtedness one owes to him. So the rough meaning is 'someone worthy of respect.' No implication of 'Living Buddha!' So the Chinese created this confusion through Chinese translations."

It was rare indeed for him to say anything against the Chinese, whom he goes out of his way to forgive and try to understand. And I knew that he had no need to go into the issue in just offering a formal response to my simple question. But clearly the matter was of such importance to him that he was determined to explain his position fully, with a tenacity that I'd seen him apply to many points of scholarly precision.

"Some Western books," he went on, "also say 'Living Buddha' when they describe me, or 'God.' Totally wrong!" As he said this, I recalled that I had used versions of the term many times in writing a profile of him eight years before, and my editors in New York had added insult to injury by titling the piece "Tibet's Living Buddha." Perhaps he was just trying to ensure that I didn't make the same mistake again? Living Buddhas, after all, are seldom seen fleeing from their thrones on hybrid yaks and arriving in the outside world suffering from the highly ungodly condition known as dysentery.

To call the Dalai Lama more than human is, for non-Tibetans, to demean him in a way—and to demean ourselves, by suggesting that what he does we cannot do as well.

I duly recorded his amendment and wrote a new article taking in the series of discussions we had had. When it appeared in the same New York magazine, it was given—what else?—the title "The God in Exile." Humans, as he might have told me, are not always keen to give up on their fairy tales.

If nothing but the bright side of characters should be shewn, we should sit down in despondency, and think it utterly impossible to imitate them in *any thing.*

— SAMUEL JOHNSON (to Edmund Malone)

THE ICON

The first time I met the Dalai Lama in person, I was a seventeen-year-old schoolboy being reluctantly dragged on a trip around my ancestral roots by my parents and introduced to the uncles, grandparents, cousins I had barely seen before. India was of no interest to me then, except insofar as it flavored and colored the psychedelic songs and fashions that were popular in my English high school, and I did what I could not to be moved or engaged by its kaleidoscopic swirl but to hold on to my privacy and my secret wisdom, as any teenager eager to be misunderstood might. When my father took me on a two-day trip up into the mountains to meet the Dalai Lama, I was determined not to betray any interest in him; the man was, after all, just a friend—or colleague—of my father's.

I succeeded quite well in my intention. We took the overnight train from Delhi to Pathankot, and then jammed into a taxi for the long drive toward Upper Dharamsala. For hour after hour, so it seemed, we drove in and out of clouds, shifting levels of grayness.

Dharamsala is notorious for the intensity of its rainfall in the summer, and all I can recall now is pine trees, switchback turns, clouds, and more clouds. Then we arrived at a battered little settlement of a few huddled huts and, following along a narrow road above a valley, came to the house at its end and went in to see a man in red and saffron robes.

What he said then, I really cannot remember, though our conversation went on for an hour and a half or more (not many people were knocking at the Dalai Lama's door in 1974). All I remember is his using the word *bodhichitta* (which he translates as "a good heart infused with wisdom"), a term he would use again the next time I visited him, alone, in that room. In the fullness of my seventeen-year-old's wisdom, I knew nothing, of course, about the fact that this monk had been in constant negotiation with China and Mao Zedong for a quarter of a century by that point, was hoping to send delegations to Tibet before too long, had recently told his Khampa guerrillas to lay down their arms, after President Nixon and Henry Kissinger had opened the door to China and Nepal had decided it would help the coming power in Beijing. All I knew was that there were clouds everywhere, in the room and around it, swirling in and out of the space where we talked, and the world was very far away indeed, not visible through the mist.

We were on a mountaintop—I had never been so high in Asia at the time—and a deposed ruler in monk's robes was talking about Emptiness and Reality, and outside the large picture windows there were no signs of human habitation. We had taken leave of the real world altogether.

It has been one of the small miracles of my life to see the Dalai Lama come down from the mountaintop, as it were, and out of the mist and become as sharply defined a member of the global community, and as widely heeded, as the singer-activist Bono or that other hero of oppressed peoples, Nelson Mandela. His face appears on bumper stickers in surfer towns ("Be Stoked"); in-flight magazines tell us (in an article on "cool") that "the Dalai Lama is cool because he is." The eccentric film director Werner Herzog brings out a book on him, and Hunter Thompson includes him in his "Honor Roll" of gonzo heroes. This bringing together of such different worlds (a larger reality and a smaller, perhaps) offers an opportunity and poses a question: when a monk comes out in front of the swarming cameras, how much do we see the monk, and how much only what the cameras construct?

By the summer of 2005, I had grown accustomed, almost, to finding the Dalai Lama used as a comic prop in nearly every other Hollywood movie; in the space of two months I saw him alluded to in *Monster-in-Law, The Wedding Crashers, In Good Company,* and *Uptown Girls* (in which a bored Manhattan princess, applying for a job at the Fifth Avenue boutique Henri Bendel, gives as a reference "The Dalai Lama, Tibet"—a rather poignant error in light of the fact that Tibet barely exists now and the Dalai Lama hasn't lived there in almost half a century). You can buy $200 limited-edition dolls of the monk these days, and a Broadway producer is talking of having a vampire dress up as him, for farcical effect. "Formerly," as Oscar Wilde's Gilbert noted more than a century ago, "we used to canonize our heroes. The modern method is to vulgarize them."

Yet what surprised me, repeatedly, in the middle of all this was that the Dalai Lama clearly saw things in a much more spacious way than I would: everything in the world could be used for some good was his position, even the publicity machine, the celebrity circus, the ever more intrusive media. It's customary for some of us to think of the spiritual world, the realm of the monk, as pure, while the world of the flashbulb and the sound bite is compro-mised at best. And certainly liberties were taken with the Buddhist that I could rarely imagine being taken with the pope or even, these days, an Islamic cleric. But one of the striking arguments being advanced by this most visible of monks, as by a few like-minded souls, was that even these things of the world could be transformed by the purposes we bring to them. There is nothing good or bad, as Hamlet has it, but thinking makes it so.

In the spring of 2004, therefore, I flew to Vancouver to see how the Dalai Lama would deal with clamorous crowds and media scrutiny much more intense than in low-key Nara. I wasn't especially interested in his personality, glowing and moving though that personality was, in part because I didn't feel he was very much interested in it and, more, because his public virtues were really just symptoms of the private practices and stillness that underlay them. But for decades now I had been interested in how globalism could acquire depths, an inwardness that would sustain it more than mere goods or data could, and how even the media might be able to address something more than just the passing events of the day. If our new way of living were to offer any real sustenance, I'd long thought, it would have to be invisible, in the realm of what underlies acceleration and multinationals.

Weeks before I even set foot in British Columbia, the Web site specially set up for the event (as for just about every visit the Dalai Lama makes around the world these days) informed me that the city was already in a frenzy of excitement; the global order's godfather, as he sometimes seems, had not been to Canada in more than a decade. His general talks on how to lead a kinder and more attentive life had already been relocated to the largest public arena in town—the Pacific Coliseum, long home to the ice-hockey–playing Canucks—after tickets had gone, months in advance, in just twenty minutes, and eight thousand people had been left disappointed. In Toronto, on the same trip, the Dalai

Lama was scheduled to give a talk at the cavernous fifty-thousand-seat SkyDome, generally host to major rock groups and baseball games. Whichever direction I turned in, on the rainy April evening when I arrived, there were pictures of the Dalai Lama, fluttering from the lampposts of Vancouver (or those lampposts not given over to banners of the Canucks). It was as if, as the press frequently put it, a president was visiting, in the company of Mick Jagger.

The Dalai Lama was coming here, rather typically, at the invitation of a Chinese friend who had stumbled into his home in 1972, in black cape and Fu Manchu goatee, with no idea, really, of where he was going. The traveler, Victor Chan, had just been abducted in Afghanistan, along the hippie trail, with two women, and when the three of them had escaped, one of them had recalled that she was in possession of the name and address of a hospitable Tibetan who lived in a forgotten hill station in northern India called Dharamsala. The Tibetan in question, of course, turned out to be the Dalai Lama, not much known in those days, and now, thirty-two years on, this countercultural Chinese Heinrich Harrer, as it might seem, Victor, was bringing him to Vancouver to speak on peace and reconciliation with two of his longtime friends and allies, Desmond Tutu and Václav Havel, as well as with the most recent Nobel peace laureate, Shirin Ebadi, the female judge who had fearlessly stood up to the theocratic regime in Iran.

Everywhere I looked, traveling up to the event, George W. Bush and John Kerry were debating on TV, in anticipation of the presidential election six months later, and as soon as the two men in suits had stopped talking about war, other men in suits—my media colleagues—appeared on-screen to talk about what the men in suits had been saying about war; the nature of modern broadcasting is that nothing is feared—not bombast or repetition or bile—so much as silence. In just a generation—since my first trip to Tibet, in

fact—the world seemed to have moved from having too little information about itself to having too much, and what the soul cried out
for, I began to think, listening to the men chattering on all those
screens, was something that could put the clutter into a larger perspective. Where once information had seemed the first step to
knowledge, and then to wisdom, now it sometimes seemed their
deepest enemy.

By seven o'clock the next morning, when I arrived at the Chan
Center for the Performing Arts at the University of British Columbia (the city had become something of an outpost of China, and
this Chan was no relative of Victor's), long, long lines of people,
mostly silent, were trailing all around the building in the rain, and
deep into the recesses of the campus. It was, as is the case almost
everywhere the Dalai Lama speaks, a de facto global gathering:
women in formal Tibetan dress, the powers that be of the local
community, journalists from what looked to be Japan and Taiwan
and maybe mainland China, a hundred different means and ends.
The media alone were so numerous that we were assigned a separate theater from which to follow the proceedings on-screen and
so, asked to arrive two hours in advance for security reasons, we
filed into a large auditorium where the living laureates would be
turned into images, oversized icons in a virtual world.

It was a little strange in this context to have read, among the
many stipulations sent out in advance, that "for the purpose of
these events, the Pacific Coliseum is considered a church"—and
yet in some ways it seemed a perfect model of what these visitors
hoped to do: to turn an entertainment complex into a place for
entertaining (with due humor and humility) a sense of conscience
and awareness and something more than just the self. As the great
student of comparative religions Huston Smith has noted, ours is
the first age that archaeologists have found that does not have a

temple (but has, rather, a stadium or a shopping mall) at its center. Another stipulation, though, reminded us that even churches are by no means sanctuaries, outside the real world and its conflicts: "Dolgyal worshippers and those propitiating Dolgyal are asked not to attend the teachings."

The precisely worded request was a reminder that every opening brings its complications, and the Dalai Lama was still as entangled in local political disputes as any other spiritual or political leader might be. He stands, for every Tibetan and Tibetan Buddhist (those in Mongolia, say, and now Korea and Taiwan and elsewhere, too), as a visible embodiment of their faith and, quite literally, a god—an incarnation of Chenrezig, deity of compassion—so beyond the common realm that Tibetans are too awestruck even to address him directly; and yet in recent years, those who propitiate a Tibetan deity called Dorje Shugden, sometimes known as Dol- ✓ gyal, have taken to picketing his public events because they felt he was discriminating against their particular corner of Tibetan Buddhism. Like many of the debates within the Tibetan world, this one goes back centuries, and yet, like many of them, too, it is hardly an abstract or remote affair: seven years before, three members of the Dalai Lama's private monastery, including the head of his Institute of Buddhist Dialectics, were found murdered in their beds only a couple of hundred yards away from the Dalai Lama's home, and it was generally assumed that the killings were connected in some way with a string of bloody threats from the followers of Shugden.

So as I settled into the media auditorium, what I felt I was really watching was how these individuals from very different situations would handle the challenges of publicity, of celebrity, even of enmity. In theory, all of them were here to receive an honorary doctorate from the university before their serious discussions began, and to inaugurate the Contemporary Tibetan Studies Program on the campus. Yet really, I felt, they were here to try, in a limited time, to offer a fresh perspective, the one that says that revolutions begin at home. The Dalai Lama liked to talk of "human beings," nearly always preceded by the pronoun "we," but what he was really talking about was "human becomings," and the ways each one of us could travel along the open road to becoming more compassionate and responsible. A global peace reached by men who are themselves still restless or frightened or jealous is not going to be much of a peace at all.

 The only real peace could arise from stilling something in yourself, going back behind the self, to someplace where you had no sense of "us" and "them" but instead saw everything linked in a pulsing network, which reminded you that the boss you cannot abide may in fact have been your mother in a previous lifetime— or, indeed, might become your mother in a future life. The only revolution, in that sense, came from reevaluation; to change a society or a system, you had to push back to its root causes in the mind. "Hate," as Graham Greene memorably puts it in *The Power and the Glory,* "was just a failure of imagination."

I knew, to that extent—as did almost everyone in attendance— what the visitors would say in advance, and we knew, all of us, that none of it was remarkable or new: "What hope can we have of finding rest outside of ourselves if we cannot be at rest within?" Saint Teresa of Avila had asked of herself and the world four centuries ago. Yet what was exciting about their presence—the hope of transformation they brought with them—was the fact that all of them were experimenting with highly practical forms for these lofty ideas: Ebadi by actually safeguarding and writing the laws of her country, in the face of a regime that wanted to rewrite or override them; Tutu by setting up a Truth and Reconciliation Commission in his native South Africa after the end of apartheid, so that old crimes would neither be forgotten nor merely avenged; and the Dalai Lama by to some extent leaving his technical Buddhism at home on such occasions to advance his favored "secular ethics." Havel (who had had to cancel at the last minute because of illness) had even appointed a scholar of Woody Allen to be his ambassador to Washington when he came to power, as a way, perhaps, of advancing a politics that did not rest with politicians.

It was as if what they were really bringing the audience, even in this ritual exercise, was a frame to place around the events of the day, so that we could see them in the settings of something more lasting and expansive ("Creation," Desmond Tutu would perhaps call it, and "justice," maybe, for Shirin Ebadi, and "ultimate reality" or "human potential" in the Dalai Lama's dictionary). By their nature, ideally, an archbishop, a monk, and a judge ask us to see the news of the moment in the light of principles that last much longer than mere moments.

Look at America's involvement in Iraq, Ebadi was effectively saying in her public statements, not just in terms of Washington's relations with the Middle East, of the murderous Saddam Hussein and the crusading George W. Bush, but in terms of some principle of the sovereignty of states and the concerns that every nation might face if such principles were overrun. Look at your own life and all that you have suffered, Tutu was saying in his commission, not as something so large that it blocks everything else out, but from the perspective of the heavens, in which it is a mere speck on a canvas extending across centuries and continents. Look at Tibet's dialogue with China, the Dalai Lama always said, not only in terms of this leader or that loss but, rather, in the context of an almost endless series of causes and effects that stretches indefinitely into the future. China and Tibet would always be neighbors and their destinies would always be intertwined; in taking care of the needs of the Tibetans, therefore, you could not afford to overlook the priorities and needs of the Chinese.

As soon as Tutu was called to the front of the stage to receive his doctorate, accompanied by a large black tasseled cap, he recalled how he had received another such cap at West Point. It turned out to be many sizes too big, he said. "Now, any normal wife would at that point have said, 'I think we need a smaller cap.' But of course my dear wife, Leah, who has known me for so long, said, 'This shows that my husband has much too big a head!' "

The audience chuckled with delight; such self-effacement was exactly what it expected from a man of the cloth, and Tutu knew how to work a crowd just with the way his voice went up and down, melodiously. And yet, I thought—since men of God, as much as monks and lawyers, tend to be careful with their words—the joke contained, like much around it, a useful point. Don't expect the world to fit its needs to accommodate you; work your needs around the circumstances of the world.

I could imagine what some of my colleagues would say in response to all this—and a journalist's job is to entertain such voices (as, the Dalai Lama might say, is a Buddhist's). All three of the peace laureates were idealists, in the happy position of spinning out moral principles instead of dealing with a real world in which we more often have to choose between wrong and wrong than between right and wrong. All three of them had suffered, to be sure, and weathered their suffering with dignity, and yet suffering alone was no guarantee of wisdom, let alone of political authority. There was a reason why church and state were generally separate, and it was that church operated in the eternal world of justice, and politics acted in the much more qualified, temporizing world of men.

But then I recalled the words I had read at the very beginning of

Tutu's most recent book, and they were words that had taken me aback at first. "I am not an optimist," he wrote. "Optimism relies on appearances, and very quickly turns into pessimism when the appearances change. I see myself as a realist." Instead of just placing a Band-Aid on a wounded society, he was trying (as his Tibetan friend might echo) to undertake radical heart surgery. Living for sixty-two years without being able to vote in his own country had trained him in the hollowness of just wishing things might be otherwise, and when he had urged the world to boycott his country, he had essentially been saying that he and his parishioners were ready to go without everything if it could finally effect a change in a government that could transform their lives at the core.

I looked at Ebadi, sitting firmly in her chair, and recalled how she had, at times, in protecting dissidents, uncovered lists of troublemakers to be assassinated on which her own name featured prominently; death threats were her daily bread. And I saw the Dalai Lama craning forward in his seat and picking out faces in the crowd, and recalled that he was still traveling, after almost fifty years, on the yellow identity certificate of a refugee. Prayer, I recalled reading in Emerson—and it was perhaps the best definition I had met—is merely "the contemplation of the facts of life from the highest point of view."

The very notion of a "spiritual celebrity" is an odd one, of course, and yet in a world where celebrity is ever more a global currency, the spiritual celebrity is the one who can actually change the coin of the realm into something more precious or sustaining. All three of the visitors were here because they refused to turn away from the clatter and commotion that is the real and daily world; and yet all three were also here because they were determined to find in that clatter the seed or outline of something more worthwhile. Their job now was to give this audience a human, living sense of contact that no audience could get from a screen (the crowd, after all, had been waiting for this day for months); and yet they had to leave behind them something that would outlast them, and maybe help people return to the clatter and commotion a little differently, in part by seeing how they could change the world by coming at it from a different angle.

After Tutu has sat down, the president of the university comes up to the podium and reads from a prepared statement. "There is no one in our society today," she intones, "who represents love, compassion, and altruism as much as the Fourteenth Dalai Lama." Then she invites him to step forward. A fairly routine formulation, I think, but what moves me is that "our": if the Dalai Lama has some relevance to those in Vancouver, it will come only if they see him as part of their world and he sees them as part of his. Precisely, in fact, the kind of connection that was impossible when Tibet was set behind the highest mountains on earth, a fantasy place for most of us, and full of people who perhaps saw the rest of us as not quite real.

The Tibetan steps to the front of the stage and offers a few words in English, always a handy way of at once putting his listeners at ease and reminding them, with his uncertain grammar, that he's just one of us, no different. Then he says, "I need a walking stick for my broken English," and summons to his side his translator for the session, a famously learned Tibetan scholar and philosopher, with doctorates from both Tibetan institutes and Cambridge, who now lives in Canada, trying to bring Tibet to the world and vice versa. "So long as space remain, so long as sentient being remain," the Dalai Lama says in English, invoking his favorite prayer, from the eighth-century Indian philosopher Shantideva, "I will remain, to serve."

"I believe that," he continues. "That is my fundamental view. This is not holistic view; this is selfish view. Because thinking about others, I feel tremendous satisfaction. Serving others, best way get one's own deep satisfaction. In realistic way, I try to promote human values."

"Realism" again, I think. And complex ideas broken down into simple building blocks, as in a child's construction kit (the Dalai Lama loved playing with Meccano sets as a boy in the Potala). In the five minutes he has, he must try to give the audience something practical and clear enough that people can both remember it and take it home.

He speaks then, as ever, of his new favorite theme, of how Buddhism can offer something, perhaps, to "cognitive science and the study of consciousness," and the fact that certain properties of mind and the emotions do not belong to his tradition but, tests are showing, to all mankind. We see a rope in our room and take it to be a snake, the Tibetans say, and we are terrified; but as soon as we look more clearly and see that it is just a rope, all our fears are calmed. Our terrors are of our own creation. The world itself is not so frightening, if only we can see it correctly. Then he speaks of his old friend Tutu. "I have only one difference," he says, turning around to beam at the beaming archbishop. "Creator! But, same aim." The audience is transparently won over by a transparent sincerity and lack of shadow: just one man obviously speaking from the heart, with no apparent wish to sell any position or philosophy, let alone himself.

Yet what strikes me as much as the matter of the speech is its manner. The Dalai Lama begins his sentences in English, often, with "So, therefore," as if to double-knot his propositions in a tight sequence of cause and effect. At the same time, he often ends his sentences with "That's my view" or "That I really believe," as if to acknowledge that this is only his thinking, not absolute truth. His sentences are crowded with careful qualifiers—"generally," "perhaps," "I think"—much as, in normal conversation, he always cites dates, and, on one occasion, making a small claim for Buddhism, he scrupulously offered me seven "maybe's" in a single answer. The words he returns to over and over, I notice again, are "calm," "sincere," "healthy," and "authentic," and two of the words he also uses constantly are "heartfelt" and "unbiased," as if, once more, to tell us that he seeks scientific objectivity, but not at the expense of the human heart.

He also seems to be reverting often, this particular day, to the New Agey word "holistic," which someone must have told him is the best way to capture the central Buddhist idea that everything is interconnected and nothing has an independent existence. It may be the right word for the idea, but still it sounds strange from a man who regularly writes off the New Age as lacking in rigor. "Wholeism" is really what he's talking about.

His translator, after twenty years of collaboration, conveys the few words of Tibetan into English very fluently, a small figure with almost crew-cut hair next to his bulky boss. As a onetime monk and professional philosopher, he knows how to keep up with the sometimes intricate and rarefied ideas behind the simple words. As he does so, the Dalai Lama, as in Nara, peers around the room, almost visibly taking notes, then looks up, with conspicuous eagerness, at the ceiling, for all the world like a small boy suddenly finding himself in a natural history museum. At one point, though, as the translator is speaking of "conversations with scientists," the Dalai Lama breaks in quickly and I see that he has been paying attention all along. "No," he says briskly. "Dialogues!" It is, I gather, an important term for him.

In Tibet, and among Tibetans around the world, not least in his exile home of Dharamsala, the Dalai Lama is revered as a god, quite literally; every shop in Dharamsala has at its center a framed picture of him, and even the most renegade Tibetans, jiving before Western girls to the latest song from the Red Hot Chili Peppers, grow silent, almost teary-eyed, if asked about the Dalai Lama (who is, to some extent, their homeland, as well as their faith and their sense of self). In the Tibetan community the Dalai Lama still officially settles every institutional dispute, has ordained a whole generation of monks, and carries such ritual authority that even the most cocky, Columbia-educated Tibetan kids (I have seen) are too nervous to translate for him and reflexively bow their bodies before him, as subjects used to do before kings. In exile, more than ever, he's the Tibetans' main external asset.

But in the larger world the Dalai Lama is merely an icon, a secular divinity of sorts, and for that there is less precedent. The Dalai Lama remains intensely pragmatic about the uses the world makes of him—if it helps people to use his smiling face as a screen saver, he says, or if it does some substantial good to broadcast his speeches on the dance floors of London discos, then let them use him or anything that is "beneficial"; beyond a point he can't control the ideas people have of him or the hopes they bring to him, and a physician's job is to try to offer help wherever he is needed. Still, one effect of this is that he offers forewords even to books about young Tibetans' impatience with his policies and, as one close friend asserts, "answers questions he shouldn't answer."

It might almost, I sometimes think, be a kind of riddle that people of this kind pose for us: how much will we respond to their essence, the changeless core of what they are saying, and how much will we merely read them through the keyhole of our own priorities? I remember, in my own case, being moved and humbled, meeting him the day after his Nobel Prize had been announced, when the Dalai Lama spoke to me as openly and directly as if we were equals, not even stopping to remove any barrier between us, as if he seemed to see none. But the incident I probably spoke of more widely that year was his fifty-fourth birthday party in the hills of Malibu, a few months earlier, when mortals like me got to stand for hours next to such figures of glamour as Cindy Crawford and Tina Chow. Everyone we meet we tend to cast in the light of our own tiny concerns.

As I watch the Dalai Lama and Tutu proceed out from the large auditorium and follow them into a small room nearby where they will be conducting two TV interviews (with Ebadi, also) for consumption across Canada, I cannot help but notice how they speak for the "same aim" but in radically different voices. Tutu uses the whole register of his rolling, musical voice in English to call upon powers hidden in the language that bring Shakespeare in union with the King James Bible; he gets the audience to move in by making his voice very soft, and then he steadily raises the volume so we climb and climb with him. The Dalai Lama speaks, especially in English, much more slowly and carefully, in precise, rounded phrases, as if offering the stones out of which he's built his thinking. Tutu is a figure of jokes and flights, of silvery expansiveness and shine, and the effect of listening to him, as he repeats and repeats phrases, is of seeing light stream through a stained-glass window; the Dalai Lama speaks as logician more than as poet and (true to his Buddhist principles) offers statements that seem almost simplistic until you dig beneath each word to see the reasoning behind it.

And yet the biggest difference between the two visitors, at this point in history, is simply that they're standing on opposite sides of the struggles they stand for. Archbishop Tutu's task is to some extent over; his battle has been won. Thanks to his efforts, and those of Nelson Mandela and many others in South Africa and outside, apartheid has been lifted, and although the violence and danger and confusion in the country may at times be even worse than before, the outside world has done its bit to put power back in the hands of the majority. So when he goes up to the podium, what he says is "Thank you. Thank you, thank you, thank you." Thanks to those in Canada and elsewhere, he says, South Africa is celebrating its tenth anniversary of freedom a week from now. It's hard not to glow when such a dignified man offers thanks.

The Dalai Lama, by contrast, is saying, "Please." Please help my people in Tibet even though you may seem to lose the support of the world's largest nation in the short term. Please rise to your highest selves in seeing that responsibility is an assertion of enlightened self-interest. Please try to see that if you think we really inhabit a global universe, then your welfare depends on that of Tibet, as much as its welfare depends on you.

No one likes to hear a plea, especially from a guest, and least of all from a man she likes and respects; the natural impulse is to look past the plea to the liking and respecting (especially if that man seems so in command of himself and his philosophy that it's easy to imagine he can help you much more than you can help him). The very fact that the Dalai Lama tells the world he needs it moves many in the world to assume that he must, in fact, be above it.

And yet, for all these underlying strains, it's touching to see the Dalai Lama with his old friend and colleague, relaxed, perhaps, and playful, as we can only be when in the company of someone who knows what we are up against and shares our aims. As the TV interviews proceed, I notice how the Tibetan chooses examples that are as unexpected as they are precise: in arguing how force can sometimes be used for the good, he cites the Korean War, which he followed in his teens, suddenly thrown into a full-time struggle with China; and in mentioning how there are practical ways of improving the world, he cites the rivers of Stockholm, where marine life was once dead and now fish are everywhere. Coming to places like Vancouver, I realize, is how he refines and updates his observation of the world.

None of it is new again, and sometimes that almost seems to be the point: the Buddha, after all, came not to proclaim a new doctrine or to announce a revelation so much as to find and then to remind us of what we all know and hold inside ourselves already. The Dalai Lama knows how to tell TV cameras where to set up by now, and has learned that what they seek from him is sound bites, not ten-minute philosophical disquisitions; but what also strikes me, as I come upon my father's account of his first meeting, more than forty years before, is how much the twenty-four-year-old monk with the brush cut who'd just arrived in India sounds, in every particular and gesture, like the aging man I'm watching now.

"He did not claim to be, one never thought he was, perfect or infallible," my father had written at the time, "but in his company I felt the freshness of immense personal purity." The Dalai Lama had asked my father searching questions about how he saw the larger world, and he had stressed that it was important to keep talking, even to one's presumed enemies, because one day they would wake up. "Ageless," as my father saw him, and able to "assume a variety of poses, utterly without affectation," he had "his eye on the essentials."

As the interview ends, the only other journalist in attendance, a likable and clearly sincere soul who covers religion, offers me a ride into town. "I don't know how exactly to say this," he says as we drive through the traffic, every other surface projecting the Dalai Lama's face, "because I don't want to believe it, but do you get the impression that the Dalai Lama is not exactly the brightest bulb in the room?"

He's a doctor of metaphysics, I think, and a famously accomplished philosopher speaking in a second language; what we've seen in his address is the equivalent of Jimmy Connors hitting the ball around with a small boy at a celebrity tennis tournament. If anything, his inclination is to speak at too high and technical a level if he does not take care—as he did this morning—to remain aware of his audience and find the words that will make the most sense to it.

"It's funny," the man goes on (and I begin to see his real concern—gushing about the Dalai Lama is getting tiring for all parties), "there are a lot of people who don't believe in anything, but they will die just to see the Dalai Lama. It's almost like they feel if he touches them, if they get his blessing, they're set up for life."

"Exactly what he tells them not to think." A true Buddhist, he's always saying, more than anyone has no faith in either blind piety or personality. Trust and respect might almost be described as the opposite of undiscerning faith. And yet I know exactly what my new friend is talking about. At this stop—at every stop—on his global travels, people will tell me excitedly how they were "meant" to bump into the Dalai Lama, how they caught his eye and saw he was talking only to them, how he disclosed the meaning of the universe or read their souls just by looking at them, as if he didn't have many other things, much more pressing, on his mind. When we hear him talk about projection and delusion, we do not, most of us, have to look very far to find examples.

When the Dalai Lama first arrived in exile, he was, inevitably, an innocent in the ways of the modern world and its latest technologies;

but as I watch him go through his schedule in Vancouver, I notice how much he's learned to adjust to the times. The first time I saw him in the New World, at Harvard on his first American tour, in 1979, he seemed still like a figure from another planet, spinning out philosophical discourses that almost none of us could follow; when I attended press conferences of his in New York in the 1980s, only a handful of journalists would show up, and nearly all of them would be Tibetan.

I think of how he told my father, more than forty years ago, that when the spiritual aspect of Tibet was being stressed, it was necessary to talk about the political—and vice versa—and how "we need to translate spiritual and religious truth into a political and social forum," and I begin to see how carefully, with his habitual empiricism, he's schooled himself in the language of the world, not changing his fundamental positions but constantly finding new ways to make them approachable. After he arrived in India, his first priority was organizing all the Tibetans who flooded out with him and setting up a Tibet outside Tibet. But then, old friends say, he threw himself into his studies and went on extended retreats as he could never have done in old Tibet, turning the neglect of the world to advantage, and very quickly the fresh-faced student in his twenties grew into a much more poised and electric figure.

It was as if he learned how to speak to the world by stepping away from it and then, with fresh purpose, began to engage with it anew. In 1967 he made his first trip outside India and China and Tibet, to the Buddhist nations of Japan and Thailand; six years later he undertook his first journey to Europe. After he finally received permission to visit the United States, six years after that, he initially visited Tibetans, but slowly extended his pilgrimage to take in newspapers, politicians, the houses of Congress, and, ultimately, the White House.

As he found that those who listened to him were less likely to act on his discussions of the situation in Tibet than to follow his more general moral prescriptions, he started shifting his emphasis to ethics (while always trying to meet leaders privately in every country, to talk about Tibet). More recently, having found that charm opens doors but does not always win real-world assistance, he has seemed to be speaking more and more from the strong and even wrathful aspect of his being, as if to clean out the house before he leaves it, and replacing the image of the jolly smiling traveler with something much more focused and unsparing.

When he went for a lunch with the *New York Times,* he startled (and perhaps opened up) his hosts by going over to chat with a waiter; at a moment of great ceremony with François Mitterrand, he began talking to some bodyguards he remembered meeting many years before. And in Dharamsala itself, whenever I went to see him, I would notice that the figures before me in line might include a frightened Taiwanese student (since the Dalai Lama is especially keen to keep his door open to those of Chinese descent) or a ragged pair of backpackers (who can inform him about Tibet).

And yet for all of that, it's impossible, as Buddhism would suggest, to control the perceptions that other people have of us, and it's very difficult, as experience tells us, to get the better of the media.

I remember one book I encountered in which the CEO of a large company, clearly a sincere man eager to do something useful with his power, engages the Dalai Lama in a series of discussions. Early on, speaking of leadership, he suddenly asks the Tibetan monk whether he feels closer "to John Lennon, the dreamer, or to Gandhi, the politician" (the Dalai Lama's answer, in the translated version I read, was transcribed as "?!"). The man perseveres, and gets him to read out the lyrics of John Lennon's anthem "Imagine."

The Dalai Lama, asked again and again what single role he chooses for himself says, "I don't know."

Then, suddenly, he starts talking about his work with his people and says, "This makes me very sad." He has "neither power nor country," he says, "but I can't help it—I feel responsible for all these Tibetan refugees who have such a close connection with their country."

He can't be what the interviewer wants, he might be saying, and he isn't always able even to be what his people ask of him. He's human.

As the stay in Vancouver draws to an end, all the curiosities that attend almost every foreign trip of the Dalai Lama's, and make some outsiders look askance, begin to mount. Elegant women in off-the-shoulder dresses and men in well-pressed Nehru suits gather outside a downtown theater for a Peace Concert, pushing their way past the homeless people curled up in bundles on the sidewalk in the rain, only blocks away from where crack addicts are selling themselves for pennies. A multicultural chorus of kids in rainbow T-shirts bursts into a specially written chorus—"*Om Mani Padme Hum, Dalai Lama Hum*"—and then begins singing, "Prayer flags in the breeze, / Floating laughter . . ." while images are projected on giant screens on both sides of the stage of the man and his monks (although floating laughter has not been the distinctive characteristic of Tibet in the last fifty years). Only a few hours later, the three Nobel laureates show up again, soon after dawn, at Christ Church Cathedral downtown, to receive an honorary degree from the other large university in town, Simon Fraser; the nineteenth-century cathedral, otherwise closed for restoration, is specially opened up for this convocation.

A great procession of grizzled Marxists, beaming Bengalis, First

Nations leaders in pigtails, rectors and ministers and city council-
lors proceeds up the nave, and in the midst of the global parade
comes the visiting trio, the Dalai Lama dressed in a long red gown,
an odd blue cap perched on his head, yellow tassels hanging down
from it, so that he looks a little, unfortunately, like a jester from a
Shakespearean comedy. (The photographers will again have no
problem filling their front pages.) A "Kyrie Eleison" sounds from an
upper gallery, and as the dignitaries move forward, pace by pace, a
stylish Iranian man beside me in an elegant suit and tie extends his
palms out, movingly, in the classic Islamic gesture of petition and
worship. "I hold before you an open door" is the apt motto of the
cathedral.

Again, as the day before, each of the three is given five minutes
to speak, and the Dalai Lama, aware that he is now in a place of
worship, and not a university, says, conventionally enough, "Of
course, to myself, Buddhism is best. But this does not mean that
Buddhism is best for the world. No! Each person, each individual
can find the best. Like medicine. You cannot say, 'Just because I take
it, it is the best medicine.' For some people, Christian is best,
because it is most effective." (When I asked him later about the
biggest surprise in his life, he would mention, admiringly, how the
new pope, Benedict XVI, had stressed that in the Christian tradition, "faith, reason must go together.")

The word "practice" that Buddhists use, I think, as he says that
"meeting with people from other traditions has deepened my own
practice," suggests the notion of hard work and discipline (practice
makes less imperfect)—and of getting ready for a final exam (in
this case, perhaps, death). And the use of the word "way," like the
"carry" he loves to deploy, offers the sense of different roads, all
leading, perhaps, through wildly different paths, to a somewhat
similar destination.

Much as Tutu said the day before, he ends, "With an honorary

degree, I do not think this person is something special. I am nothing. But the activities—maybe there has been a small service."

Then Tutu himself comes up to the microphone and delivers the
most heart-shaking, roof-rattling speech I think I've ever heard.
He begins, again, with thanks, his voice growing soft and softer, so
the audience leans in toward him, draws closer, as he says, "Thank
you, thank you. Thank you. Thank you." He teases the audience for
being nice and quiet—Canadian—and passes a hand across the
crowd to turn its members, he says, into Africans, who love to sing
and dance. He teases himself and says, a wicked gleam in his eye,
that inviting him up to a lectern in a beautiful church is temptation
indeed for a man who loves to deliver sermons.

And then, just as I am thinking he has wrought a spell over us
and that I am listening to something like a modern equivalent to
Martin Luther King, he says, " 'I have a dream,' said Martin Luther
King. But God has a dream for us, for all of us," and he extends his
message and his voice to the straight, the gay, the lame, the infirm
(there are loud claps from some of the queer theorists onstage), till
finally it feels as if he has carried us all up to the heavens, and for a
brief moment we are not on the ground looking up but on high
looking down, as an all-forgiving, eternity-dwelling God might
look. For a moment, he has carried us up into a vision of perfection.

And then his voice comes down again and brings us back to
earth, leaving us gently in our seats, and there is a silence across
the whole illuminated space. I glance at the friend sitting next to
me, shaking my head in silence, and try to look down so he won't
see the tears of exaltation.

When I walk out into the rain—fervent Canuck fans are cavorting
in their team colors among Tibetans and Tibetophiles, many of

whom (the daily paper has told me) have driven fifteen hundred miles to hear the Dalai Lama speak—I try to steady myself and put things in perspective. These men are in the inspiration business, after all, and, like any professionals, they're good at what they do. As Tutu had jokingly implied, a podium, a church, and a microphone are for him as a hockey stick, a net, and some ice might be for a professional Canuck. Again, the main interest of the event to some degree is the contrast in their voices: the Dalai Lama takes us into ourselves, where all the power and the responsibility (for a Buddhist) lie, delivering his words with a settled gravitas. Tutu, by comparison, carries us up and out of ourselves and to where we seem joined in a heavenly choir in what could be taken to be our rightful home.

Just one week later, though, at a small town two hours from Seattle, I happen to bump into a young teacher whom I had got to know in the basement of Christ Church Cathedral just before the ceremony for the honorary degrees. My new friend Christian gives me a copy of an article he wrote about the occasion and says, "You know, it really made a difference. As soon as I got home, I went around and introduced myself to all my neighbors. It's not, I know, like changing the world, but it's a first step, I think. I'd never done that before."

As I listen to him, I realize how little any of my ideas about celebrity and the media have to do with the days just passed. Really, what I've been thinking about was my world much more than the Dalai Lama's. A pickpocket encounters a saint, the Tibetans say, and all he sees are the other man's pockets.

IN PRIVATE

It's a bit embarrassing to have been concerned with the human problem all one's life and to find at the end that one has no more to offer by way of advice than "Try to be a little kinder."

—ALDOUS HUXLEY

THE PHILOSOPHER

I magine, for a moment, that you are a body (not difficult to do, since in part that is what you are). You have eyes, ears, legs, hands, and, if you are lucky, all of them are in good working order. You never, if you are sane, think of your finger as an independent entity (though you may occasionally say, "My toe seems to have a mind of its own"). You are never, in your right mind, moved to hit your own foot, let alone sever it; the only loser in such an exercise would be yourself.

Instead, you likely take measures to ensure that every part of your body is healthy. You clean your teeth regularly (the Dalai Lama, characteristically, pulls out a toothbrush even at ceremonial occasions and brushes away, as if everywhere were home). You exercise. You ensure that you get good sleep and try to maintain some control over what you put into your system. At some level, you strive to make sure that your right foot knows what your left is doing; if they're moving in opposite directions, you'll fall on your face.

This is all simplistic to the point of self-evidence. But when the Buddhist speaks of "interdependence" (the central Buddhist concept of *shunyata*, often rendered as "emptiness," the Dalai Lama has translated as "empty of independent identity"), all he is really saying is that we are all a part of a single body, and to think of "I" and "you," of the right hand's interests being different from the left's, makes no sense at all. It's crazy to impede your neighbor, because he is as intrinsic to your welfare as your thumb is. It's almost absurd to say you wish to get ahead of your colleague—it's like your right toe saying it longs to be ahead of the left. You can't say you wish to devastate China, because China is your right eye (and Tibet is your left); different, to be sure, unequal—one may be 20/40, one 20/20—but all part of the same mechanism, fundamentally working toward the same end. Many Buddhists have seized on cyberspace, the ecosystem, on globalism itself as merely a perfect equivalent and metaphor of how they see the world: a complexly linked worldwide web that in classic Buddhist philosophy is sometimes known as "Indra's Net."

Perhaps it's not surprising, then, that the Fourteenth Dalai Lama is famous for his laughter, the sudden eruption of seemingly helpless giggles or a high-pitched shaking of the body. Seen from the vantage point of one who meditates several hours a day, traveling to the place where everything is connected, much of our fascination with surface or with division seems truly hilarious. Quarreling over money is a little like "robbing Peter to pay Paul," in the Christian metaphor; it's like taking a ten-dollar bill out of your right-hand pocket and then, after a great deal of fanfare and contention, putting it in the left. Talking about friends and enemies is a little like holding on to this hair on your arm and claiming it as a friend, because you see it daily, and calling the hair on your back an enemy, because you never see it at all. Talking of how you are a

Buddhist and therefore opposed to the Judeo-Christian teaching is like solemnly asserting that your right nostril is the source of everything good, and your left nostril a place of evil. The doctrine of "universal responsibility" is not only universal but obvious: it's like saying that every part of us longs for our legs, our eyes, our lungs to be healthy. If one part suffers, we all do.

Simple, you may say, but "it takes more courage than we imagine," as Thomas Merton wrote, "to be perfectly simple with other men." And from this basic proposition flow many other truths, as naturally as the fact that $2 + 2 = 4$ tells you that $2 + 2 + 2 + 2 = 8$. Of course you will want to forgive others, in the same way you will want to stop punching your own side. Of course you will look in terms of the larger good, the wider perspective (the word "wider" is a favorite of the Dalai Lama's), because a hair may be cut off tomorrow, but the body as a whole can keep functioning no worse than before. There's no great need to mourn the loss of that toenail; the foot as a whole is still moving and, besides, at some point every part of the body is going to grow old and die.

This mention of an extended sense of kinship, even identity, is as global, as ecumenical, as loving your neighbor as yourself. But where Buddhism differs from other philosophies is in saying that the architect, the administrator, the guardian of this whole body is not Allah or God or the swarm of deities of the Hindu pantheon; it is a network of which we are part (that is a part of us). That is why the Buddha did not speak of "praying ceaselessly," as Saint Paul did, but of "striving ceaselessly." Buddhists do not (or need not) seek solutions from outside themselves, but merely awakening within; the minute we come to see that our destinies or well-being are all mutually dependent, they say, the rest naturally follows (meditation sometimes seems the way we come to this perception, reasoning the way we consolidate it).

If you believe this, human life offers you many more belly laughs daily, as the Dalai Lama exemplifies. Why run around the world, to Lourdes or Tuscany or Tibet, when in truth the source of all your power, your answers, lies right here, inside yourself? Why give yourself a hard time and proclaim your own worthlessness when in fact the keys for transformation are within? Why despair, indeed, when you can change the world at any moment by choosing to see that the person who gave your last book a bad review is as intrinsic to your well-being as your right ear is?

To understand the Dalai Lama, or any serious, full-time follower of the Buddha, especially if (as in my case) you come from some other tradition, perhaps it's most useful to see him as a doctor of the soul. The Buddha always stressed that he was more physician than metaphysician; when you find an arrow sticking out of the side of your body, he famously said, you don't argue about where it came from or which craftsman fashioned it—you simply pull it out.

A practical, immediate cure for suffering and ignorance is what he offered; when asked about the existence of the soul or other lofty philosophical questions, the Buddha customarily said nothing, as if to suggest that such disquisitions were beside the point when a patient was lying on his deathbed and you had the chance to help him. As Somerset Maugham, the onetime medical student and lifelong traveler who had a rare gift for entering other characters, put it, the Buddha "made only the claim of the physician that you should give him a trial and judge him by the results."

The Dalai Lama, always so faithful to his source, often uses the image of medicine, as he did when receiving his honorary doctorate at Christ Church Cathedral in Vancouver, and tells people that there is no "right" religion for anyone, though some find Buddhism helpful, some Christianity, the way some patients choose radiation therapy, some chemotherapy, and some, perhaps, Chinese herbs.

Besides, as he told an interviewer in 1989, "we have enough religions. Enough religions, but not enough real human beings. . . .
Don't let us talk too much of religion. Let us talk of what is
human."

Like any doctor, he's not concerned with pressing on strangers
his view of the universe; the important thing is diagnosing what
the problem is and suggesting a possible cure. If there's no problem, then, as he often says, he can go home; there's no need of a
house call. Ideally, he prescribes the kind of preventive medicine
that might be called meditation or philosophical training. But,
however charming or lovable or intelligent he is, a doctor's presence is only as good, really, as his ability to heal our pain.

If someone asks the Dalai Lama about a problem in her sexual
life, he is likely to say, as many a doctor might, "That's out of my
domain. You'll have to consult a specialist." If he is about to join in
a discussion with an abbot in Nara and he spots a girl sitting in a
wheelchair nearby, he will instantly break from his discussion the
way a physician, if suddenly there is a car crash outside, will leave
his dinner companions and see if he can be of help. Though trained
in the technical and complicated history and implications of dis-
ease, his job is to take that recondite learning and translate it into
simple, concrete instruction for his patients. The most important
thing we ask of a doctor is that he not hide the truth from us, out
of kindness or sympathy, not dress it up in euphemisms or
periphrases, but just tell it to us straight, so we know where we
stand.

A doctor is not presumed to be all-powerful. He has a private
life, we know, and though his part in our life is to give us the fruits
of his specialized training, we do not expect him to be an expert
when it comes to playing tennis or taking photographs or being a
father. "If you have come here with expectations of the Dalai

Lama," I heard the Dalai Lama say before a large public audience in Switzerland, "you're likely to be disappointed. If you think the Dalai Lama has special powers, you're wrong, unfortunately. If I had healing powers"—he broke into a series of coughs—"I wouldn't have this sore throat right now." A doctor has sides of his life that are not covered by his training, but at some level every doctor is on twenty-four-hour call for life.

Like any doctor, the Dalai Lama tries to remain abreast of all the latest discoveries and breakthroughs in the field, and travels constantly to interfaith meetings and labs around the world. Often, even on social occasions, he is asked for his advice—as we, when meeting a doctor, may say, "I'm sorry to bother you, but my cousin's wife has this pain . . ."—and he has to be careful not to offer advice in those fields where he's not qualified. To a physician who takes seriously the Hippocratic oath, the notion of a celebrity doctor is a little comical. He may have a good bedside manner, he may be called in on TV shows as a pundit, he may have published many books, but all he is doing, really, is applying a knowledge that is universal, outside of him, and available to anyone who works in the same field. When he retires, another doctor comes along and, generally, offers us the same diagnoses and prescriptions (not least because medicine is an objective science where diagnoses are arrived at through empirical tests, records of famous cases, and statistical probability).

Most of all, a doctor has to be clear-eyed; he cannot avert death forever—sooner or later he will lose many of his patients—and all he can do is to try to ensure that every day is spent as fruitfully, as happily as possible. He doesn't care, ideally, whether his patient is a backpacker or a head of state (the diagnosis is the same); and he isn't concerned about surface issues (asked how he feels about discos around the Potala Palace, the Dalai Lama always answers, instantly, "No problem"). The words he will use—and this, too, perhaps sounds familiar—are "beneficial," "useful," and "positive effect," generally qualified by the wise disclaimer "generally."

One day I was talking to the Dalai Lama about his ceaseless traveling around the world meeting with politicians (the most frustrating part of his job, he said, because "the problem is so big that even if these leaders sincerely want to help, they cannot do anything," and yet not to meet with them was to achieve nothing at all). "To me," he said, "I treat every human being, whether high officials or beggars—no differences, no distinctions.

"But newsmen, reporters," he went on, maybe because he was speaking to one at the time, "always ask. They consider whether I meet the prime minister or not the most important issue! At some point, I get quite fed up. I am Buddhist monk, I am a follower of Buddha. From that viewpoint, it's nothing important. It's much more important, one simple, innocent, sincere spiritual seeker—that's more important than a politician or a prime minister.

"So," he said, of newsmen, "I feel it is a reflection of their own mental attitude. These reporters, usually they consider politics as something most important in their mind. So meeting with a politician becomes very significant." For himself, "meeting with public, ordinary people, at least there's some contribution for peace of mind, for deeper awareness about the value of human life. When I see some result, then I really feel, 'Today I did some small contribution.' "

On a recent trip to South Africa, he said, he had met Nelson Mandela and a man regarded as the mentor of Mandela, in Soweto. He wanted to visit a typical home in Soweto but understood it might not be easy, so he waited in a car while an official found a home that was interested in meeting a visitor from Tibet.

One such house was found, "and it was really a human family, a human home: very friendly, very clear. Very innocent. I asked about their livelihood, their difficulties, their education—everything. And also the murders, the crime. Then later one person joined, I think better-educated, and he expressed to me sadly that they feel—the South African black person—that the potential of their intelligence is inferior to that of the white. Then I really felt sad.

"And then I argued, or explained, 'This is a wrong concept. You should not feel like that. All human beings have the same potential, the same potential of intelligence. Here we need self-confidence.' Now, I explained, the main thing about my own situation is that the Chinese attitude to Tibet—they always look down on Tibet as inferior, backward. But when we Tibetans have the opportunity, we even carry better than Chinese. So there's no basis to believe you're inferior.

"And then, after a lengthy explanation, all his face changed. Then, with a tear, he told me now he believed what I said. 'Now my attitude has changed.' He feels more confidence, he told me. And I really feel a great sense of achievement: one person, one simple person, in his late thirties, I think. Till that day, deep down he feels, 'We are poor, we are inferior, we have less potential.' With this kind of mental attitude, there's no chance of making competition. And without competition, you can't progress. And I think genuine mutual trust must be built on the basis of both sides' self-confidence. Without that, if one feels inferior, how can you develop mutual trust? Very difficult.

"So, therefore, after changing his mind, I really felt, 'Now I made one contribution.' "

To recall that the Dalai Lama is, as much as anything, a man trained to heal specific infirmities (of ignorance and the suffering that arises out of it) is to recall that the man himself is not all-important: he stands for a body of teaching that can be advanced and applied by many other hands; he stands, most of all, for the sense that each of us can play a significant part in healing ourselves. A doctor's paradoxical wisdom, often, is to make himself redundant; do thirty minutes on a treadmill, he says, eat salmon and avoid fatty foods, have an apple every day, and all being well, you won't have to see me again. Indeed, in the Buddhist context, a doctor (of philosophy, say) is not just telling people that they can heal themselves but also reminding them that, if they wish, they can read the medical textbooks themselves, and go to the source of all knowledge about the self. The wisdom being imparted has little to do with the mortal, fallible being who's imparting it, and, indeed, the more it has to do with him, the less reliable it is.

Many of the great doctors in history have distinguished themselves and come to inspired diagnoses in part by seeing the connectedness of things, the way a problem in the head may affect the performance of the body, or how what you put in your mouth can alter the acid in your stomach. The body is a single organism in which one push here may have a strong effect there. So it is, too, the Dalai Lama says, with the world—and our very concerns about it are all intertwined, impossible to solve separately. It's no good offering people peace, he suggests, if those same people lack food and water; and it's no good offering them food and water if our forests and rivers are polluted. It's no good, even, to clean up our environment if we're still polluted within. In short, the solution to all our problems, economic, environmental, political, spiritual, can only be addressed by going back to fundamentals, the change of attitude that can create a change in everything the attitude inspects. Reforms on the surface make no difference whatsoever.

This stress on the powers within us is part of what makes

Buddhism so hopeful, even if some observers, noting only the absence of God from its worldview and the mention of suffering (or, as it has been better translated, "discontent"), call it "fatalistic" or pessimistic. After all, it's hard to change others, but nearly always possible to change ourselves. It's all in our head, as a doctor might say, though in this case "it" refers not only to a problem, an illusion, but also, as a sequel, to a possibility, an ability to cut through illusions. "In a sense, a religious practitioner is actually a soldier engaged in conflict," the Dalai Lama said at a New Jersey monastery on one of his first trips to America. But the practitioner's enemies are "internal ones. Ignorance, anger, attachment and pride." The devil, as many Christians note, is not something outside of us.

Indeed, the beauty of Buddhism, as the Dalai Lama might see it, is precisely that it is not exclusive or rarefied; much of what it is showing us is exactly what people throughout the centuries have told us, whether they call themselves Vedantists or Muslims or nothing at all. "They that be whole need not a physician," as Jesus famously says in Matthew 9:12. Epictetus told us, centuries ago, that it is not pain that undoes us but our response to it, the way we let it keep lingering in the mind. Confucius, an exact contemporary of the Buddha, spoke in exactly the same terms as the Buddha about the virtue of moderation, the need for detachment in a world of constant change, the truth of interdependence, and the way we must care for the larger whole. Gandhi himself, a Hindu sometimes described as a "Christian Muhammadan," said that his mission was not "to deliver people from difficult situations" but, rather, to show that "every man or woman, however weak in body, is the guardian of his or her self-respect and liberty." To call these truths Buddhist, the Dalai Lama is often quick to imply, is as strange as calling the law of gravity Christian just because it happened to have been formulated by the Christian named Isaac Newton.

◎

I puzzled all this out, the way I might once have tried to unriddle a complicated mathematical equation, and felt that I was coming at last to a beginner's (and outsider's) view of how Buddhism made sense. And then—quite fatally—I went to see Ngari Rinpoche, the Dalai Lama's younger brother, again, and all the understandings I'd come to were just a source of mirth to him.

"We're really such a tiny speck in the universe," I pronounced as we sat out on his terrace in the spring sunshine, overlooking miles and miles of the Kangra Valley receding down below. "Hardly more than a wisp of smoke." Secretly, I was proud of myself; I'd begun to grasp something of the Buddhist distinction between the false self, which we construct, and the true self, which is just a stream of energy within a network of such streams. I put down the book on self, reality, and reason in Tibetan Buddhism he'd lent me the previous week, to show him that I'd read it.

"Why?" he said, almost jumping out of his chair. "Are you telling me I should be a vegetable—like some Zen meditators in Japan? We need some conceptual thought, if only as a monitor to keep ourselves honest."

"Another person, you mean?"

"Surveillance." He stopped for a moment. "Something to watch over the mind that's investigating itself."

I didn't say anything in return; he'd caught me off guard, just as I thought I'd got my head around an elusive truth.

"Look at it the other way," he said calmly, as if laying down a law. "Perhaps we are the center of the universe. The problem if you see yourself as a speck is that you lose all self-esteem."

I thought of the Dalai Lama's heartfelt story about the man in Soweto; I thought, too, of the Tibetans all around me, who regularly said that they were nothing and should leave all power in the hands of the Dalai Lama.

"If you are proud and likely to argue," he said, "then you need to realize that the self is nothing. If you are lacking in self-esteem, then you have to think about your potential, how much power you have inside yourself."

The phrase one always heard around Dharamsala was "Middle Way," in deference to the Buddha's guiding principle of walking along the road at the center, not veering toward extremes. As the *Diamond Sutra* put it, in what sounds like an affirmation of perpetual mobility, "The bodhisattva develops a mind that alights nowhere."

"Someone's got to blow the whistle," he continued, as we looked out over the valley. "People don't like me because I rock the boat. I'm argumentative. But our people need to be challenged, to think harder."

"Not only your people." He was doing the same with me, I thought, reminding me of the grooves and assumptions I fell into, then trying to wake me up as I wandered into his philosophy.

"There's no larger force out there," he went on.

"What about karma? Isn't that supposed to be a process that's larger than us and works through us?"

For a long moment Ngari Rinpoche was silent; like anyone who enjoys a good argument or fight, he happily conceded when a point hit home. And whenever anyone came to him with a problem—I remembered him listening in rapt attention to Hiroko the evening of the storm—he became a doctor again, leaning forward in evident sympathy.

Most days in Dharamsala, when I strolled across the busy intersection at the bottom of the slope outside my guesthouse and walked into the central temple, I stumbled into a scene out of classical Tibet. On every side, the shady courtyard between the temple and the Dalai Lama's house, the main walkway, the parapets looking over the valley, the stone steps leading up to the temple were crowded with young monks, their red robes turning the scene into a garden of questions. They were standing in clusters of three or four, and sometimes in pairs, under a tree, against a wall, in the part of the temple where a painting of the Potala Palace hangs. And everywhere what looked to be a furious fight was going on.

One monk would be standing above another and, every few moments, he would lunge forward, striking his left palm against his right in a thunderclap as he shouted some machine-gun sentence at the other. The one sitting on the ground would remain completely unperturbed and answer quietly, as if literally unmoved by the challenge. The standing monk would come at him again and again and again, with one shotgun question or assertion after another—"If matter is immaterial, how does anything die?" "If you say, 'I don't trust the mind,' what is this 'I' that's separate from the mind?"—and the other would sit where he was, offering some words in response. Then he might get up and they would change places.

These daily sessions were, I learned, the equivalent of homework for the monks being instructed in the monastery or the Institute of Buddhist Dialectics, ways of at once training them in the central Tibetan art of debate and of refining, deepening, challenging their grasp of basic philosophical questions. It was a peaceful form of armed confrontation—mind-to-mind combat, you might say—and corresponded in its way to the in-your-face flourishes and trash-talking of the games of basketball the monks often played on the other side of the valley, dribbling behind their backs while taunting their opponents, or harassing them constantly on defense. It also, I noticed, made each novice a master of both still-ness and movement.

In the eighth century, the book Ngari Rinpoche had lent me explained, Tibetan Buddhism came to a crossroads that reflected, in a way, its difficult geographical position: should it follow China (the Chan tradition of Buddhism, which would later go to Japan and become Zen, stressing meditation and a kind of no-nonsense this-worldliness) or should it follow the giant on the other side of it, India (a more philosophical, metaphysical approach)? A great public debate was held in Tibet's first Buddhist monastery, at Samye, from 792 to 794, and after the Indian tradition won the debate, Tibetan Buddhists took the leading philosophers of India's Nalanda University as their teachers, many of them embarking upon a full-time pursuit of logic and reasoning, a little, perhaps, as Jesuits do in the West. Within Tibetan Buddhism, the Nyingma and Kagyu schools incline more toward meditation and mysticism, but the Gelug school, to which the Dalai Lama belongs, is firmly rooted in debate and scholarship. I remembered how the one time the Dalai Lama had contradicted his translator in Vancouver was when the eloquent younger philosopher had used the word "con-versations" and the Dalai Lama had broken in with "Dialogues!"

This tradition of debating had always struck me as Tibetan Bud-dhism's way of keeping itself honest and on its toes, alert to every challenge, not hardened into dogma or a sense of certainty. One of the powers of Catholicism, to an outsider like myself, was how fearlessly its more thoughtful practitioners give life and flesh to everything that unsettles us: Graham Greene chose to center his stories around frightened, lonely men who are asked suddenly to act better than they are; the rock band U2 gives drama to its inter-est in a life of conscience by actually pantomiming onstage the appearance of a devil and all that tempts us toward glamour or wealth or pride. Flannery O'Connor dreamed up a character who shows his interest in Jesus by denying the existence of Jesus, and Martin Scorsese serves up movies that examine a life of clarity and direction through its absence and plunge us into a counterworld ruled by Milton's Satan, to give flesh to his belief, as one character says, that "you don't make up for your sins in church. You do it in the streets."

Tibetan Buddhism's equivalent to all this is the ritual of debating, which so thoroughly becomes second nature in its practitioners that every time I spoke to either the Dalai Lama or Ngari Rinpoche, I heard them say, "Look at it from the other side" or "If you believe this, what about this?" (the opposite of a profound truth, as Niels Bohr once said, is another profound truth). The Dalai Lama, in fact, is said most to enjoy those sessions where he gets together with advanced monks and takes them on in hardcore dialectics. He will offer a reading of a classical text and then invite the others to hammer away at it; or he will ask one of them to offer an interpretation and then will lavish criticisms from his own position. More than just a way of sharpening the instrument that is the mind, and learning how to defend one's positions, it is a way of moving in the world in a flexible, unbiased way.

The most passionate and articulate dissident in Dharamsala once told me, over tea on a sunny lawn in the spring, that he had actually, when young, been offered a scholarship to go and study (of all things) medicine in America. As a young man of conviction and rebellious tendencies, though, he wanted to join the CIA-trained guerrillas then fighting for Tibet.

He went to see the Dalai Lama to inform him of his choice, and, he told me, his leader was furious that he would give up the chance to acquire useful training (and, besides, imperil the chance for future Tibetans to get such scholarships abroad). "I think I can help

Tibet more by seeing the people and culture I am struggling for," the rebel said, not one to bow down. Instantly, in his telling, the Dalai Lama relented: since there was a conclusively thought-out position behind the decision, he would respect it.

This training in reasoning (which is, really, a training in cutting through externals and going back to a first cause, the founding principle from which everything else follows) explains, perhaps, the speed with which certain Buddhists slash through almost everything to what they see as essential. All the money in the world cannot deal with mental disturbances, the Dalai Lama has said, in suggesting why there is some value in exploring our inner resources. Looking at the surface is only going to take you away from the cure if the problem is within.

Only a fool, a Buddhist might say, would rage at the fact that $2 + 2 = 4$; that is a principle of life that one has to accept in order to work with. And for rationalists like Tibetan Buddhists of the Gelug school, the main law of cause and effect that runs through the universe like a wheel is the one I'd mentioned to Ngari Rinpoche: karma, that elaborate, latticed form of connection, as strong as Newton's laws, that stretches back over lifetimes and suggests not just that everything is intertwined but that, in some way too complicated for us fully to understand, we will reap what we have sown. That is why, Tibetans believe, some children are born with AIDS, though clearly they have done nothing wrong in their lives—it is the working out of something from a past life. It is why a nun who has given her whole life to helping children is suddenly—senselessly, as it seems to us—struck down by cancer. It is why, as some see it, Tibet was abruptly overrun by China; this arose from practical mistakes (declining to join the League of Nations when an invitation was extended in the 1920s; not modernizing and building an army, as the Thirteenth Dalai Lama had suggested;

remaining too isolated), but it might also have sprung from causes
and conditions too intricate for most of us to follow. In William
James's terms, we are like dogs barking at the injustice of the universe when our keeper goes out, to buy us some more food.

The Gospels, revealingly, tell us little of Jesus's spiritual formation and concentrate mostly on his words and actions. The Buddha
story, by comparison, places most of its emphasis on how Siddhartha came to enlightenment—the process (which anyone can
follow, even today, in principle)—while the particular details of his
subsequent teachings and wanderings are often barely mentioned.
Even non-Christians may know some of Jesus's words, while
typical Buddhists may know hardly any of Buddha's specific discourses. Buddha is a precedent more than a prophet; and where
Jesus came to earth as the way, the truth, and the life, the Buddha
came to suggest that the way is up to us, the "truth" is often imper-
manent, and the light comes and goes, comes and goes, until we
have found something changeless within.

Around the temple, meanwhile, and the Dalai Lama's house, there
were lepers permanently gathered and a blind man wailing, a
small boy by his side as if to protect him. As soon as I walked
toward the courtyard where the debating was taking place, men
with no arms came up to me, and others whose growth had been
stunted, while women taking shelter under the roof of their saris
cried, "*Namaste!* Sir, sir!" As across all of India—though here there
were more importunities, because of the large proportion of foreign tourists and of Tibetans who believe they gain merit by giving
things away—women and their babies, next to ancient-looking
men in rags, were assembled in straggly groups along the side of
the road, feeding their tiny fires after dark, and, when the rain

came down, trying to keep themselves dry or warm under the awnings of precarious houses. In places like Dharamsala, talk of healing and suffering, questions about justice and why people had to bear such burdens, were never entirely academic.

The Dalai Lama, then, follows the teachings of the Buddha as faithfully and carefully as a doctor follows *Gray's Anatomy.* When his younger sister lost her husband in a car crash, he offered her constant support and comfort, she records in her memoirs, but he also told her, as many a Buddhist monk might, to remember that she was not alone in the world, death, perhaps, being the sort of event that joins us with others at least as much as it separates. Of losing his homeland, he says, as mentioned, "It is not the time to pretend things are beautiful. That's something. You feel involved with reality," sounding a little like a physician who refuses to dress up a diagnosis (our very lives, some Buddhists say, are akin to a burning house). And even when, sometimes, he talks somewhat sorrowfully about all the expectations brought to him by his people, he is, like his forebear at times, perhaps, a doctor in a war zone wondering how expectation can deal with problems that can only be solved within.

All this, though, is only what the job demands: all Buddhist priests, and certainly all thirteen Dalai Lamas before him, have had to deal with their flocks in this way. What makes the present incarnation unique—again, what gives him a new fascination and fresh potential across the globe—is that in bringing his teachings to foreign cultures, the Fourteenth Dalai Lama is doing most of his instruction in translation, as it were, to people who know next to nothing of his tradition, and so it becomes doubly important to leave complexity behind and try to speak to and for some universal concern. He is a doctor, to continue the analogy, addressing a classroom of schoolchildren, in a language not his own, about issues that are to him of life-and-death importance. It's no surprise that much of what the children hear (I think of the reporter in Vancouver and his understandable disappointment) sounds like childishness.

Very soon after the Dalai Lama began traveling to the West, he saw, as earlier noted, that he achieved little by giving the sorts of highly technical lectures on epistemology and metaphysics he delivered in 1979. The Buddha himself was acclaimed for his "skillful means" and, especially, for his ability to talk to those who did not know or even, perhaps, distrusted his teachings (finding the right way, for example, to cool down parents upset that they had lost their children to him). Thus the Fourteenth Dalai Lama slowly shifted toward delivering lectures on "basic human values," as he puts it, that could be of use to anyone who listened and equipped listeners not with new theories but with practical measures for everyday life. These fundamentals—that anger backfires against the one who feels it, that kindness helps us if only by making us feel better, that ignoring another's perspective is to create problems for yourself in the long run—are as basic, to the Buddhist, as the earth's being 93 million miles from the sun. Every culture has its own words for the figures, even its own symbols, but the law universally applies.

Even now, when I attend his annual teachings in Dharamsala (or at other places around the world), all I can hear through my headphones is translated talk of how the self may not exist, or may *not* not exist, as apprehensible to me as the numbered propositions of Wittgenstein might be. Yet as soon as the same speaker is addressing a general audience, a few hours later, he translates himself into a breathing clarity whose simple precepts (universal, and delivered now in English) are given weight and authority in part by the bearing of the person who's delivering them. "There is no need for temples," he characteristically says, "no need for complicated philosophy. One's own mind, one's own heart, is our temple."

In his typically coruscating late novel *Magic Seeds,* V. S. Naipaul sends his confused hybrid hero, W. Somerset Chandran, the drifting son of a self-styled Hindu wise man, an Indian Maugham perhaps, into the jungle to become a revolutionary and then into prison to enjoy the revolutionary's fate. In prison, Willie is greeted by a sign saying, HATE SIN NOT THE SINNER, which, ever mixed up, he doesn't know whether to ascribe to Gandhi or the Gospels. Later he meets other such slogans on the wall: "Truth always wins" and "Anger is a man's greatest enemy." Placebos of sorts, we are made to understand, that are no more substantial than the revolutionaries' slogans, used only to try to make the prisoners feel better. "To do good is the greatest religion," "Non-violence is the greatest of all religions."

All these "pieties," as Naipaul calls them, are in fact not so different from statements of the Dalai Lama's that are disseminated across the world—bromides, as it may seem, that tell people no more than any Golden Rule or Boy Scout's manual might. The Dalai Lama knows, of course, that life is more complicated than such sentences, knows (to revert to the image of the body) that sometimes we do have to rely on one extremity more than another (as when we're standing on tiptoe), knows that sometimes there are genuine differences between the parts (the mind hungry for the spicy Thai curry that the stomach distrusts). The little apothegms of his that get marketed on buttons and bumper stickers make no more sense than a single thread taken out of a Persian carpet, an intricate web, and pronounced to be beautiful. When once I mentioned a celebrated text on "The Paradox of the Age"

found on T-shirts and posters everywhere (even in Tibetan temples), one of the man's longtime translators could barely contain
his impatience. "It's nonsense!" he roared. "All these things you see
ascribed to him, others are just making up!"

Yet the Dalai Lama, like anyone bringing a gift to a host,
sees that it makes sense to bring only those things that the
other person can use. Complex, technical Buddhism is of no value
to typical non-Buddhists or beginners; indeed, it can take them
away from the task at hand. People may get so caught up in the
issue of whether mind exists that they ignore the hungry person
knocking at their door. Nobel physicists in my hometown sometimes visit junior high school classrooms, and their intelligence
there is measured not by how brilliantly they talk but by how
simply.

The Dalai Lama, in any case, is not saying, "All you need is love,"
and if he were, his own life would remind him of the inadequacy of
mere good intentions. Tibetan temples do not swarm with wrathful
deities for nothing, and even when one is told that the triumphal
dances of skull-headed ghosts across their walls represent only the
victory over ignorance and delusion, one cannot soon erase the
images of violence. As Abraham Joshua Heschel, who constantly
explored the paradoxes of the spiritual life through the twentieth
century, has it, life is often war, and "a war which cannot be won by
the noble magic of merely remembering a golden rule." Reason, for
Heschel, "is a lonely stranger in the soul, while the irrational forces
feel at home and are always in the majority. Why bear hardship on
behalf of virtue?"

I noticed, as I followed the Dalai Lama around, that he often got
dismissed when he spoke in English, in compressed and simple
terms, by people who had come expecting fireworks; and yet, con-
versely, when he took to the high road, in Tibetan, with intricate

philosophical arguments worthy, as one Christian professor told me, of Aquinas, he generally got ignored. In six weeks of being in Dharamsala during one spring of daily teachings, I heard only two people talk about what the Dalai Lama was saying; the rest spoke more generally, as Tibetans might, of "presence" and warmth and goodness. Often, the easiest thing was to say that he spoke just with his person, his actions, making sure the old man at the back of the room was given a place to sit, cheerfully putting on an extremely unflattering orange-visored baseball cap while talking on "Stages of the Path," as if to make himself seem less exalted or remote.

For myself, as someone born in the West and trained in some of the higher universities of skepticism, I often found it very difficult to follow the philosophical complexities that were his bread and butter. But as I looked around me in the streets of Dharamsala, or traveling to Yemen, to Bolivia, I sometimes did begin to see that discontent was the only reality we knew, and such possibility as we found would have to come out of it. As I sat at my desk, day after day, I really did find that everything was a product of my inner weather, the page that seemed so radiant yesterday looking dead and lusterless today. And as I thought about how I might better get on with the people I knew, my circumstances, I saw that everything really did depend on how I looked at it: call someone a friend, or turn to her better side rather than her lesser, and something useful might result.

One day, a little like my new friend Christian, I noticed that in the midst of a long disquisition on Tibetan history, the spiritual and temporal leader of the Tibetans had caught (before I did) the fact that my cup of tea was empty. I recalled that the person who had most vehemently challenged the prices charged for a Dalai Lama teaching was, in fact, the Dalai Lama. And I remembered that it was he who had once brought up to me the instance of his endorsing the later deranged Japanese cult leader Shoko Asahara—which was proof, he said, that "I'm not a 'Living Buddha'!" Something changed in me each time I left his company, even as I was telling my friends, heatedly, that humans never really change.

Below what we think we are
we are something else,
we are almost anything.

— D. H. LAWRENCE

THE MYSTERY

One day in Dharamsala, I woke up and went out while it was still dark. Dogs were running up and down the settlement's muddy gullies and steep slopes, and along the narrow mountain road that winds down toward the valley figures could be seen moving quickly in clusters—Tibetans, I soon saw, loaded down with white scarves, and the outlines of monks. I followed them down through the darkness to the scramble of largely dilapidated buildings that mark the government in exile and its library—"Voice of Tibet (Voice for the Voiceless)," said one door, and "Tibetan Torture Survivors' Program," said another. Then I was at a small temple, between the yellow-walled library and the valley below, where a long line of mostly ragged pilgrims was snaking around the outside corridors.

I could have been in Tibet again, so unglossy and atavistic was the scene: toothless old men in cowboy hats made for the high plateaus, and women whose eyes seemed innocent of towns, unused to being in any buildings save ones like this. The long, winding trail of petitioners and nomads grew longer every second, while the blue-black sky across the valley began to pale, and the youngest monks of the temple, boys of seven or eight, began laboring past, carrying huge gray buckets and great swinging kettles, out of which they dispensed cups of Tibetan tea and clumps of rice.

Very promptly, at a few minutes before seven a.m., the large, gold-studded red doors of the temple swung back and the few foreigners in attendance (and almost no Tibetans, for some reason) were let into a small chapel, thick with the smell of melted butter and the usual, everyday furnishings of incense sticks protruding from cans of Coke and Fanta bottles. Maybe eighty or so in all pushed into the close space—the president of Kalmykia and his entourage seated cross-legged at the front—and only one Tibetan couple joined us, as wild-eyed and raw as the others. Very soon—I couldn't help but notice—the woman was howling, rolling her eyes around and falling about in convulsions, while her husband, seemingly unconcerned, sat by her side as if this happened every day.

At the stroke of seven—things weren't always so punctual in Dharamsala—a side door opened and one of the temple's monks came out, with a few others in attendance. He looked to be an unusually mild and gentle sort. He stood beside the raised throne at the center—everyone was silent—and as he did, three attendants started affixing to his body layers of clothing, covered by a rich gold silk brocade, and attaching to his chest a circular mirrored breastplate, ringed with pieces of amethyst and turquoise. A silver quiver followed, and a three-foot-long silver sheath and sword; then a kind of harness, seventy pounds in weight (I would later learn), was placed on him, and a huge headpiece weighing thirty more pounds. The unwieldy figure—less a man, he now seemed, than a piece of walking regalia—was placed on the throne and strapped in, as it appeared: the odd impression was of an astronaut being prepared for a long and dangerous journey, less into outer than into inner space.

Then nothing happened. The quiet-faced monk sat where he was, absolutely still, his eyes closed, and for ten minutes or more— the whole room was silent—you could almost see him descend into himself. It was like nothing I had ever witnessed, as if we were watching him go down and down, into the inner reaches of the well that was his soul. It was as if he was gathering himself, collecting force, and disappearing before our eyes as he returned to whomever he was beneath the surface.

Then, without warning, the strange figure jerked back. He started moving of his own accord, convulsively; three monks raced in to grab and steady him, and he lurched to his feet and began shaking back and forth. The terrible, implausible impression was of a child in a tantrum, his face crumpled as if a balloon had been punctured. The lips and eyes were misshapen, so it looked as if he were sobbing after being denied a favorite treat. Then the figure began moving around spasmodically and jets of water issued violently from his mouth, the attendants dabbing his cheeks clean while the huge, barricaded presence shook himself out of their control.

The Tibetan woman who had been falling back onto the hard floor as if in a faint and shaking her head furiously was now reaching new levels of transport, rolling her head around and letting out bloodcurdling shrieks, audibly becoming someone else as the state oracle was set again on his throne and people began lining up to jostle past him and receive a blessing from the shuddering form. The hysterical woman was the first to come before him—was she possessed? was this a kind of fit?—and then the whole crowd pressed forward, every person extending a white scarf toward the figure on the throne and lingering for a moment or two before the clenched, puffing face, out of which still came jets of spit. Some-how, in his derangement, the man offered reflexive blessings to each white scarf that went past, and dropped little handfuls of brown seeds into every passing hand; then he stood up again, abruptly, and clattered through the hall, out onto the sunny out-door terrace, where he sat down on his transported throne, in full view now of the great assembly of Tibetans, and began muttering words as bodies pushed and shoved about him.

The other monks took up positions around his seat, two crowd-ing very close to relay what he was saying, while a third stood at attention and scribbled furiously, covering page after small page. The dictation seemed to go on and on, for ten minutes or more, and then, suddenly, the great caparisoned group stumbled back into the chapel and the great doors closed behind them. Whatever the deity who oversees Tibet wanted to convey through his human medium had been delivered.

The Dalai Lama uses his oracles (of which the most prominent is Nechung, whose trance we had just witnessed) as he might his left hand, he says, and he uses his Cabinet as he might his right, bal-ancing visible and invisible worlds—the conscious and the sub-conscious realm—much as the Middle Way would suggest (though he also admits that he regards the medium who speaks for Tibet's protector deity as his "upper house" and his regular political coun-selors as his "lower," perhaps because the oracle speaks for a wis-dom that is beyond the human, and beyond the reach of human meddling. It was Nechung, after all, who told him when he was only fifteen that he had to assume temporal power early, as the Chinese advanced into Tibet; and it was Nechung who told him in 1959 that he had to flee Lhasa—and gave him the route to do so—that very night). The Dalai Lama stresses that the oracle is in fact a

healer and a protector, something more than just a spirit that can
divine the future, but the fact remains that the spirit clearly lives in
a domain very different from that of the lucid, analytical, doctor's
logic that marks the Dalai Lama's mass public talks around the
world.

Like any being, Tibetan Buddhism has a daylight and a night-
time side, a part that belongs in the public, visible world and a part
that belongs to the realm of dreams and premonitions and everything that exists outside the conscious mind. Most of us associate
the Dalai Lama with the daytime—waking up before it is light and
going to sleep soon after the sun goes down—but when he sleeps,
he readily admits, he enters a different part of his practice, one that
reaches even into his dreams. As I watched him carry Tibet and its
form of Buddhism around the world, I noticed that he always
stressed the New Testament side of the tradition, as it were, more
than the Old, downplaying the complexities that Heschel described and Job lived out in favor of more elementary and practical
principles. He tended to shield the wider world from the esoteric
side of Tibetan Buddhism the way one might keep a loaded gun
in a locked cabinet, so the kids don't start to play with it and it
doesn't fall into the wrong hands. But that did not change the fact
that this more mysterious, nonrational side—the part that existed
beyond the realm of mathematical formulas—remained as intrinsic to his practice as logic and debating; you have only to look at
any Tibetan temple wall or *thangka,* swarming with skull-headed
beings riding monsters, and copulating deities (the female figure
milky white, the male more dark), or look at the mandalas nearby
in which all visible and invisible worlds are distilled into a single
mystical diagram, to realize that Tibetan Buddhism has taken the
nonanalytical side of the tradition, as well as the analytical, to some
of its richest extremes.

One of the conundrums I watched the Dalai Lama face as he

traveled around the world was the fact that it was this explosive, esoteric, specialized side of Tibetan Buddhism—full of the "magic and mystery" of which such explorers as Alexandra David-Neel excitedly wrote—that has long been the main source of fascination to outsiders; those who are turning away from the Sunday School traditions of their own faiths do not want to give them up just to receive Sunday School wisdom from Tibet (or, in fact, to receive talk of analytical scholarship and scientific rigor and hard work, as the Dalai Lama stresses). The Dalai Lama carefully unfolded across the globe principles for selflessness and compassion, examples of responsibility drawn from the Buddhist notion of interconnected-ness and an emphasis on practicing humanity, as it were, without having to think constantly about religious rites and scriptures. But what many a foreigner in his audience wanted (and perhaps saw, whether he provided it or not) was fire and smoke.

I once went to my local university library to read up on Tibetan Buddhism, and, not to my surprise, the shelves were crowded with books with titles like *Civilized Shamans, Oracles and Gods of Tibet,* and *Travellers in Space;* over and over they served up what could be called the spiritual side of the fairy-tale Tibet we've Orientalized for so long, which can be seen as a faraway monk with his back turned to the world, developing inner strengths and charting an interior landscape—the geography of the mind—while the explor-ers of Queen Victoria were searching for the source of the Nile and mapping the canyons of Afghanistan. And certainly Tibet, like any person who spends a lot of time alone, seemed to have plumbed its inner resources, examined its mind and its dreams, so intensively that the result was what could look to the outsider like genius or madness or, most likely, a confounding mixture of the two.

Even seven centuries ago, Marco Polo was entertaining his read-ers in Venice by writing of Tibetan lamas who made a khan's cup rise to his lips, and even in the last century David-Neel was electrifying audiences by writing of monks keeping themselves warm on the icy Himalayan plateau just through the strength of their meditation, or running for two hundred miles at a stretch while in a trance. The very uniqueness of the school of Buddhism that Tibet had taken to its highest pitch—Vajrayana, or the "Thunderbolt Vehicle"—lay in its extraordinary claim that if you were able to master certain extremely advanced and secret techniques, you could actually attain enlightenment in a single lifetime.

The Dalai Lama always spoke of daily practice, on and on through lifetimes, of not expecting rewards for millions of incarnations, of not looking for the bright lights and instant powers that some beginners hoped for in the exotic discipline; yet even he, when asked, said with characteristic directness that if you meditate for long periods every morning, you can improve your memory and "finally you can develop clairvoyance," and even he, in his second autobiography, admitted that much in Tibetan life and culture confounded his scientific mind: at one point, he reports seeing a piece of a rinpoche's skull that had somehow survived the fires of cremation (as Tibetans believe is possible) and on which was clearly visible the Tibetan character representing that rinpoche's particular protector deity. Whenever I read such sentences, it was as if the human, appreciably accessible figure I saw and touched had vanished in a second behind a closed door.

For Tibetan Buddhists, as for scientists like Michael Faraday, the world is made up not just of matter but of fields of energy, currents that for Tibetans link what they call "subtle vestures" to "gross vestures," hell realms, or the land of hungry ghosts, to the world of protective spirits and deities. To the real practitioner, to say it again, all these figures are symbolic: as the Dalai Lama stresses, the beings carrying skulls brimming over with blood, the naked figures entwined around one another, tongues alive, are just unusually graphic representations of the forces that play out inside us and, in some cases perhaps, of the forces we need to summon within to repel the lures of hatred or ignorance or greed. Yet on a remote plateau three miles above the sea, where people live huge distances from others, in a charged, almost otherworldly atmosphere where the heavens seem very, very close and each of their changes and moods has strong and distinct implications on earth, none of the iconography probably seems entirely pictorial.

That is the other element of Tibet that leads to all the books called *Out of This World* and *Dreamtime Tibet* and *Tibet the Mysterious;* due to its intense and high isolation, and because its monks and scientists of self were developing inner techniques while other countries were working on cars and airplanes, it seems to belong to an earlier time that feels to many of us like an almost preconscious memory, an ancestral wisdom that we have lost (in part through all the great technological innovations we have gained). Until very recently, and even now in places, Tibetans have lived in a domain eerily similar to that of the early Christians, amid what Gibbon called "an uninterrupted succession of miraculous powers, the gift of tongues, of vision, and of prophecy." Tibetan culture is much closer than our own to the world of Shakespeare, in which every comet or cloud formation is a direct message from the gods (and the king of the day, James I, was celebrated for his book *On Dae-monologie*); Tibetan religion keeps intact a system we nowadays associate with the ancient Greeks or Romans, in which the connection between other worlds and our own has not been broken. It was only a few centuries ago, after all, that murderers in Europe hoped to escape capture by eating meals on the bodies of those they'd killed and housebreakers stole into homes in disguise, bearing tapers made of the fingers of stillborn infants.

"Below and beyond the conscious self," as Aldous Huxley wrote, examining the eruptions of hysteria and witch burning that arose in seventeenth-century Catholic France, "lie vast ranges of subconscious activity, some worse than the ego and some better, some stupider and some, in certain respects, far more intelligent." Almost as a function of not embracing modernity till recently—and in spite of an analytical tradition that can debate philosophical abstractions with any Platonist or positivist—Tibet still seemed to have at least one foot in this other world. Its scientists of the mind speak of seventy-seven thousand chambers of the "subtle body" and eighty-four thousand "negative emotions" in the human sphere (as well as eighty-four thousand "doors of transformation"); Buddhism is always committed to reality, but reality, as Picasso reminds us, is made up not just of what we see but of all that we make of it, the dreams and impulses that arise out of it, all the ways an external, visible landscape plays out in an inner, invisible terrain. To be only rational is not, you could say, entirely reasonable.

After the great debate at Samye, in which Tibet decided to follow the philosophical Indian path more than the pragmatic and more meditation-based Chinese, and especially after Tsong Kha Pa created the Gelug school of Tibetan Buddhism in the fifteenth century, many Tibetan monks gathered in monasteries that were, among other things, great philosophical laboratories for examining and perhaps extending the ideas of Nagarjuna and Shantideva and the other seminal Buddhist philosophers. Yet equally inevitably, many other monks wandered off across the vast emptiness of the Tibetan plateau, meditated for years on end in caves, and developed spiritual faculties that belong more to the realm of religion than to pure philosophy. The Dalai Lama presents a practical Buddhism that is striking for its sanity, its balance and lucidity, its appeal to common sense as much as to the other senses; but many other Tibetan lamas, for many centuries, have practiced a much wilder and more radical kind of Buddhism that can manifest itself in what has been called "crazy wisdom," ideas and acts so far beyond the norm that most of the rest of us don't know what to make of them (and certainly lack the tools to pass any judgment on them).

Tantra, as esoteric Buddhism is sometimes called, is, according to the Dalai Lama, a very specialized and secret training for death, and the kind of inflammable practice that can be pursued only under very careful supervision and expert guidance. It takes much of what Tibetans see as belonging to the "gross" levels of mind—sex and drink and illusion—and tries to raise them to the subtle, the way, I once heard the Dalai Lama say, Ayurvedic doctors take mercury, which, untreated, works as poison, and use it as a medicine. Far from the talk of compassion and selflessness that the Dalai Lama often gives to outsiders, Tantra celebrates the dangerous fact that the human is not the humane and that transcendence, by its very nature, remains far beyond conventional notions of right and wrong. "To give up one's concept of being good," as William James put it, "is the only door to the Universe's deeper reaches." Tibet itself is said by its folklore to have emerged from the union of a bodhisattva and a demoness.

The result, as an American political scientist put it in 1979—introducing Buddhism to the New World—is that you can find in Tantrism "almost everything that is connected with the popular Western conceptions of magic. Secret teachings, scriptures in code, the practice of drawing symbols on the ground and uttering spells to call up deities, supernatural powers that could be used for good or evil." As another Western scholar calmly (and typically) describes it, you protect yourself against leprosy, or the possibility of being poisoned, in classical Tibet by visualizing a goddess and then visualizing your own body as a fat corpse. Then you imagine the goddess severing the corpse's head and throwing the skull into a container, into which are also thrown chunks of bone for another supernatural being to come and devour raw. In the high, thin air of Tibet, with the animist spirits of the traditional Bon religion still alive, the burning of effigies is common, as in many a folk tradition, and even high officials make decisions on the basis of throwing dice, casting pieces of dough up in the air, and other forms of traditional divination.

This is not so different, perhaps, from talk of a prophet who raises men from the dead, turns water into wine, and walks across the waters; in seventeenth-century France, as Huxley has it, it was regarded as a terrible form of impiety *not* to believe in witches (since not to believe in Satan, and thus the prospect of a fallen angel, was almost the same as not to believe in God, and thus the possible purity of angels). A Catholic church that still practices exorcism or the kind of faithful Christian who reports feeling his body growing warmer (sometimes uncomfortably so) when he recites the Jesus Prayer should not express surprise at this; accounts of the great Christian mystics' lives also belong to a realm of ecstasy and physical intensity that lies beyond our reason.

Yet when I watched the Dalai Lama carry his tradition, very carefully, out of its centuries of isolation and into the glare of the modern world (always stressing that he thought that his culture needed to be less solitary and in closer contact with modernity), I felt I was watching him walk across not just continents but centuries, and carrying into broad daylight some of the dusty secrets of the human family that had, as it were, been locked up in some cobwebbed chest in the attic for many centuries. When he gave advanced Tantric teachings, there often came a moment when he asked those who had not taken the appropriate vows or committed themselves seriously enough to Buddhist practice to leave, because he would be giving empowerments and initiations that could be dangerous if the right motivation was not present. As it was, he had given more Kalachakra (or Wheel of Time) initiations than all thirteen previous Dalai Lamas combined, many of them in places like Toronto, Barcelona, and Madison, Wisconsin.

In effect, he seemed to be bringing out into the world two sometimes unrelated treasures, each of them explosive: one was Tibet and its particular culture, often hard to translate into other tongues, and the other was his brand of Buddhism. To mass general audiences, he always stressed "uncrazy wisdom," as you could call it, because philosophy seemed a way to cut through all divisions to some universal human core. ("Sectarianism is poison," he writes, in an unusually violent statement in his second autobiography.) When he spoke of "Nalanda Buddhism," in honor of the ancient Buddhist university in India from which his tradition's great philosophers had emerged, he was essentially suggesting that reason and universality could offer places where Gelug practitioner and Kagyu, eastern Tibetan and central, American and Chinese could come together.

Yet at the same time he was bringing a very complex series of rites and visualization techniques and mandalas into our midst, all of which took him behind closed doors again; he traveled with certain *thangka*s and statues that clearly had esoteric value, and locked boxes that had to do with the private requirements of the Dalai Lama, not open to the gaze of scientists. More than once, when I asked him whether Tibet's recent sufferings were the result of its collective karma, he answered, "It's complicated" or "Mysterious," as if, in effect, to say that it belonged to worlds I wasn't in a position to enter or understand.

As I watched him carry all this around from Harvard to Japan, for thirty years, part of what intrigued me was seeing him almost visibly gathering evidence everywhere he went as he noticed how different parts of his teachings hit home or distracted, how they got misunderstood or in some cases distorted, and constantly adjusted his approach accordingly. He took, as the years went on, to urging more and more foreigners not to abandon their own traditions and become Buddhists (if only because he had seen by then what misunderstandings could arise); he often downplayed meditation in the West, maybe because he felt that it was one of those exciting and even exotic techniques that could take people away from their everyday responsibilities and the need for simple mindfulness and kindness. When he did talk of meditation, he always stressed the hard work involved rather than what he called "mystical gifts." He also began warning foreigners more and more against Tibetan lamas and teachers who, perhaps, were practicing a "crazy wisdom" amid newcomers who did not have a context for distinguishing craziness from wisdom. I once told Ngari Rinpoche that I'd heard that many Chinese were studying under Tibetan lamas. "They'll get disenchanted soon enough" was the Dalai Lama's younger brother's characteristically provocative response. "Unfortunately, it's often the same old story."

It was a register of his confidence and the trust he had won that the Dalai Lama seemed to feel increasingly comfortable telling foreign audiences exactly what they didn't want to hear; yet I sometimes recalled how even the Buddha, by some accounts, had not always been able to determine or affect all that was said and done in his name. For five centuries after his death, people by and large respected his wish that no images of him be created (because images take us away from his teachings and, besides, imply that he was something more than a regular human who is moving and inspiring precisely because of that humanness). When he was depicted, it was sometimes as a footstep (walking along the open road), sometimes as a tree (offering us shade—and reminding us of where he found enlightenment), sometimes even as a wheel (the wheel of Dharma teachings rolling along the Eight-Fold Path).

Yet when Buddhism reached the edges of Asia—became, you could say, the victim of its own popularity—it found its way into the hands of Greek statue makers, who started to depict the Buddha's own face (which looked strikingly similar, in their renditions, to Apollo's). Later, Chinese craftsmen added a crown to the head. By now there are so many giant Buddhas in so many temples— starting with Todaiji, in Nara, which I had visited with the Dalai Lama—that it may be hard to recall that the Buddha was speaking, more than anything, for the illusion of form and the imperma- nence of everything, not least the human figure.

"We Tibetans are not real Buddhists," Ngari Rinpoche said one morning as I took my place on his terrace and he served me tea, along with a plate of cookies. "Too many spirits, too many deities. We're always looking for something outside ourselves to come to the rescue. That's not Buddhism."

"But it's human," I replied. "You can't expect people to live with- out prayers or talismans of some kind. We may be high-minded in theory and talk of clinging to nothing at all, but in practice people need something to help them through their fears." I recalled how the Dalai Lama himself had told me that, twice, as a child he had been so frightened in the dark that he'd seen a cat jumping across the room (later, when he'd checked the cats nearby, he'd realized they were all of a different color).

"But that's not Buddhism. I think there should be a police force to go into all these organizations, all the Tibetan centers around the world, and take care of the ones who are encouraging this." I could see from his smile what was coming next. "And I would like to be the one to volunteer for the job!"

He broke into a huge, infectious explosion of laughter that set his body shaking—the very laugh that his older brother had made famous around the world. Tibetan Buddhism often balances Avalokitesvara, the god of compassion, with Manjushri, the god of wisdom, generally depicted with a sword raised in order to slash through our illusions. Kindness without wisdom is sometimes no kindness at all.

"But it wasn't so different in Tibet many centuries ago. It's no different in Japan—or Thailand, or any Buddhist country. Even in India, where the Buddha came from."

"But we Tibetans are the worst offenders," he said, not ready to be placated; the other man's grass is always less polluted. "We have all these *puja*s, these rituals, but we don't know the meaning of Lord Buddha. We can't say we're Buddhists."

He looked at me in the quiet morning, his eyes holding mine while I thought of a response. High above the valley, we could hear barely a sound from the road below. A piece of paper rustled in the wind, and I reached for one of the cookies on the plate.

"It's good to sway," he said in a very different voice, much gentler, so that I recalled that devil's advocacy was part of his self-created job description. "Next time you see me, I'll be doing or saying something completely different. Everything's always changing, always moving. That piece of paper, you, me, this terrace—nothing is the way it was even a second ago."

While we spoke, scientists at Berkeley and Princeton and Wisconsin and elsewhere—as the Dalai Lama had told the academics in Nara—were working on a series of experiments, conducted over decades now and reported on in *Nature* and *Proceedings of the National Academy of Sciences* and many other of the most respected scientific journals, that, remarkably, suggested that the wildest stories passed on by Alexandra David-Neel were not so wild after all. Senior monks and seasoned meditators really could dry wet sheets in less than an hour, experimenters had found, and resist extreme cold just through the force of their meditation. One monk had reduced the rhythm of his heart to an almost unimaginable five beats a minute, and brain scans showed, visibly and quantifiably, how certain monks had reached levels of calm and self-possession that were, quite literally, off the charts.

Meditation was now being taught at West Point—perhaps as a result of what had been conclusively proven about how it could contribute to both health and composure; the findings of such researchers had been featured on the cover of my longtime employer, *Time* magazine. An issue of the *Harvard Law Review,* of all things, had been devoted to the practice of sitting in one place and stilling the mind. The Dalai Lama, in fact, seemed to be stressing science more and more as the twenty-first century began, perhaps because—again—it offered to take us out of a domain where one side of the world used the Koran to justify terrible acts of violence, while another used the Bible. The "essencelessness" that quantum mechanics stresses, Heisenberg's uncertainty principle, the very way relativity and quantum mechanics dissolve the separation of subject and object—all were ideas he felt should be intrinsic to a Tibetan monastic curriculum.

In a curious way, in fact, globalism was supporting some of the principles of Buddhism, as much as the other way round. Fifty years ago, an American visiting a village in Tibet might have been taken to be a magician, even a sorcerer, if he had pulled out a Polaroid and snapped a picture then and there, or produced a tape recorder and played back to the villagers the sound of their own voices. And they, in turn, might have seemed to be uncanny fakirs or wonder workers if they had showed the American how they could reduce their oxygen consumption by 64 percent in deep meditation, or bring down their entire metabolism. These days, what had once looked like a miracle just seemed to be a particular capacity of the mind or body developed unusually intensely, and Tibetans could see that it wasn't magic—only real life and training—when they turned on their TVs and watched Olympic sprinters running at nearly twenty-three miles an hour, or Carl Lewis jumping over the equivalent of a nine-yard pond.

When William James, then a Harvard professor, went to research various mediums on behalf of the American Society for Psychical Research, he confessed that he found the investigation of these seeming charlatans "a loathsome occupation" and (as he put it later) "a strange and in many ways disgusting experience." As a hardened empiricist and a lifelong student of chemistry, comparative anatomy, and physiology, James rejoiced whenever one of the mystics popular in his day was exposed as a fake, her secret doors revealed.

Yet, as a serious scientist, James was committed to keeping his mind open and drawing no conclusions that could not be fully supported. This left him at a loss when, on at least one occasion, a dozen visits and all the protocols of research failed to find a flaw in a medium he inspected.

"I have hitherto felt," he wrote a friend of his father's, "as if the wonder-mongers and magnetic physicians and seventh sons of seventh daughters and those who gravitated towards them by magical affinity were a sort of intellectual vermin. I now begin to believe that that type of mind takes hold of a range of truths to which the other kind is stone blind." This new feeling left him "all at sea," he confessed, "with my old compass lost, and no new one" to replace it. To a Buddhist it would just mean that a form of ignorance had been removed; the "wildest dreams of Kew," as Kipling put it around the same time, "are the facts of Khathmandhu."

Two hours east of the Dalai Lama's home in Dharamsala, passing along small country roads running between trees and tea plantations, the snowcaps shining brilliant in the blue skies above, I turned one day off the narrow main road and onto an even rougher path, which gave onto a hidden valley of sorts. Houses were clustered on a ridge halfway up the slope, and in a moment I had left India behind and was in a country of whitewashed houses with the golden turrets of a temple looking over them. I got out of the car in a dusty courtyard and followed a path along the slope to a temple with a front courtyard perhaps the size of a kindergarten playground.

Old Tibetan women were already sitting on the ground in front of the courtyard—though it was barely eight a.m.—and the prayer halls were full of young monks bustling about and running hither and thither. Visitors began to assemble from all around the area, till soon the space around the courtyard was completely packed, and newcomers had to peer over three or four heads to see what was going on.

The answer to that inquiry was that Tashi Jong Temple, home to a group from the Kagyu order, whose head is the young Karmapa, was holding an annual "lama dance" that makes the hidden forces of Tibetan Buddhism manifest and gripping over the course of eight days. Very soon the courtyard was full of lamas from the temple moving their arms and legs in a highly choreographed, very slow dance. The rhythm was almost hypnotic—the opposite of dramatic—and all the ready smiles and air of improvised jollity that surround a traditional performance of Tibetan folk dancing or opera were absent. Every gesture held a precise meaning, and the whole ceremony was at once a kind of exorcism and a petition to certain gods.

In an elevated chair—a kind of throne—to one side of the courtyard the young rinpoche of the temple looked on. Behind him roamed a much wilder figure, in much paler robes, the coils of his dusty hair piled on the top of his head like a sleeping snake. This was, I heard, a yogi—a monk who had meditated for years at a time in a cave. His top-knot represented the years he had spent far from society, not cutting his hair while he meditated.

Now this figure was the unofficial head of the temple, a tutor to the rinpoche and, almost literally, the power behind the throne. Figures came onto the scene from the inner halls of the temple wearing masks that looked grotesque to me, and representing various old kings and spiritual figures. Above the courtyard stood a building in which monks were going on sustained retreats even now. Farther up was a pleasant, brightly colored cottage with a garden where I would meet another yogi, close to death, whose years of meditation were evident in his gaze. Nearby was the now celebrated Englishwoman who had become a nun and meditated alone in a cave, through avalanches and visits from wolves and stalkers, for an unbroken twelve years. Later in the afternoon I would climb up to a retreat hall high above the temple courtyard where people could take off for months-long explorations of the interior. I had never been in any place (outside of Tibet) that felt so much like Tibet, so removed from the daily world I recognized.

At moments like this, I was always reminded, forcibly, of how the Dalai Lama, to summon the metaphor again, was constantly coming in and out of his temple, emerging to greet the outside world and talk to it and then disappearing once more into what was a private and almost unimaginable Tibet (just as, during the teachings he gave in Dharamsala, he emerged twice a day from his compound and walked, smiling and greeting petitioners, behind his texts and accompanied by various objects and ritual figures, to the chair from which he spoke; and twice a day he walked back again, into his strictly guarded domain). Much of the time he and his monks practiced a highly cerebral debating that, to some extent, argued about how many symbolic angels could dance on the nonexistent head of an imaginary pin; yet the rest of the time they functioned in a world that acknowledged that philosophy cannot, as is classically said, cure a toothache, and even that, to the nomad in his lonely tent, fifteen thousand feet up, all the figures that swarm across Tibetan *thangka*s were real, painfully real.

The Dalai Lama, besides, could never write off the world beyond logic entirely when it was that very world that had brought him (and a few hundred other incarnate lamas, down from what once had been a few thousand) to the chair on which he now sat, thanks to the consultation of cloud formations, reflections in a mystical lake, and various dreams. The very system of incarnate lamas, or *tulku*s, found through such secret symbols just after their birth, might almost have been a careful mixture of shrewd logic and Tibetan anti-logic: its beauty, after all, was in bringing to power tiny boys (and, occasionally, girls) who had had no chance to be corrupted by the world and had no interest at all in self-advancement. Its shadow side was the very fact that by placing two-year-olds in power, it was effectively, for a few years at least, putting real power in the hands of regents and senior tutors, or relatives of the child, who were by no means immune to power brokering and political chicanery. For Tibetans, I was surprised to learn, having a *tulku* born into the family was not a source of celebration; it was believed that, in worldly terms (and through a kind of complex compensation, perhaps), it usually brought bad luck.

The Dalai Lama generally, as already mentioned, referred to the Dalai Lama institution as if it were just a set of clothes—of duties and responsibilities and titles—he was born to wear (and he referred to death, engagingly, as equivalent to "a change of clothing"); as his younger brother put it to one writer, "He is a simple man whose job it is to be Dalai Lama." This separation of the spirit and the container was made evident by the fact that some Dalai Lamas were fat, some thin; some were very mild-mannered, some fierce. The Great Fifth Dalai Lama is generally credited with establishing Tibet as it was until recently (and building the Potala Palace, for example, as a great symbol of church and state in one); yet the Dalai Lama who followed him famously spent much of his time cavorting in the taverns outside the Potala's walls, shed his robes, and left, before his mysterious disappearance, a set of erotic poems that are beloved by Tibetans but susceptible to all kinds of interpretations.

Yet, even in this context, things were never so clear, or so easily written off, as I would like. One day I picked up a book concerning Tibet and the Thirteenth Dalai Lama by Sir Charles Bell, the nononsense British diplomat who became the first Westerner to grow very close to a Dalai Lama, and who actually stayed for a year near his palace. Bell's account was as clear and practical as you would imagine of an officer reporting back to headquarters. The Thirteenth Dalai Lama was "singularly frank," Bell wrote in 1924, and often dismissed his officials so that he could talk to his foreign friend alone (and even seek out his counsel). "His Holiness has always disliked ceremony," Bell went on, and, in fact, when he was forced into exile in 1910, in India, as China's rulers advanced on Lhasa, the Thirteenth clearly rejoiced in the freedom he suddenly enjoyed to take walks in the forest and move around as he could never have done in Lhasa. "He is fond of horses," Bell wrote, "dogs, and animals generally, but especially of birds. And flowers are an abiding joy to him."

All this was straightforward enough, and an invaluable source of information about the first Dalai Lama to move out into the larger world and to begin to draw Tibet into modern times. Yet what I found startling, reading it eighty years on, was that in detail after detail, phrase after phrase, Bell's description of the Thirteenth Dalai Lama could not have been a better description of his very different successor, the Fourteenth. One of the many reasons why I thought there was no call for much physical description of the person and personality of the current Dalai Lama was that it had been given, quite powerfully, eleven years before he was born, by a man who was describing his precursor.

"He is impulsive, cheerful, and gifted with a keen sense of humor," Bell wrote of his friend. "His eyes twinkled as he described to me the strategems by which he evaded the pursuit of the Chinese soldiery." He was "a shrewd judge of character, quick in understanding" and always ready to show his feelings, though "innate courtesy never wavered." Surprisingly, perhaps, the head of Tibetan Buddhism was not enthusiastic about Buddhism being carried around the world, although he genuinely respected anyone who sincerely pursued a religious practice (and was taken aback, he confessed, by the Chinese he met who didn't).

"The God-king is intensely human" was Bell's conclusion, and got up to meditate sometimes at three a.m., not even breaking from his meditations when traveling on trains. He gave his secretaries fits with his eagerness to make good use of every moment, and he always seemed to hunger for details of the outside world, having the English papers translated for him and following the tense situation in 1920s Germany. At the very least, he seemed to have much more in common with his successor than even a George Bush had with a George W. Bush. The one detail that Bell didn't include (because he could not know of it) was that, as a boy being taught calligraphy, the Fourteenth Dalai Lama was made to write out the Thirteenth's chilling last testament over and over, so that, one might guess, he finally had it by heart.

Even in old Tibet the incarnation system had never been an unambiguous blessing; the finding of new lamas and the protection of them against rival candidates or others with different ideas had never been easy. But like everything in the Tibetan world, it had become infinitely more complex now that the culture was scattered across the globe, and incarnate lamas were being presented in Seattle, in Spain, all over the place. The head of the Nyingma lineage had become the subject of much speculation in the West after he announced that the martial artist Steven Seagal (a generous contributor to his cause) was a high Tibetan incarnation, and then said the same of a four-times-married former psychic from Brooklyn. Besides, traditional monastic search groups looking for new incarnations now had to travel across Tibet and into other countries, with secret faxes sent back and forth and no one sure of whether the new lama would be found in China or Tibet (where he would not be able to see the Dalai Lama) or be born in exile, and therefore unable to meet the vast majority of his people.

The second-highest incarnation in all of Tibetan Buddhism—one of the main figures responsible for finding a new Dalai Lama—is the Panchen Lama, whose traditional home is Tashi Lhunpo Temple in Tibet's second city, Shigatse. But the Tenth Panchen Lama had remained in China when the Dalai Lama fled to Tibet, and not even Tibetans were of one mind as to how much he had collaborated with the authorities in Beijing, how much he had used his position in China to try to help Tibet from within. In 1989, a healthy man of fifty, he made a long-planned return to Tashi Lhunpo to inter the remains of previous Panchen Lamas, only five days after saying, outright, that the Chinese had brought more harm than gain to Tibet. Suddenly, only days after his return, he collapsed one morning and died, and rumors of a poisoning began to fly.

For six years the search for his successor was conducted via a complex series of communications between Tibet and Dharamsala, until finally, in May 1995, the Dalai Lama announced that a little boy had been found in Tibet who was the Eleventh Panchen Lama. As soon as he did so, incensed perhaps that a Tibetan exile was daring to authorize incarnations in Chinese territory, the Chinese came up with their own candidates and, in a divination ceremony at the Jokhang Temple, in Lhasa, that partook of all the ritual they so often mocked (including boys choosing pieces of paper from a golden urn), they announced their own little boy (the son of Communist cadres) as the true new Panchen Lama. The Dalai Lama's choice, six years old, was placed under house arrest, and has not been heard of since.

Among the other highest incarnations in Tibetan Buddhism—in fact, the oldest incarnation in the philosophy—is that of the Karmapa, the head of the Kagyu lineage. When the Sixteenth Karmapa died, in 1981, a search was undertaken, and two young candidates emerged, each backed by one faction of the previous Karmapa's followers. One boy was in Delhi, the other (the Dalai Lama's approved choice) in China itself, though, in the first days of the new millennium, as in a fairy tale, and months after the Dalai Lama turned sixty-five, the fourteen-year-old from China, having pulled off an astonishing escape, dramatically appeared in Dharamsala. Tibetans by now know that no fairy tale comes without a shadow, or some aspect of the real world, and so while some people embraced him as the new hope of exile Tibet, others wondered how the most conspicuous Tibetan in Tibet could have escaped under the eyes of a Chinese government that was able to intercept even the simplest peasant.

The Dalai Lama greeted the boy and gave him a place to stay near Dharamsala, since the Indian government, fearing he was a Chinese spy, refused to allow him to take up his ancestral residence in Sikkim. But the confusion perhaps intensified the Dalai Lama's wish to stress, as he had done since 1969, that there might be no Fifteenth Dalai Lama at all. There would be another Dalai Lama, he always said, only if that Dalai Lama was of help to the Tibetan people.

Meanwhile, the world of protective deities and spirits, of rival groups within Tibetan Buddhism and ancient enmities that had always cast shadows over old Tibet now came out into the global order. In 1996, the Dalai Lama began, as I'd seen in Vancouver, to tell audiences not to propitiate a particular deity called Shugden, because he felt that it was proving harmful, and that certain of the tenets involved in its propitiation went against the principles of Buddhism and the very tolerance and reason he was trying so hard to promote. In response, the followers of the spirit, gathered in the West around a Tibetan in England who ran an organization he called the New Kadampa Tradition, started protesting the Dalai

Lama's talks (hence the warning that had greeted me in British Columbia), claiming that he was violating the principle of freedom of religion; they even allowed themselves to be co-opted to some degree by the Chinese.

Again, one had only to tiptoe across the threshold of the dispute to find oneself in a furious, febrile world of curses and threats and almost medieval intrigue. In the letters certain Shugden supporters sent the Dalai Lama's government in exile (released in a brochure put out by that government), the sentences pullulated with references to "donkey officials" and "poisonous and shameless" rivals. At one point, a package had been sent to a monastery in India containing a knife and the message "We were unable to meet you this time but we hope to get you next time." A senior monk was beaten up and a barn and granary went up in flames. Then the head of the Dalai Lama's own Institute of Buddhist Dialectics was found stabbed in his bed, along with two younger monks, apparently cut up as if for exorcism.

The letters from the Shugden group (and, its members would no doubt suggest, those sent back to them) open the door on a set of spirits not so different from the grinning skeletons and dancing monsters of a *thangka*. Some of the correspondence I read spoke of "turning the milk sea of Tibet into a sea of boiling blood," of "eating the three carcases" (presumably belonging to the three who had been killed), and warned of more carcases to be found soon. There was no talk of calm logic or scientific investigation, least of all of a doctor's wish to heal.

One hot day in August 2005 in Zurich, at an eight-day set of teachings on compassion the Dalai Lama was offering, the public-address system suddenly declared—in German, Tibetan, and English—that followers of Shugden should take care not to attend the following morning, when the Dalai Lama was going to be offering some special initiations. Flyers were handed out to the same effect, and the announcement was broadcast again. Then, as he was nearing the end of his daily *explication de texte,* at four p.m., the Dalai Lama suddenly said, "Today I am going to speak for thirty extra minutes. If that makes problems for you, please feel free to go. But I hope you will not mind my going on a little late today." The audience, which could never get enough of him—many of its members had traveled across the world for these teachings—was clearly delighted.

Slowly at first, in long and forceful Tibetan sentences—rendered into German by a scholarly man onstage next to the Dalai Lama (and into other languages by unseen translators speaking into our transistor radios)—the Dalai Lama began to explain why he did not wish any followers of Shugden to attend the special initiations, even if some of them had chosen, in spite of requests, to attend the other days' teachings. For them to be present during these esoteric ceremonies would potentially impede the progress of everyone else, he said, and even do harm to the person giving the initiations, himself.

His voice began to rise, and soon he was speaking like thunder. Argument after argument followed as to why Shugden supporters should not come, and his bearing was as wrathful as I had ever seen in public. Occasionally, his words would trail off, and the mild-mannered Swiss professor in jacket and tie by his side would start translating the sentences; then, before the man could continue, the Dalai Lama would start up again, drowning him out.

The audience laughed at such moments, though not with delight.

"In no way are the Dalai Lamas attached to the Shugden deity," the Tibetan leader said, going through history to show how previous Dalai Lamas had spoken of the spirit. "This has been a problem for three hundred and sixty years. I initially was involved with this deity, but then through some analysis, I realized there was some kind of harm in it, some kind of problem. Then I referred this issue to two of my tutors."

His junior tutor, however, Trijang Rinpoche, was widely believed to be a follower of Shugden himself. Indeed, there are said to be more than one hundred thousand in the Tibetan community who propitiate the deity. Trijang Rinpoche, the Dalai Lama now said, was to be revered for his great contributions to Lam Rim, or Stages of the Path, teachings. But it was his own job, the Dalai Lama stressed, "to continue the line that the two great Dalai Lamas, the Fifth and the Thirteenth, have taken. And the Fifth actually denounced the Shugden deity as a harmful spirit."

On and on the passionate tirade went, like nothing so much as a prosecuting lawyer's final summation. Some people began to look at their watches. Always he was working for harmony between the schools of Tibetan Buddhism, the Dalai Lama said. Yet a Shugden teacher had said that if a Gelug practitioner follows a Nyingma teaching, he will be killed by the Shugden deity. What did this have to do with the clear philosophy laid out by Lord Buddha? And if you looked at the Nalanda teaching, the great work of the Indian philosophers Shantideva and Nagarjuna, which he was explicating now, what did that have to do with propitiating deities?

It was as if a door had swung open behind him and suddenly one could see something of what this man (a tiny figure at the far end of a huge rock-star auditorium, flanked by two giant video screens that projected his face around the building) was sitting in front of. When finally the Dalai Lama stopped speaking, the eight thousand people in Hallenstadion filed out of the day's teachings very quietly.

In the end, I thought, it was probably not so different from what you find in any relationship, even with those you have known for an entire lifetime: at the core there is likely to be a mystery. And all that you know and learn about a person does not take away from the vast amount you cannot and will never know. "Our knowledge," as Isaac Bashevis Singer, wise chronicler of spirits and golems pointed out, "is a little island in a great ocean of non-knowledge." In the Dalai Lama's case, bringing a complex and sometimes secret set of rites out into the world, this was especially true, since so much of what belonged to his tradition could make little sense to another culture. And so he offered a carefully watered-down form of general teaching centered on basic human truths—science plus ethics, in effect—and true to his central contention that at every moment you should try to do some good, but at the very least should do no harm.

He'd told me once how surprised he had been, on meeting a Christian in Europe, to hear the man say that "the self is a mystery." And God, too. For someone coming from the Indian philosophical tradition, he said, with its three thousand years of investigating the self, the self seemed eminently knowable, a series of laws and connections that could be investigated as any other aspect of nature or consciousness could. And yet for all of that, the rites or practices by which the mind conducted these investigations, examining the self and even its unreality, involved techniques or customs that to the outsider were at least as mysterious as any other matter of incarnation.

Often, I recalled, in the years after his death, the Buddha was represented by just the image of an empty throne.

In order to be not remembered or even wanted I have to be a person that nobody knows.

—THOMAS MERTON

THE MONK

At the beginning of the twenty-first century, a Swiss photographer named Manuel Bauer spent more than three years following the Dalai Lama on his travels around the world, making more than thirty trips in all and recording every moment of his day the way a modern photojournalist chronicles a presidential candidate on the campaign trail. He took pictures of him as he prepared for bed, sitting in his undershirt, and he took pictures of him as he woke up in the morning and began his hours of meditation. He took pictures of him weeping onstage, conducting private ceremonies with his oracles, watching TV bare-chested, and pouring tea for Václav Havel. When Bauer showed his subject proofs of the book to see if any of the four hundred images had violated privacy or inadvertently overstepped some boundary, the only one the Dalai Lama questioned was a picture in which, because of the perspective, it appeared that he was sitting higher than one of his teachers.

It's startling, often, for outsiders to hear the Dalai Lama say (as he always does) that he's had eleven teachers in the course of his life, or fifteen, as he said later, or even nineteen, as one of his more recent interviews had it; many of us from abroad, knowing only that he's the head of Tibetan Buddhism, are unaware that he's not even the head of his own Gelug order (merely its highest incarnation). Yet his stress on his many official teachers, his memories of the whips they mounted on the wall in Lhasa to keep him in order, his turning to lamas in the crowd during public addresses to ask them for their more informed readings of a text all work to remind us that he's a monk.

The very purpose of a monk, in any tradition, is to be an all but nameless cog inside a machine, precisely fixed within a hierarchy and committed to obedience to his practice, his seniors, and, most of all, the doctrine he's given his life to. In Tibet this is all further complicated—or made obscure to us—by the system of incarnate lamas, which throws all notions of conventional hierarchy on their heads: when the Dalai Lama's senior tutor during his formative years—the man he often calls his "best friend"—died in Dharamsala in 1983, a young boy was found some years later who was said to be the new incarnation of Ling Rinpoche. The result was that the Dalai Lama could be seen all but bowing before a very small toddler—and, at the same time, beginning to instruct him a little in certain of the doctrines in which he had been instructed himself by (Tibetans believe) the boy's previous incarnation.

By reflex and training, therefore, the Dalai Lama is still as much student as teacher, and his intimates say that whenever he has a spare moment on the road, his favorite habit is to pull out a book of stories about the Buddha and read first the Tibetan commentaries and then the Indian. Outlining for me once his habit of "radical informality," he confessed that he felt emboldened to practice it only because his senior tutor had watched him in action once and

given him a kind of imprimatur. The radicalism of his lack of interest in ceremony and ritual arose out of some careful reasoning, the
tutor felt, and so was not mere revolution for revolution's sake. The
leader of the Tibetans sounded, when he told me this, like nothing
so much as a schoolboy told by an admiring teacher that he could
study beyond the required texts and walk out of the school's narrow bounds.

This absolute freedom in shaking up his philosophy, using exile
as a way to reform Tibetan Buddhism from within, can be deceiv-
ing. The Fourteenth Dalai Lama has swept away a lot of the need-
less pomp and even feudalism encumbering Tibet in its past; he
has allowed that a woman could quite possibly become the next
Dalai Lama, "because of different circumstances"; he has tried to
dissolve many of the centuries-old divisions that separate one
group of Tibetan Buddhist monks from another, often to the rage of
other Tibetan leaders (he has in his own studies incorporated elements of Nyingma and Kagyu teaching traditionally at odds with
his Gelug school, all in the interests of declaring that Tibet's new
mission is to put its petty differences behind it and join in some
larger, global community). But this irreverence toward surfaces
arises only, one feels, because he remains deeply rooted within.
Textually, the Dalai Lama is a conservative, a sincere and wholehearted follower of the Buddhist doctrine, and very straight in his
observance of what he calls the "original, classical, authentic teachings," and here many of his admirers in the West, products of the
rebellions of the 1960s and eager to be free of all the hierarchies
and laws they associate with their own traditions, run quickly into
a wall.

The Dalai Lama, for example, does not endorse homosexuality,
because one old Buddhist text speaks out strictly against sexual
penetration in the mouth or the anus (such was the state of

thinking in those days that it said nothing about women). He deplores anyone who exercises prejudice against homosexuals on the grounds of their sexual orientation, but he feels that for him and his fellow monks, at least, the old laws have to be adhered to. A friend of mine, long a Tibetan Buddhist monk and sometime translator for the Dalai Lama, told me that a group of gays and lesbians held a meeting with the Dalai Lama once in San Francisco to raise the point with him. In fact, my friend (a Tibetan scholar) said, the famous injunction against oral or anal intercourse was a late addition to a text that spoke only against adultery; Tibetan Buddhism at its heart prescribed no such doctrine, which would exile male homosexuality. The Dalai Lama, true to form, said that if his friend could produce the text and show him in completely convincing scholarly terms that he had misjudged the old texts, he would certainly be open to changing his mind, but till then he could not go against the code he had inherited.

In the same way, he will not endorse intoxicants or sexual license, and is tough on the subject of divorce, because it makes young children the victims of their elders' uncertainties or immaturity. He has "a little bit of reservation," he told me once, about all the incarnate lamas popping up in every corner of the globe, some from non-Buddhist families, as well as about the reverence brought to certain Tibetan teachers and lamas abroad, some of whom were not regarded as very great scholars within their own community. He delights listeners everywhere by being the rare spiritual figure to say there's no need for temples or scriptures, let alone for an immersion in his own tradition; but then he disappoints them, often, by suggesting that there is a need for old-fashioned ethics and all the things your grandmother told you were good for you.

By curious circumstance, one of the first Western visitors to travel all the way to Dharamsala to see Tibet in exile, and to report at length on his discussions with the Dalai Lama, was the Cistercian monk Thomas Merton, who headed off from his monastery in Kentucky in 1968 to talk to some of the teachers and philosophers in Asia he'd been following from afar, with such interest and sympathy, for so long. There is a large extent to which only a monk can really appreciate and read a fellow monk, as only a ballet dancer can assess a fellow dancer's performance, catching the subtleties and minutiae the unprofessional watcher would miss, and Merton's account of the Tibetan leader served to open the door for the West to a being who had previously appeared to belong to exotic books in a foreign tongue. (The fact that Merton was found dead, apparently of electrocution, only six weeks after his stay in Dharamsala, in his hotel room in Bangkok, gives an added piquancy and perhaps weight to the encounters that to him threw such a fresh light upon his long vocation.)

When Merton arrived in Dharamsala, via the overnight train from Delhi (the first train ride, he reported excitedly, he'd taken since joining his monastery twenty-seven years before), he came upon a whole settlement of monks, as his eager eyes conceived of it. The valleys in and around Dharamsala were a mandala, he wrote, in which there were hermits and mystics in every corner, deep in meditation, and ten-year-old incarnate lamas being trained in their ancient practices while the laypeople of Tibet walked around and around, driving the community on with their constant recitation of chants and spinning of prayer wheels. It was raining when the visitor arrived, and thunder "talked to itself all over and around the cloud-hidden peaks." There was even a tremor of earthquakes, and Merton was moved to reflect on how, across the world, elections were bringing a new American president into office (Richard Nixon, as it happened).

Merton reported, vividly, on the Indian goatherds walking along the slopes, as they do now, members of the Naddi tribe, and the sharp, bracing air of the snowcaps overlooking the settlement. He registered, below his room, "an argument of women," the same ones whose granddaughters are perhaps arguing today. He looked in on "a rather crumby" restaurant (his unorthodox spelling revealing, touchingly, how far he lived from the colloquial world) and used the day's newspapers for toilet paper. In the distance, he heard "the report of a gun from down in the valley," a reminder, startling, of how the Indian army lived, as it still does, at the very edge of the Tibetan community.

Yet the heart of his visit, fully reported in his letters back home, was the series of discussions he enjoyed with the Dalai Lama, then only thirty-three, and perhaps as excited as Merton was to get to meet a monk from another tradition. "The central presence," as the American put it in his journal, "is a fully awake, energetic, alert, nondusty, nondim, nonwhispering Buddha." To the visitor's relief, the young leader seemed much more solid than all the talk abroad of the magic and mystery of Tibet had led him to anticipate.

"The Dalai Lama is strong and alert, bigger than I expected" was Merton's first response and then—clearly speaking of something within as well as without—he added, "a very solid, energetic, generous, and warm person." The sense of solidity (the idea that recurred) was confirmed when, in their second discussion, the two of them talked of epistemology, then of *samadhi,* or one-pointed concentration, the Dalai Lama striking Merton as "very existential" and quite "scholastic." The Dalai Lama's "ideas of the interior life are built on very solid foundations and on a real awareness of practical problems," Merton reported, and the Tibetan ended their second meeting with the injunction to his Western visitor to "think more about the mind."

In their third and final encounter, the Dalai Lama—as he has become famous for doing—bombarded the foreigner with questions: about the process of initiation for monks in the West, about the process of enlightenment, about whether Trappists could watch movies, whether they could drink alcohol, whether they were vegetarians. You can hear, in Merton's reports, the sound of a professional in his field, still more isolated than he would like, seizing on the chance to grill and exchange ideas with another professional passing through. The Dalai Lama, Merton decided, was really "interested in the 'mystical life,' rather than in external observance."

The Cistercian left Dharamsala, as so many would do, feeling he'd found a true friend, even a kindred spirit. Yet he realized, even then, that the young lama was "very sensitive about partial and distorted Western views of Tibetan mysticism and especially about popular myths." Over and over the Dalai Lama stressed the importance of hard work, of rigor, of putting in grueling training before thinking, say, of Dzogchen practice (a form of advanced, intense meditation). Reading Merton's reports now, one can feel that one is hearing a veteran of contemplation and metaphysics (the Dalai Lama) wondering why and how anyone would wish to play professional football, as it were, before he's even learned how to put on a helmet (he'll get hurt, he'll throw off everyone else, he'll get in the way of real spiritual progress, if he thinks that spiritual practice somehow requires any less training than does any other discipline or job). And already, Merton notes, "the Dalai Lama has to see a lot of blue-haired ladies in pants—losers. And people looking for a freak religion."

It's never clear how much Merton was writing as he always did and how much in the light of his meeting with the monk who reflected back to him some of his own qualities, but it was while he was in Dharamsala that he began to formulate the idea of "the metaphysician as wounded man. A wounded man is not an agnostic—he just has different questions, arising out of his wound."

A monk is a figure of fascination to some of us, even of inspiration, precisely because (in theory, at least) he turns his back on what most of us find important and chooses to interpret success, wealth, power only inwardly, seeing the self as more of an instrument than an end per se. Where some of us try to make a name for ourselves, he begins by discarding his very name, and where some of us try to follow the news, he roots himself in the old, through which he can make sense of everything new that happens. The Christian monks I know who gather in their cloisters on Sunday evenings to watch John Cleese movies, the Tibetan rinpoches who have no patience for Westerners' careful pieties can afford to be irreverent only because their sense of what they owe reverence to is so precise and so sharp.

I often felt that the heart and soul, quite literally, of the Dalai Lama's life existed in precisely the parts that most of us couldn't see. "The truth," as Meister Eckhart put it, "is that the more ourselves we are, the less of self is in us." Like the most impressive experts in any field, the Dalai Lama tempted us to forget that he had studied for eighteen years and faced an oral examination by thirty scholars of logic, thirty-five doctors of metaphysics, and thirty-five experts on the Noble Path; indeed, his warmth and everyday humanity meant that many of us spoke to him as if he were truly one of us—no one asks the pope whether he has dreams of women or what makes him angry. Yet the fact remained that, like every Tibetan Buddhist monk, he was bound by more than 253 different vows.

I asked the Dalai Lama once how things had changed for him since the last time we'd met in his room, and he said, "Less hair, I think, both of us," to get rid of all reserve at the outset, and broke into gales of wholehearted laughter. Then he answered my question, saying that nothing much had changed except for a small problem with his throat. "And my spiritual practice," he went on, "not much. But as usual, I carry it."

Nowadays, he said, as a result of ongoing studies and the new requirements that came with each new teaching, "my daily prayer, especially what I have to recite and go through, that normally takes about four hours."

"Every day?"

To answer, he took me through his day: meditation, prostrations, reciting special mantras, then more meditation and more prostrations, followed by reading Tibetan philosophy or other texts; then reading and studying and, in the evening, "some meditation—evening meditation—for about one hour. Then, at eight-thirty, sleep. Most important meditation. Compulsory meditation for everyone—even some birds. The most important meditation, not for Nirvana, but for survival!"

A joke, of course, to defuse the onerous sound of the activities, and to bring in everyone, even those birds, and yet what I was brought up against again was an almost unimaginable otherness at the center of him. Most of what he did, I was reminded, was invisible.

I have spent much of my adult life in monasteries, interested in watching how these often silent revolutionaries turn the world inside out, subverting our assumptions, rooting themselves in what can't be seen, and then disappearing at regular intervals behind the sign that says, MONASTIC ENCLOSURE. PLEASE DO NOT ENTER. The Greek word *askesis*, from which "ascetic" comes, refers to the training of athletes, and monks are, at least in principle, spiritual athletes who put themselves through almost unfathomable training practices to make their minds as sharp and effective as the bodies of professional sportsmen are.

On Mount Hiei, behind Kyoto, near where I write this, so-called marathon monks embark on prolonged stretches of meditation and, in a few cases, go for days on end without sleeping, spending every night, all night, racing along the narrow paths of the sacred mountain, a dagger at their side; they have sworn they will take their own lives if they drink a single glass of water or eat a crust of bread in the course of nine days. At the end of their ordeal, the monks of Mount Hiei look as if they've passed through death itself and emerged at the other end like human candles, illuminated outlines of themselves, aglow (photographs are taken of them after their intense austerities, as if to record the inner equivalent of a three-minute mile). On Mount Hiei a monk is said to be able to hear ash dropping from a stick of incense in the next room; in Catholic hermitages, according to the Benedictine brother David Steindl-Rast, an ascetic aspires to a state in which a "drop of spring water" is full of flavor.

When we see the Dalai Lama pick out from a crowd a face he has not seen for fifty years, or recover a statement he heard thirty years before, what we are seeing, in effect, are the fruits of his long exercises in collecting himself, the ways he has brought his attention to a point in meditation so that it burns as a magnifying glass might burn a piece of paper in the sun. Students at the Gyuto Monastery in Tibet, to take an almost random example, used to have to memorize 600 pages just to gain admission to the monastery, and then embarked on learning another 2,500 pages by heart, apart from all the other chants and recitations they had to master. The purpose of such exercises is not just ritualistic; it is a way of sharpening the mind so that it opens out into what might seem a gigantic filing cabinet or computer hard drive (thus the Dalai Lama, for example, when talking about rural development around the world, will, as in Taiwan in 2001, recall the mayor of Shanghai forty-six years before, who—with impressive prescience, as the Dalai Lama sees it—told him that he was devoting as much energy to developing the villages around Shanghai as to the city center, so as not to deepen the gap between rich and poor). This is not magic but—the whole point, really—something anyone can choose to do if it may be of help.

You can see all this in the way the Dalai Lama speaks. Monks tend to be sparing with their words, precise—few "um's" and "er's"—because they have cut away everything that is inessential and their words emerge from an abundant silence. Often the Dalai Lama will say nothing for what seems like minutes after I ask him something, and I can almost see him gathering himself and sorting through his mind to find the central principle.

He starts speaking slowly, usually, like a car in a residential neighborhood, and then gathers speed and continuity, as if accelerating onto the open highway, going back to develop points he's made before, picking up new examples and facts, often returning after an hour or so to offer an addendum or ignoring my next question to go back and amplify his previous answer. (One time he even used driving as a good practical example of how all the book knowledge in the world doesn't help until we practice—and the more we do practice driving, the less dangerous it will become.) The answers tend to be rich, fully paragraphed philosophical treatises, complete with subclauses and qualifications, and broken down almost visibly into points 1, 2, and 3; though they end, very often, in some comical example that sets him off on gusts of infectious laughter and, to some degree, brings us back to earth. Humor in the Dalai Lama arises, frequently, from setting the world around us against the logical principles he's just explained.

It's no coincidence, I sometimes think, that the Dalai Lama is often photographed peering down a microscope in some foreign lab; as with most of the monks I know, he tends to bring a concentration to things that means a large part of him is living below the surface. Often I will take something he's said to be almost a truism, solid and inert as it comes to me; but as soon as I go over my notes or start to think more about it, I realize that "the mind is its own master," say, has special and rich implications for those who believe that the "mind" is something different from the self, and that mastery is a way of speaking of discipline and craft, as well as power, and that the very word "master" is the same word often used for the Buddha. A student at the Institute of Buddhist Dialectics, next to the Dalai Lama's house, one of its teachers told me, spends two years studying just four lines written by Tsong Kha Pa. He then spends the next four years on a single phrase.

When someone like the Dalai Lama says—as he constantly does, in a brisk, unhesitating way—"Impossible!" or "Impractical!" or "No problem!" or "Not important!" what he is really doing is refusing to be distracted, and reminding us what is central. And when he goes to meetings with practitioners of other religions, he's not just taking in the latest discussions and techniques in the field but also becoming a deeper Buddhist, as he said in Vancouver, by talking to a Christian. Reading Saint John's account of the meeting between Mary Magdalene and Jesus after the Resurrection, talking on the parable of the mustard seed and the Transfiguration before a group of Christians in London, the Dalai Lama moved many of his listeners to tears, even as he constantly, carefully, stressed that Christianity and Buddhism were not just different ways of explaining the same truth, and that to try to combine them was like trying "to put a yak's head on a sheep's body."

Indeed, even though all monks are committed to the same task, deep down—as doctors or hospital construction workers are—the details of their practice are as different as their wildly divergent times and cultures. A Christian generally longs to be rooted in the home he's found in God; the Buddhist, more concerned with uncovering potential, is more interested in experiments and inquiries, always pushing deeper. In fact, Christianity works from very uncertain beginnings toward a specific end (redemption and a life with God); Buddhism starts with something very specific (the Buddha and the reality of suffering he saw) and moves toward an always uncertain future (even after one has attained Nirvana). The image of the open road speaks for a perpetual becoming.

In either case, though, the monk aspires to bring the perspective of his silence into the chatter of the world, looking past events to all that lies behind them. Thus, when terrorists attacked the United States on September 11, 2001, the Dalai Lama lost no time in sending a letter of commiseration to George W. Bush and his people, and he did the same on the first anniversary of the attack. Yet he also took pains, true to his principles, to say that everything has a cause, and that nothing will be resolved until the fundamental cause is taken care of. Simply to respond to violence with violence is like hitting a man in a hospital; he is unlikely to act kindly until he is made better. On the first anniversary of the attack, he reminded the U.S. president that in a world of flux, "today's enemies are often tomorrow's allies."

A doctor's religion may not be important, but which teacher he studied under is often of great importance, and the Dalai Lama always stresses the depth of his debt to Ling Rinpoche ("an acute philosopher with a sharp logical mind and a good debater with a phenomenal memory") and, even more, of the closeness with which he attends to the figure he sometimes calls his boss. "As followers or students of this great teacher," he told the American Buddhist magazine *Tricycle*, in 2001, speaking of the Buddha, "we should take his life as a model. His sacrifice—leaving his palace and remaining in the forest for six years. He worked hard to be enlightened. When the Buddha started his teachings, he considered his audience's mentality, their mental disposition, then accordingly found teachings." It was hard, reading these words, not to think that the man delivering them had himself been forced to quit his palace in his twenties; had worked, day and night, for fifty years to try to bring light to a tangled situation; and, when he appeared in public, was famous for being able somehow to communicate with small children, grandparents, atheists and Christians alike.

Whenever I read about the Buddha's life, in fact, I felt a strange frisson of déjà vu, uncanny, which made sense only when I recalled that I had been watching someone who traveled so carefully in his footsteps. It was as if the Buddha, walking along his road, had left signs and messages for those who came after, to advise them how to get over that high gate, or which was the best way to get around the large boulder in the middle of the road. Everyone ended up taking his own, slightly different route, but the aim, as much as moving forward, was to offer what you had learned to those coming after. Once you have crossed the river, in the Buddha's favorite example, you can leave the raft behind. And Tibetan Buddhists, true to this idea of progress, believe that there are fourteen fundamental questions ("Are the self and the universe eternal? Are the self and the universe transient?") that even the Buddha left unanswered, for those who came after to take on.

One of the striking things about Siddhartha Gautama was that after coming upon his enlightenment under the pipal tree, he had no wish to spread his discoveries, since he didn't feel confident that they would be of use or interest to anyone else; the essence of his teaching, famously, was "Be lamps unto yourselves" and "Seek no refuge but yourself." But when he became convinced that there might be some virtue in talking of his own experience, he spent the last forty-five years of his life ceaselessly traveling across the Gangetic plain, among the new cities that were coming up there in a time of flux that also brought, as one biographer, Karen Armstrong, writes, a sense of "spiritual hunger." Although he engaged in public debates, he repeatedly shied away from cosmic questions as distractions, perhaps, from the main concern.

"Forget about next life," I once heard the Dalai Lama say on a tape as I was browsing in a bookshop within his temple. "This very life should be useful to others. If not, at least no harm."

"I do not give knowledge," the Buddha said. "If you can believe anything, you get caught in that belief or distraction." Zen monks, famously, took this distrust of images to such an extreme that they burned Buddhas to keep themselves warm in winter and said, "If you meet the Buddha along the road, you must kill the Buddha."

The correspondences between the teacher and his far-off student were sometimes so startling that I did not know whether to call them coincidence or continuity or a mixture of the two. The Buddha is said to have had his first moment of insight when his nursemaids left him alone as they went to watch an annual ceremonial plowing of the field and he noticed that some young grasses had been torn up for the ceremony, destroying insects and their eggs. No television interviewer who has seen the Dalai Lama break off an answer because he's noticed a bird falling to the ground outside and wants to tend to it will be surprised. When the Buddha practiced austerities, all he achieved, in the dry accounting of Karen Armstrong (once a nun herself, and now a scholar of religions), "was a prominent rib cage and a dangerously weakened body." When the Dalai Lama tried to become a vegetarian for twenty months around 1965, he contracted hepatitis B and almost died, his doctors telling him, as his mother had done, that his Himalayan constitution could not survive without meat. The Buddha is said to have cried out in pity when he heard of a yogic master who had spent twenty years learning to walk on water (he could just have taken a ferry and used his energies for something else); the Dalai Lama has said that "the best thing is not to use" any magic powers, not least, perhaps, because they take most of us away from what is more sustaining.

Even Thomas Merton, during his visit, was struck by how "always and everywhere the Dalai Lama kept insisting on the fact that one could not attain anything in the spiritual life without total dedication, continued effort, experienced guidance, real discipline." In later years, however, the Dalai Lama has begun talking even more about "hard work," "determination," the importance of not giving up. Indeed, it's not uncommon to see tears come to his eyes, even in a huge arena, when he speaks of the Tibetan poet-saint Milarepa, say, meditating and meditating for years in a cave, or of any of the great Tibetan figures who almost killed themselves in their exertions. (I remembered how a tear had come into his eye even when Hiroko once said that she had tried, really hard, to learn from his books, but it was difficult.)

One other thing moved him to tears, even in public, I heard from an American monk who had been living in the Dalai Lama's monastery for twenty years. That was when someone asked, during a public address, "What is the quickest, easiest, cheapest way to attain enlightenment?" And, the Californian monk went on, "these days in the West there's nearly always someone who asks that question."

Every monk is the same monk, in that he is working to dissolve his sense of self, in part by surrendering to something larger; and every monk is a radical, insofar as he works from the root (*radix* in Latin). For the Buddhist, though, this has especial truth, since his first concern is the interior landscape, where awareness or its obscuration lies; faith for him is really self-confidence, and prayer a form of awakening latent energies.

The Dalai Lama is in these respects truly just another monk, "a little bit anxious," as he confessed to me, when he has to give a talk before senior monks, many of whom have much more time for study than he does, and obliged to spend months doing "a lot of homework." He comes to important meetings in flip-flops (for interviews he generally sheds his shoes and sits cross-legged in his chair, sometimes holding his interlocutor's hand), and when he's backstage at a modern theater, I have seen, he eagerly cross-questions technicians as to how the lights work. "Utilize modern facilities," is his practical position, "but try to develop a right kind of attitude." It seems apt that he has a remarkable memory for dates and faces, but is altogether less good with names.

It's a happy aspect of his circumstances that he takes as his political model a Hindu (Gandhi), works very closely with many Christians (Tutu, Václav Havel, Jimmy Carter), and lives in a country (India) that has the world's second-largest Muslim population. Many of the scientists he collaborates with may pride themselves on having no religion at all. Yet even as he has made dissolving distinctions his life's work, he is careful not to speak for a "world religion," if only because we need different approaches and different languages, as it were, to deal with the different kinds of people there are in the world. "Sometimes," I heard him say in Europe, "people, in order to have closer relations [with other traditions], stress only the positive things. That's wrong! We have to make clear what are the fundamental differences." In almost the next sentence, though, he added that whenever he saw an image of the Virgin Mary, he was moved: which human being does not have a mother?

Because of the "fast pace of life" in the West, he told me once, monks in the East may have a small advantage over their counterparts in the West when it comes to meditation (though no sooner had he said this than he remembered some Catholic monks he'd visited in France who seemed unsurpassable in their single-pointed concentration); yet Buddhists, he said, perhaps had something to learn from Christians and others when it came to social action and bringing the fruits of their practice out into the world. As he said that, I recalled how Bono, the ardently Christian lead singer of the group U2, had been asked in 1990 to write a song for a Tibetan Freedom Concert and had come up with a haunting ballad about how we share "one love, one blood, one life, you've got to do what you should," and yet concluded, again and again, "we're one, but we're not the same." The song had become one of the group's talismanic anthems, which I'd heard sung in the dusty Current Event café in Dharamsala, and was a favorite at modern weddings. And yet, Bono always stressed, the song was about divisions, inherent differences—the fact that we can never be as one as we would like.

Every monk is the same monk insofar as he journeys into a similar silence and a parallel darkness—the blackness behind our thoughts we find in meditation—and every monk is the same monk as every lover is the same lover: it doesn't matter whether the object of your devotion is called Angela or Jigme or Tom, whether she existed in Sappho's time or right now. Yet every monk is most the same monk because his journey into solitude, community, and obedience is a way, really, for him to bring something transformative to the larger world, in the attention he brings to it.

"Be not *simply* good," as Thoreau wrote in his first letter to Harrison Blake, "be good for something."

Perhaps the most moving moment I ever witnessed in Dharamsala came in 1988, when I was invited, during the Tibetan New Year celebrations centered on the Dalai Lama's temple, to stand in on one of the meetings the Dalai Lama holds with Tibetans who have just arrived, after treacherous flights across the mountains, to see him again. Many of these people had risked their lives traveling three weeks across Himalayan passes in midwinter to meet with him for a few minutes and then would cross back over the mountains, perhaps never to see him again.

The people who were gathered in the room, maybe thirty or so, were strikingly ragged, their poor clothes rendered even poorer and more threadbare by their long trip across the snowcaps. They assembled in three lines in a small space, and all I could see were filthy coats, blackened faces, sores on hands and feet, straggly, unwashed hair.

When the Dalai Lama came into the room, it was as if the whole place began to sob and shake. Instantly, among almost all the people assembled on the floor, there was a wailing, a convulsive movement, a release of all the feelings (of hope and fear and concern and relief) that had been building inside some of them for over thirty years. The man sat before them, seeking them out with shrewd, attentive eyes, and none of the adults before him could even look at him.

"Even we cannot watch this, often," said the Dalai Lama's

private secretary, who had stood by his side, imperturbably, as calm as the monk he once was, for almost a quarter of a century at that point. The Dalai Lama sat firmly in the middle of the tumult, though later he would tell me that although "generally, sadness is manageable," even he was sometimes moved to "shed a tear" when he saw all the hopes that these people brought to him, and all that they had suffered.

"Sometimes we try to find someone else to do this for us," the secretary whispered to me where we stood. "It's just too much."

The Dalai Lama tends to be more brusque with Tibetans than he is with Westerners, partly because he knows that this is what they expect of him, and partly because he knows that they would be discomfited by too much familiarity from their godhead. But now he went down the lines, greeting each person in turn, asking (I could guess) where this person came from, how things were in her local area, what might be done to help. Each person, in answer to the questions, looked down, or just began to howl and shake with sobs.

Only a few children sitting in the front, the smallest in the party, answered the questions, their high, piping voices telling him they came from Kham, or their father was a farmer, or the trip had taken them twenty-three days. Only the children had not been storing up their hopes for all these years, with only this one chance to release them. Then, after making sure that all the refugees would be properly looked after, and given new homes here if that was what they wanted, the Dalai Lama told them to keep their spirits up and their hearts intent on how they could help others.

The four hours every morning of meditation were, I saw now, straightforward compared with the house those foundations supported.

IN PRACTICE

You must invent your own religion, or else it will mean nothing to you. You must follow the religion of your fathers, or else you will lose it.

—HASIDIC PROVERB

THE GLOBALIST

To make your way to Dharamsala, the strung-out settlement south of the Himalayas to which much of the world seems to be beating a path these days, you need a lot of determination and a strong dose of reality. You can fly to Amritsar and then take a five-hour drive from the Sikh city. But the Golden Temple, which sits shimmering on a pool at the center of Amritsar, the holiest shrine for all Sikhs, bears bullet holes from a near civil war twenty years ago when Indira Gandhi's troops stormed the sacred space to try to rout the militant Sikhs calling for their own nation. And even the road up to Dharamsala is far from unworldly: I once saw four separate cars smashed along the road, some with bloody bodies laid out beside them.

You can also fly to Jammu and take a five-hour drive from there. Jammu, however, sits in the heart of Jammu and Kashmir state, another restricted war zone where fighting has broken out repeatedly for fifty years or more; the last time I visited the small airport there, practically the only other passengers I saw were blue-helmeted peacekeepers sent by the United Nations to try to heal the wounds of Kashmir. Most travelers going to Dharamsala from Delhi take an overnight train to Pathankot, followed by a three-and-a-half-hour drive, braving the station in the Indian capital where figures swarm around foreign passengers, hands extended, many of the beggars going to sleep in the same hallway through which you pass. The final alternative is to drive, for ten hours or more, from Delhi, through narrow country roads ever more crowded with bicycles, cars, trucks, scooters, cows, and people, so jam-packed around every town that no car can move through what is in effect a mob. This is the route, for security's sake, the Dalai Lama usually takes.

There is, on paper, an airport only a few miles from Dharamsala, but on most days it is closed; sometimes it seems to be closed for years on end. When occasionally a small plane does take off from there, there is often no room for luggage, so that the few passengers arrive at the other end to learn (as in a Buddhist story about death) that none of their possessions have accompanied them. The wonky twelve-seater run by one of India's new start-up airlines is such a shaky prospect, on this route between the mountains, that even the Dalai Lama's celebrated calm is said to be unsettled by it.

The town itself, when you arrive, conforms to none of the rosy notions many visitors have entertained—of temples set among picturesque valleys and meditating monks in an otherworldly location. There are such temples, often dramatically placed, and there is always snow on the mountains that rise up to fifteen thousand feet here, the foothills of the Himalayas; Tibet is barely a hundred miles away. But what greets you, as you get off a bus or step out of your taxi from the airport or far-off rail station, are some very muddy little lanes with open sewers running beside them, and a jumble of broken shops, overseas phone parlors, and guesthouses tumbling up and down the unpaved slopes (the last time I counted, there were eighty-one guesthouses in this settlement of only twenty thousand people offering rooms for less than seven dollars a night). The signs say "Dreamland" and "Lost Horizon" and "Tibet Memory," flyers on the walls sing of Shiva Full Moon Parties, and everywhere, along the grimy lanes, are the world's young and the seekers of five continents, being besieged by Indian taxi drivers and purveyors of wisdom, and Tibetans who stand outside shops called "Kundalini Cosmic Souvenirs" or roadside stalls offering "spiritual gems."

You have ended up, you may well imagine, in some wild bazaar of the sacred and the profane. Notices around town advertise "Traditional Tibetan Universal Massage," remind you that "Harmonising with the Moon Courses Are Taking Place at House Om Tara," ask for news of a man from near Seattle who's gone missing. The British alighted on Dharamsala in 1849 and set up the little Anglican church, the army cantonment, the cottages called Ivanhoe and Eagle's Nest, which are still the first things you see if you arrive by bus. But an earthquake destroyed the settlement in 1905, and hardly had it begun to recover than Partition, in 1947, sent up to 70 percent of its people away. McLeod Ganj, the area the Tibetans have settled, at fifty-four hundred feet, a few miles above the everyday little Indian town of Dharamsala, was a ghost town when the Dalai Lama and his family arrived here in 1960, and to this day many people believe that Prime Minister Nehru offered it to the exiled Tibetans as a way to put them out of view, only three hundred miles from Delhi on the map but, in practice, tucked away in another universe.

The town that has arisen around the Tibetan leader has the feeling, therefore, like so much in the Tibetan situation, of an inner diagram or an extended symbol. You hear that inscriptions mentioning a Buddhist monastery from more than two thousand years ago have been found in the Kangra Valley below; when the Chinese traveler Hsuan Tsang passed through in the year 635, he reported seeing fifty monasteries, with two thousand monks in them. You learn that the very word "Dharamsala" means, too fittingly, "a place of shelter," often for pilgrims. You gather that the house where the Dalai Lama first lived when he arrived here, alert for visitations of bears and leopards and deer, is now, too perfectly, a "mountaineering institute." But what hits you most about this highly improvised, unorthodox assemblage of houses and hopes is that it seems to stand for so much else. Foreigners like to call it "Little Lhasa" and come here in search of the Tibetan wisdom that had never been available to the world till it came out of China in 1959 and landed in this neglected area. Tibetans struggle across the Himalayas and settle here because it is the home of their beloved leader and, therefore, the home of their hearts, the next best thing until Tibet itself can be recovered. Indian holiday makers and honeymooners flock into the flimsy, many-storied, wedding-cake new Indian hotels perched on slopes because they have heard it is a cool place where they can get a whiff of both West and East.

Dharamsala, built, in effect, by a man who is talking about the impermanence of nearly everything and the folly of desire, can seem very much like a community founded on longing, on homesickness and restlessness and dreams. The Tibetans who live here to some degree wish, more than anything, that, like a sand mandala, it can be dissolved and they can return to the place of which it is a mere replica; many foreigners who visit are exiles of a deeper kind who hope to make a home in this foreign culture, surrounded by customs that are not their own. The Tibetans look to the Westerners, often, as emissaries from the land of abundance and freedom they dream of; the Westerners gather around the Tibetans to hear about antiquity and mysticism.

To get almost anywhere in Dharamsala, you have to scramble up steep, steep slopes made of nothing but mud and jagged rocks and cow dung, so dark after nightfall that even a flashlight or small candle does not prevent you from falling on your face or lurching suddenly into a ditch. Pathways twist around the side of mountains, over pieces of industrial piping, through small forests where, it is whispered, women often get attacked or confronted by exhibitionists. And the weather changes precipitously, as if, in the classic Buddhist metaphor, standing for the mind (different, shifting clouds in front, and deep blue sky always within).

Dharamsala is the single rainiest spot in all of monsoonal India, and in the summer it is notoriously sludgy, the unstinting downpours turning everything into a damp cave of sorts; in winter, snow and ice lie on the ground, and the little lanes are dark and forlorn for much of the day. And then, out of nowhere, the sun begins to shine and picks out the marigolds outside the bright houses, the flowering honeysuckle in the spring, the gold turrets and yellow walls of the temples set on hillsides and in valleys, and you can easily feel as if you have landed in a realm of enchantment.

The Tibetans are an outdoors people, coming from a land where temperatures may differ by forty degrees Fahrenheit in the shadows and under the high Himalayan sun. They love to congregate on lawns for picnics, to climb up to their rooftops, to sit on terraces; they decorate their homes and temples in festive, fresh shades of gold and white and blue. Dogs yap from the open spaces of the roofs, nuns sit in the sunlight shaving one another's heads or studying sutras, games of basketball start up in one of the settlement's many courts. Anything seems possible in the clarifying mountain light.

Optimists note that the sun always breaks through again, especially in April, May, and October, and few places are better suited to the light than these mountain settlements of long views and open space. Pessimists note that every breakthrough of the sun—of course—is followed, out of nowhere, by another torrential downpour that knocks out all the lights across the valley, renders phones mute, and takes you, in effect, back to a world that seems medieval. Both notice that getting anywhere here—to the temple, post office, or meditation center—involves the conquest of a lot of obstacles.

Whenever I am staying in Dharamsala, I wake up just before dawn and go out into the blue-black night, the only sound at that hour wild dogs barking along the muddy lanes, and perhaps a few domestic dogs answering their barks from indoors. Very few lights are visible in the Dharamsala night, and what one feels more than houses are the presences of the mountains above, the untamed nature of the entire region. A few figures will be proceeding along the main road past the central temple already, and on some days I follow along with them, walking past the entrance to that temple and down to a path that cuts between the pines. The people all around me in the dark are generally the same I'd see in Lhasa— small Tibetan women with gray braids and weathered faces, toothless smiles, their brothers or husbands beside them in strong mountain gear—all of them spinning prayer wheels and murmuring constantly as they take the Lingkhor, or roughly mile-long pilgrims' path, around the hill on which the Dalai Lama lives.

Along the tiny path Indian Buddhist monks are sometimes sitting, converted Hindus in tangerine robes, looking for alms, and a man seated in a little makeshift cave carving *mani* stones, or small rocks on which auspicious messages and prayers are painted in yellow and white and orange. Cows sometimes drift up from the trees below, and after light has begun to show above the mountains, white butterflies twirl in the brightening air. In one place, the

hill leading up to where the Dalai Lama sleeps (and now is meditating) is crisscrossed with rows of prayer flags, generating their
good wishes into the increasingly blue skies; juniper is being
burned inside two large, *kiva*-like white *stupas,* and three monks
are sitting in a row outside a little chapel full of candles, reciting
prayers for the Dalai Lama's long life.

In Lhasa, three such pilgrimage circuits traversed the holy
places of the city, and here in exile the Tibetans who remember
Tibet are doing what they can to keep the old rites going. Around
the temple itself, on the top of the hill, monks and old men and lots
of Tibetan kids are circumambulating along a smaller circuit, chat-
ting with friends as they go, reciting sutras, hardly stopping, as the
tourists do, to admire the new light catching the windows of the
hotels along the ridge. And every Wednesday, as well as every day
when the Dalai Lama is not in town, the petitioners walking along
the outside circuit, perhaps sixty of them in all, stop by the stupa,
and the men sit down and join in with the chants, for an hour or
longer, and then everyone gets up and stands in a line, facing the
hill and the leader's house, and sings the country's national anthem. Then they all stand still and quietly recite a prayer for the
Dalai Lama's long life and good health, before throwing *tsampa,* or
Tibetan barley, up into the sky, to bring health and blessings to
their leader.

As I walk along this course early one morning, I notice, pressed
among the stones, not far from where someone has had the U.N.
resolutions about Tibet from forty years ago painted onto mani
stones, a little picture, the size of a place mat, of the Potala Palace in
Lhasa. It is already wrinkled, and the wind flaps it this way and that
as it flutters between the rocks. The next day, when I go, it is still
there, but more crumpled still. The next day, I wonder if it will tear.

Up above, in the main temple, where young monks debate, is

another painting of the former home of the Dalai Lama, the classic centerpiece of Tibet, in all its glory, sitting above the tumbling, whitewashed town of Tibetan Lhasa. In the antechamber to the Dalai Lama's audience room, there is, more realistically, a picture of Lhasa today, in which the Potala hovers, contextless, among the shopping malls and nightclubs and Jeans West outlets of a high-rising Chinese town.

As you begin to walk around Dharamsala and to grow familiar with its features, a pattern slowly emerges from the mess of scrambly, irregular paths that zigzag crazily over rough slopes and between the pines and around ridges that look down on monasteries. You realize that there is, in fact, an order, a vision, hiding out inside the seeming chaos, which comes to float above it a little like the classic Buddhist image of the lotus in the mud. The official center of the settlement, the first sight most visitors come across, is a dusty, bleary little square, just large enough for a filthy bus to drop off passengers, turn around, and then head down the hill again into the plains, a perfect, cacophonous model of the muddle of streets, pizza parlors, low-speed Internet caves, souvenir shops, and bookstores squeezed into every last corner and back alleyway of the spaced-out village. But as you stand amid this crush of enticements and desperate hopes, you can see that you are at the center of a mandala of sorts (though not, these days, the swirling mandala of monks that Thomas Merton registered).

Six little roads splay out from the clamorous little square. If you follow one of them, up through the pine forests, you come to a lake and, above it, the Tibetan Children's Village, a sprawling compound of houses and buildings that stands as the formal center of Tibetan education today, the reason many children come all the way from Tibet in order to be schooled in their traditional culture. If you take the next road up, you arrive at the gold-roofed temple, as it seems, that houses the Tibetan Institute of Performing Arts, where classical Tibetan folk opera and dance—as well as modern theater—are taught and performed to keep these forms alive. The next road along will bring you to a waterfall, past a Hindu temple, and to a clump of houses scattered across the hills where global villagers enjoy a homemade Shangri-La amid some German bakeries and wood-fire pizza joints.

A fourth road, if followed along for fifteen or twenty minutes, will take you to the center of official Tibet lore, the Library of Tibetan Works and Archives, where many of Tibet's old books and treasures reside amid the higgledy-piggledy little offices that represent the government in exile (with the state oracle's temple at one side of the cluster). Not far away is the Tibetan Medical and Astrological Institute. And another road will lead in ten minutes to the Dalai Lama's own house; the central Thekchen Choeling temple beside it; his own private Namgyal monastery, with 175 monks inside it, as it used to be around him in the Potala Palace; and his Institute of Buddhist Dialectics, housing some of Tibetan Buddhism's greatest philosophical masters, who thrash out the nature of being in something akin to an Institute of Advanced Studies in the West.

The Dalai Lama sits, metaphorically, at the center of the settlement, you soon see, "His Holiness" coming up in almost every conversation, his face beaming down from even the grocery shops of Indians and the carpet emporia of Kashmiris. He is very much the presence around which everything turns. And when you get off the bus into the clangor of competing dreams (the Eagles' "Lyin' Eyes" floating down from the McLlo café above you, tapes and cakes offered at the Rajneesh shop a few feet away, one of Dharamsala's many dirty little dives offering *Diary of a Mad Black Woman* and *Be Cool* on its DVD screen, in a tiny, ill-smelling dark room, and Nowrojee General Merchants, the one store here since 1860, still selling Andrews Liver Salt and Pears' soap, as if Lord Curzon was on his way), you realize that this is the rare city that has come up from scratch, according to a plan.

Almost as soon as he came into exile, in 1959, the Dalai Lama seized the chance to get rid of much of the red tape and serfdom that had beset Tibet in the past, and treating his new home as a tabula rasa on which to sketch a kind of new, improved Tibet—a Tibet 2.0, it can sometimes seem—that would draw upon what was best in its past, jettison the rest, and, most important, learn from its mistakes by schooling itself in the ways of the world (and of the modern, changing world at that). He set up a nursery school in his first year in exile (his commitment always to the future, which can be changed, and not to the past, which cannot), and after a while the policy was introduced that all children in exiled Tibet's elaborate network of schools would take classes in Tibetan till the age of ten or so, so they would be deeply connected with their original source, and then English thereafter, so they would be in tune with the wider world.

He oversaw the formation of a global network of settlements and monasteries and tried to urge his monks to put behind them the often poisonous animosities and rivalries that contributed, many believe, to Tibet's downfall in the past (different regions and different Buddhist schools quarreling with one another or only protecting their own, instead of presenting a united front to resist Chinese or other intruders). He began slowly, as intimated earlier, to give women, for example, opportunities they had not had before (to the point where nuns in Dharamsala can now earn doctoral degrees and are allowed to become abbots, as they never could in

Tibet, and a woman was appointed for the first time to the Cabinet). And, most of all, he started trying to give up power so that his people would (true to Buddhist philosophy) rule themselves. The very year he arrived in Dharamsala, he began drafting a charter for a new democratic Tibet, and even when Thomas Merton met him, forty years ago, he was saying that he wished he had more time for the spiritual, not the political, side of his life.

The Assembly of Tibetan People's Deputies was set up, roughly along the lines of the House of Commons, with three men and one woman from every province of Tibet, a representative from each of the main four schools of Tibetan Buddhism, and a representative of the Bon religion, as well as one person designated by the Dalai Lama as a spokesman of the arts and sciences. In 1990 he pushed the democratic process further by extending the Assembly to forty-six members, and in 2001 Tibetans enjoyed the first democratic election in their history as exiles in thirty-seven countries voted for a new prime minister to be the official head of their aspirations, choosing the gentle scholar-monk Samdhong Rinpoche. (In practice, of course, much of this is notional, since the Dalai Lama remains, quite literally, a god for the Tibetans, beyond reproach and challenge, and his prime minister can be no more, really, than his agent in the assembly of people's deputies.)

Dharamsala, the Dalai Lama seemed to be saying, would be the center of a new kind of experiment. So long as Tibetans could not enjoy freedom of worship or speech or movement in Tibet itself, they would create a new Tibet around the world, upgraded in certain ways and to some extent linked not by common soil but common purposes, a community of vision. Creating new forms as he went along, he was building up, out of necessity, a kind of virtual Tibet, a new global settlement in which people would be gathered not around a single campfire or village green but around shared hopes and a linked sense of responsibility. If it achieved anything at all, this experiment could offer a new, more positive way of thinking about their destinies for the Palestinians, the Kurds, the Uighurs, and the ever increasing number of exile groups around the world who do not have a charismatic leader and a colorful history to recommend them to the world's attention. In a way, propelled by calamity—having had to run out of the burning house that was his homeland—the Dalai Lama was suggesting that community and neighborhood could, even should, be constructed inwardly.

Centered in a ramshackle collection of huts remote even by Indian standards, joining together a group of people (no more than 150,000 worldwide) smaller than the citizenry of a typical Los Angeles suburb, Tibet in exile can at best only whisper a new possibility to the world, though the outsized popularity of its leader and the longtime talismanic appeal of the culture itself have given it a much larger appeal than it would have otherwise. The Dalai Lama's first priority always has been (and will continue to be, if there is another Dalai Lama) the protection of his people in Tibet, who still represent 98 percent of the Tibetans in existence, and who cannot, yet, participate in his democratic experiment at all. But so long as he cannot get to them, he will bring Tibet into the world and offer a Buddhist vision of policy making: reform Tibet by reforming the inner heart of Tibet.

In Tibet itself the government in Beijing has brought in, by one count, 224 karaoke parlors, 658 brothels, and one thirteen-story Public Security Office on the main streets of Lhasa alone, to create a look that would not be out of place in Atlantic City. The small capital now has a population of two hundred thousand, ten times its size in 1950, and it has been swollen to cover twenty times as much area as it used to occupy. The idea is that material plenty will liberate people from the feudalism of worship, and that modernity means having access to satellite television, sexy dance halls, and the spoils of Wal-Mart and Nike (the Chinese government even recently increased the salary of Tibetan officials by a factor of three, as if to enforce the belief that what machine guns had failed to achieve, material temptation might).

Dharamsala has all that, too—the Tibetans have always been a highly mercantile and shrewd group of traders—but it is built on the idea that modernity has to do with a set of values rather than with a set of goods, that it is the result of a cast of mind, even more than of a way of life. In their loftiest moments, those who are intrigued by the case study could even see the temples scattered across the slopes of Dharamsala as offering the beginnings of a Buddhist vision of a city on a hill (looked over not by God but, as befits the Buddhist tradition, by men).

To walk around the little lanes and the kerfuffle of dirty cafés and dusty shops, past signs saying, "the only Internet café where all proceeds go directly to the Tibetan cause" or "Charitable Trust Handicrafts," is to see how great a distance separates vision from reality—and how, indeed, vision can arise from reality only inch by inch. Dharamsala, as if in deference to the notorious filth of old Tibet, has often had almost no garbage collection, and refuse clogs its ill-kept streets; the path leading down to the idyllic Tsechokling Monastery starts next to a huge pile of trash. One day, as I walked along the always cluttered main street, barely wide enough for the single cars that barrel through it, horns screaming, I found, amazingly, a small opening in the thoroughfare, but that was only because a crowd had gathered around a space in which an Indian boy and a Tibetan were engaged in a fistfight.

One bright Saturday in the spring I went to see the Dalai Lama while he was in the midst of presenting forty-six days of uninterrupted teachings (he saw me just after he had completed his morning session of initiations and empowerments in the temple next door, on his lunch break, in effect), and I asked him how the Tibetan experiment in exile could offer a model for the world. I could tell that modesty—and realism—prevented him from making any claims for himself or his people, but at the same time he had clearly thought about the challenge as few political leaders ever had the chance to do. The minute I posed the question, he referred, with characteristic precision, to encounters he had had in Germany, in Australia, in North America and Chile, with other groups likewise addressing the issue of how to keep their traditions alive. He remembered one indigenous leader who had delivered a long, long speech demanding that all his precious land be given back to him—"Unrealistic!" as the Dalai Lama put it, with a great accelerating burst of laughter. He recalled frictions within the Tibetan community in 1951, and proposals that had been offered about how to set up exile settlements in 1959, and what to do with Tibet's small group of guerrillas in the 1970s. One idea had been advanced by a member of his family, one by a first cousin of the private secretary who was sitting by his side, but both, he remembered now (as if it had all happened four days, and not almost five decades, before), were wrong.

When first he decided that the Tibetans should set up whole settlements, with central monasteries and laypeople around them, in southern India, his people said they could not survive, he told me. The heat, the unfamiliar food, the absence of snow mountains led them to tell him they were going to die. "The next time I visited, they're still there! So I said to them, 'You haven't died yet!' " he went on, the infectious laughter breaking out again.

Much in Tibetan culture—many customs, the clothes, the long plaits, the heavy coats made for the Himalayan winter—had to be abandoned, he said, in the heat of the tropics. Since these are fading already in Tibet, "no need worry, no need effort! Cultural heritage—not relevant in today's world, so let it go." But in terms of a language, a way of thinking, the attempt to pass on to children, say, a compassionate feeling for animals, those are relevant anywhere, beneath the surface. "A young child has no idea of next life or sin or these things, but in their family tradition, from an early age, they hear 'It's not good to kill animals.' So these things are worthy of being preserved. And can be preserved."

I came out from the talk buoyed, not just by the ideas he had outlined but, more, by the precision with which he had cited specific precedents and parallels, and the modest limits he seemed to be setting for himself. He had told Aboriginals in Australia, for example, that they should keep their own indigenous names even if they were going to take on, for practical purposes, European names; in the same spirit, he actually urged some Tibetans to receive initiations from Chinese teachers, since in places the Chinese tradition of Buddhism was flourishing more than the Tibetan. In the context of trying to lead an exiled group into a new definition of itself, realism seemed at least as valuable as optimism.

Yet just twelve hours before, the previous night, I had been in a little room down the road, talking to some of the most vocal members of the new generation of Tibetans, who had experienced only displacement and a longing for a place they knew mostly through their parents' stories. Seven of us had been crowded into a single room, in a block of small cells (although the flat belonged to one of the senior members of the Dalai Lama's government in exile). The wife of the household was away in Boston, leaving her little kids to run around, barely tended by their aunt and grandmother, and one of those present, stationed abroad, was mourning the fact that his teenage daughter was entirely European in manners and dress.

The refrain of the younger Tibetans in the room—and they could have been speaking for Tibetans all around them—was loss: they were lost souls from a lost generation, with no sense of who they were or where they belonged. They spoke fluent Hindi and had grown up entirely in India, with Indian friends and tastes, but they did not wish to become Indian. They spoke good English and had contacts in the foreign world, but each step toward England or America would take them farther from Dharamsala and, most of all, Tibet.

They were Tibetans who knew nothing about Tibet, and who fought and prayed for a place that at one level they knew could not be the place they imagined.

One of them, in desperation, had stolen into Tibet for three months. Almost as soon as he crossed over into his homeland from Ladakh, Tenzin said, he was apprehended and put into detention. "They beat me every day in prison," he went on softly in the ill-lit room, "though they took care not to leave any marks." We walked out into the full-moon quiet of the spring evening, the broken offices and half-neglected rooms all around somewhat hopefully outlining a government in exile. "I was a romantic boy," he declared, though not yet thirty. "I thought I would go to Tibet and somehow win independence by myself."

Now he tried to agitate in different ways, writing poems and, when the Chinese premier was paying a visit, climbing all fourteen stories of the Oberoi Towers in Bombay to unfurl the banned Tibetan flag and a red banner that said, "Free Tibet." "We are Tibetans with Chinky faces," a friend of his said in disgust as we walked up the slope to where the Dalai Lama's house sat and slept in the clear night.

The young Tibetans at the dinner had presented me, before I left, with a book they had just brought out, the first anthology of Tibetan poetry in English, they said, in the history of their people. The book seemed mostly a mix of cries and shouts and, especially, questions. What am I, where am I going, how can I help the country I've never seen? What do I do with my Indian accent and Western dress? What is the price of going against those elders who have seen Tibet and fled from it? The most striking feature of all the poems, from young and old, from every corner of the globe (such is the state of the Tibetan diaspora today), was its lack of answers.

One poem began, somewhat typically,

> I am just a soul in a fix
> Crying for the right direction
> My mind is so mixed
> It's in total confusion.

The biographical note at the end said that the poet had been "something of an enigma amongst his small circle of friends" and had lived a "life of dreams, drugs, desperation and rift." He had died at twenty-eight, leaving behind a dark blue diary full of poems about Tibet.

Perhaps these boys, as they often were, would have written similar poems had they grown up in Lhasa at a time without occupying Chinese. Many of their gestures, the romanticism of their sorrow, sounded like what you find when you open up any collection of university poems in Bombay or Guangzhou or, for that matter, New Haven. Perhaps they'd have begun, wherever they were, with a quotation from Sartre: "Human life begins at the far end of despair." Identity crises, the search for something, a sense of pervading sadness or frustration that reaches no farther than the small cosmos of the self, are, to some extent, the universal currency of the young.

But of course there was an extra component here, among people whose culture had, not long ago, been among the most self-contained and changeless in the world, and now had been propelled into a new kind of nomadism. When we came up into the center of the Tibetan settlement at the end of the evening, many of the people around us had faces that were tomato red, having been smeared with color by Indian boys celebrating the Hindi holiday of Holi. Two days from now, in the St. John in the Wilderness church down the road, the cheerful Indian priest who slept each night on the cold floor would spring to life and, putting a cassock over his sneakers and jeans, hand out two photocopied pages with the lyrics to "Morning Has Broken" on them (and "Have a Nice Day" at the end), so that the small congregation of foreigners could join him in singing Cat Stevens's modern hymn on Easter Sunday. A cappella because the old church was lacking an organ. The boys were outsiders, really, wherever they happened to find themselves. The Dalai Lama's injunction to build a home within was like an idea they knew already but could not begin to see how to implement.

Every month, once or twice, a bus labors up the hill into McLeod Ganj, and after bumping over potholes and squeezing between the unceasing lines of pilgrims, stops at a rickety little three-story building on a barely paved slope, and fifty or sixty wild Tibetans step out. They seem to belong to a different universe from the worldly exiles all around in leather jackets and sunglasses, speaking the hipster lingo of Bombay or Delhi. The girls wear no makeup, and the boys, even in their American T-shirts and caps, bring an air of otherness into the street. Their faces are untamed somehow, their clothes torn. They seem to be blinking as they step out into a world they have been dreaming of for all or most of their lives, only to find that it is cluttered and full of signs that say, bewilderingly, "STD" or "PCO," the opposite of peaceful or exalted (at home the streets are cleaner, and much more of a piece). Their noses are running, often, and some of their clothes bear the accumulated grime of twenty days of hard travel across twenty-thousand-foot peaks and in long-distance buses, nights spent in interim shacks for transients.

When they arrive at the reception center, they will stay, sometimes two to a bed, for a month or more, getting elementary lessons in English and Hindi and waiting till the Dalai Lama is back in town and they can see him at long last. After their brief audience, the children will be assigned to schools, the monks will be sent to monasteries, the elderly will often return to Tibet, hearts satisfied, and the rest will be sent where there is room or need for them. For those who, having seen the Dalai Lama, are ready to return to Tibet, the trip back is as hazardous as the trip out, and if they are caught by police on either side of the border, they will be sent to prison, sometimes in a large building in Shigatse known, with killing irony, as "the New Tibet Reception Center."

I met a newcomer in the Dharamsala center one sunny morning, crowded among the two hundred or so sitting listlessly on shared beds or walking around the corridors, not really in any fit state to join the larger world yet, and gathered that he had managed to get out through resourcefulness alone, learning fluent English, applying for a Chinese passport, and, having taken pains to send his younger brother and sister through college before he left (since it is they who would suffer if his absence was noted), leaving through legitimate channels. Strikingly enterprising—as many in Communist systems are, especially if from unapproved backgrounds—he told me how he got jobs with foreign NGOs in Tibet, traveled all around his homeland in the spirit of a journalist, saw how, when the World Bank sent fact-finding delegations to an area, "the Chinese township cadres pretended to be monks."

He had come out, he declared now, in order to tell the world the truth about Tibet, and to me it seemed he already spoke the language of the world at large, fluent in talk of "primary health care" and stories about getting arrested along with some foreigners (one of whom tried to jump out of a third-floor window in order to protect his research materials). In Tibet, he said, "hospitals are a marketplace," and "even the doctors don't know about blood-transmitting diseases. Hepatitis. T.B." Having been trained from birth to talk in terms of "patriotic reeducation programs" and "Public Security Officers"—the phrases came trilling out—he now spoke the language given him by activist foreigner friends, members of Médecins sans Frontières.

And yet something still came through. When he finally managed to leave his homeland, the trim young man in the smart North Face "Wind Stopper" told me, "I cried. The Nepali people, they are poor, but they are enjoying basic human rights. Poor is no problem if you are free." Someone who had freedom but no food might think differently, I thought to myself, but said nothing. "I saw on the street, on a busy road in Kathmandu, there was a small temple—there in the middle of the road—and they have to protect it. In Tibet, even a huge monastery they destroy if they're building a road in the same town."

Around him, grubby children stared up, transfixed. Eight hundred and twenty-four refugee children arrived at the Tibetan Children's Village in 2004, a more or less typical year, swelling the already crowded classrooms and living spaces beyond the breaking point. Though many of them would go back to Tibet once their education was complete, they would go back as real Tibetans who knew their language and their history.

Another day, I chanced to run into Manuel Bauer, the photographer who was compiling an extraordinary archive of the Dalai Lama by following him around from dawn to dusk on most of his travels. As we repaired to a nearby restaurant for lunch, he told me how he had come to the Dalai Lama's attention by becoming the first photographer, anywhere, to chronicle the flight of modern Tibetans across the Himalayas, to freedom, risking his life to bring back the story.

It was April when his small group left, he said, just he and a Tibetan man and the man's daughter, only six years old. But already it was hideously cold. Chinese soldiers were everywhere, some of them ready to shoot simply because they were bored. Even on the brightest blue days, the wind was so fierce that it was known to blow snow into travelers' mouths, and the snow entered their systems and melted inside their bodies, causing many to die even in warm weather.

As a group of only three, he said, they moved quickly; they were able to travel by day, because they were so inconspicuous, instead of only after dark, as most refugees do, and they completed the trip in only sixteen days. But still there was derangement. "I lost my mind," the calm Swiss photographer said matter-of-factly in the quiet, sunlit restaurant. "For two, three days, I was in delirium. And in the delirium I was thinking, 'This six-year-old girl, she can move so fast. Why doesn't she carry bags? I have twenty kilos of equipment and bags to carry.' I was aggressive with her because I lost my mind."

When they crossed the Chinese border, he recalled, the trip grew only more hazardous. Many Nepali officials send Tibetans back to captivity, to satisfy the rulers in Beijing, though often they rob the Tibetans first. Even if the refugees can get to Kathmandu and the care of an official from the U.N. High Commission for Refugees, their problems are not over. "Sometimes the U.N. van, even with a U.N. person there, is stopped. And the Nepali police take everything! These refugees, they have come out with only a carpet, one bag, and they take that, the Nepali police, and send them back." The same story known around the world, among boat people from Vietnam, and Cubans, even Chinese trying to steal into America; refugees, already the most vulnerable people in the world, are perfect prey for pirates and corrupt officials.

"So you're safe only when you get to India?"

"No. I'm sorry to say this"—he had guessed my Indian heritage—"but the Indian people are not always honest. Sometimes they attack these refugees. They know they are defenseless."

"So you're really only safe when you get to Dharamsala?"

And here Manuel said nothing at all.

"When you got there, the man stayed with his daughter?"

The photographer's eyes now were red. The father deposited his daughter safely in the Tibetan Children's Village, he said, confident that she had a new life and home there, and then turned around and made the long, treacherous trip back into Tibet, alone.

There is a real excitement, inevitably, in walking through a community that has been devised by a single man, and that man not a Castro or Disney or Kim Il Sung but a philosopher and a monk:

you feel that an experiment is being conducted on behalf of one of the fastest-growing nations in the world—the land of the deracinated (since by some counts there are now one hundred million refugees in the world, part of a tribe that is twice as populous as Australia and Canada combined). There is a quickening sense—a Buddhist sense, perhaps—of things (at least in theory) being always in movement, everything becoming a work in progress; I return after two years away and find that nearly all the restaurants in the area have stopped serving beer—in deference to classical Buddhist disapproval of intoxicants—and experts are now being brought in from Sweden to help with the epidemic of wild dogs running around.

The Dalai Lama is even in the rare position, for a ruler, of trying to conduct a coup against himself, attempting to give up power as fast as his people push it back at him. At its best, to step into a community based on spiritual and not political values is to enter a world turned on its head, where—this the Dalai Lama's hope—freedom means freedom from fear and wealth means inner resources. Power, ideally, means self-sovereignty, in the democratic and the inner sense.

As I walked along the streets of McLeod Ganj, therefore, I found myself besieged by whole notions of possibility: Jewish leaders were here to tell the Dalai Lama how they kept a culture going after the First and Second Temples were destroyed, civil rights workers who marched with Martin Luther King were sitting in the drafty rooms trying to see what they could lend to this nonviolent struggle, a new garbage collection system and cleanup operation had been organized by Richard Gere. Once, talking to some young Tibetans about whether to follow their political urges or their leader's advice, I heard two young people pipe up, and learned they were Mexicans; they had come here in part to ask Tibetans how they might resolve their own differences with an insurgency in Chiapas. Another time, in the garden of my guesthouse, I found myself enjoying breakfast daily with philanthropists and government officials from Germany, Romania, America, here to do what they could to help. In its starriest aspects, Dharamsala is consecrated to the idea that the problems of one place are the concerns of every place, in our ever more linked universe.

The sixth road that sprays out from the central square at the traditional entrance to McLeod Ganj zigzags all the way down the slope, between Himalayan oaks and deodars, past the Anglican church and the "Officers' Mess" buildings, past tea plantations and terraced fields, over a bridge, and into an open space where, with the help of a local Japanese architect, the Tibetans have built a glittering center called the Norbulingka Institute, whose pathways and reflecting ponds and gold-roofed central temple and flowering trees against the snowcaps are closer to most people's vision of Shangri-La than anything in congested and noisy McLeod Ganj, forty minutes away by car. Among its pavilions and elegant classrooms, master *thangka* painters and statue artists and woodcarvers from Tibet pass down their training to new generations of apprentices, many of whom study with them for ten years or more, and out of these workshops come the golden Avalokitesvaras, the intricate mandalas, the woven snow lions that will be sent around the world. Walk to the back of the compound and pull open a little gate, and, after a three-minute stroll beside open fields, you come to the Dolma Ling Nunnery, where two hundred nuns, most of them newly escaped from Tibet, are lunging back and forth in classical debates in the quiet afternoons, taking the traditional form of the monks and making it something more murmurous, less martial.

A little down the road, in Sidhbari, the Karmapa, having

escaped from China and arrived in Dharamsala just as Tibetan hopes were beginning to fade, still stays, regarded by many Tibetans and foreigners as a new, young embodiment of Tibet's prospects, in spite of his restricted movements. And a few hours after watching the state oracle go into his trance one spring Saturday, I came down to this spot to see the Dalai Lama open a new Gyuto Temple, replacing what was for five centuries one of the most celebrated and advanced establishments in Tibet. A Tantric college set up for the equivalent of postdoctoral students of Tibetan Buddhism, Gyuto was—now is—one of the two places in the Tibetan world where monks traveled to the farthest reaches of consciousness and thought, in part by performing austerities barely comprehensible to the rest of us: for nine years in Tibet, each of the monks was not allowed to return to his own room or to take off his robes, and had to live, meditate, and sleep on the same eighteen-inch-wide pallet, using his wooden tea bowl as a pillow. Trained by such hardships, perhaps, the thirty (out of nine hundred) who managed to escape to India were able to continue their meditations when they came out into exile, in dirt parking lots and under trees, finally receiving permission to make and sell Tibetan rugs to keep themselves alive.

For years they tried to build up their temple again in India, at first not even possessing monastic robes, and at last they were able to acquire some land near Dharamsala, and to spend almost fifteen years developing and constructing a prayer hall. But even after it was completed, it took another seven years to build accommodations for the monks, and even though the sparkling new center now has six three-story blocks, including kitchens, dining rooms, and a guesthouse, it still lacks even a hot water supply. As the Dalai Lama comes down to perform the official opening—many of the monks from McLeod Ganj making their own way down, so the fields and two-lane roads of the valley run red with novices, the group of Australian Buddhists who have provided much of the financing sitting in one corner, smiling beatifically in the white scarves the Dalai Lama has just given them—he does not linger much on the completion of the task; the building, he tells the monks, is only the beginning.

Any building with nothing inside it is worth very little, he goes on; the only thing that matters, ultimately, is the construction of a more durable and living building inside, one that you can carry everywhere and that will withstand the visitations of earthquake and flood and change of government. He is talking to his monks but, as ever, the message reaches the Australians and all the rest of us gathered in the grand new prayer hall as the sun streams through the windows and thousands sit in a festival of red and gold outside. The temple is, at most, a metaphor, a gateway, a vessel, perhaps, for the inner shrine, much as could be said for all of Dharamsala.

The Dalai Lama is, I realize ever more strongly, aiming at a universal lesson, going back, as is his way, to that part of his experience that even we from Japan or California can relate to. And the more politically minded globalists at the scene may note that no previous generation had ever had a chance to see a Dalai Lama, or almost any Tibetan teacher; that in our parents' generation, only a handful of foreigners could even dream of setting foot in a Tibetan temple of any kind; that this gorgeous new construction is the result of Australian money, largely, and itself a way of transmitting Buddhism, or simple human values, to far-off cultures that previously would have had no exposure to them. With the opening of the temple, he and his followers are at once re-creating old Tibet, hoping to improve upon it, bringing it out into the modern world, and speaking to the displaced everywhere, who wish to re-create their own lost homes in some substantial and enduring way.

But the nature of globalism, as of anything, is to be a reflection of human longing, in all its many forms. And as I look around me in the afternoon of celebrations, it's easy to feel that the Tibetan leader, with his pragmatism and his hunger for experimentation, reform, a realistic radicalism, is sketching a new kind of vision; but many of the rest of us add footnotes to it, scribble notes to ourselves on it, drop tea on it and blur some of the details, or scrawl ideas across the paper till the original is barely legible.

Put more simply, Dharamsala is as compressed and bittersweet an image of the global village as I have ever seen. All the stuff of all the globe flows into its already overcrowded streets—all the ideas and fears and projections and designs—and it's never easy to see whether Tibet is getting the better of the outside world or the other way round. At certain times of the year, one of the Dalai Lama's private secretaries has told me, literally half the population of Upper Dharamsala is Israeli. A whole section of the menu at the Asoka Indian restaurant is in Hebrew, and a clock in a typical international phone parlor shows the time in Tel Aviv. So many young Israelis, just released from their compulsory military service back home, descend on Dharamsala (part of a circuit of laid-back settings and cheap drugs they have set up, from Goa on the beach to Manali and Rishikesh in the mountains) that one celebrated rabbi from New York is now in full-time residence nearby, trying to make sure that not too many of his flock are lost to Tibetan Buddhism.

The streets of the little exile settlement swarm with so many henna-haired Chileans and dreadlocked young Danes, so many Swedish girls arm in arm with ponytailed boys from eastern Tibet, and professional drifters with a somewhat glazed look on their faces, that it's hard to tell sometimes if it is a corner of Bali or one of the islands in the Gulf of Siam. The hand-lettered sign on the piece of cardboard leading to the Third I restaurant (the curious spelling itself a sign of something, some might say) offers "Origenal

Tibetan, Israeli, Indian, Chinese, Continental, pizza" and much more, all the way to "Marmite/Vegemite Toast and Mocha Shakes," and around it, in the hills, signs are painted on rocks in fluorescent blue, as on Ios in 1968, and mani stones are scribbled over with the collected wisdom of the ages: "Be gentle, be kind, this is a long journey" and "U be Bosatsu, I'll Be the Taxi-Driver Bringing You Home."

A Spanish Zen student with a shaved head is playing the didgeridoo on a rock and talking of the Indian in Rishikesh who sells didgeridoos along with tablas and tepees; the strung-out girl beside him is getting antsy because three shy Indian high school boys on a spring holiday want to come and say hello. I walk into a café in the idyllic village and ten or fifteen foreign pairs of eyes stare up at me from a series of pillows placed on the floor around a low table, crazy acid music blasting through the space and its denizens looking as if they've been on a very long trip indeed. Humus, Benotti Pie, Salom-la-Malka ("Everything with Extra Love") are all on the menu; also "Mountaineering Equipment."

To many a young Tibetan, each of these figures represents a new life, another world, a way out into a world of abundance and possibility not conceivable in Lhasa or in Dharamsala; and because the little settlement has become such a collection of foreigners of every kind, people converge from all over India to get their share of yen and euros. Yoga teachers from Goa and Kerala set up shop in the little guesthouses, offering classes on rooftops every morning and afternoon; vendors of wisdom of every stripe sell teachings that do not sound much like Buddhism at all—"GOOD NEWS," says a flyer outside the Dalai Lama's temple, and goes on to tell of a rinpoche possessed of "supernatural powers" who, here for the Dalai Lama's teachings, is ready to make his special powers available to the world. Legless mothers and lepers and urchins who crowd around you on the dusty footpaths, hands extended, come all the way across South Asia to beg for money, and some of them, longtime residents tell me, have been in the same little spot for twenty-five years or more, crouching by a slippery path each day, sleeping every night on a cold ledge beside the road, and sending remittances, often quite handsome, home to their families in the south. As I go for a walk one bright day while the Dalai Lama is offering his teachings, I see a sign that says a German woman and then a Tibetan were robbed and beaten as they took a shortcut through the trees; an Indian woman comes up to me, waving a hospital invoice; a Tibetan with a sweet, shy smile stops me and announces that he needs three dollars to have a tooth pulled out.

I could be walking through a Buddhist text, on suffering and need and decay and illusion. One day I find a list of sample sentences that a volunteer teacher, no doubt well-intentioned and idealistic, uses to help her native Tibetan students with their English.

"What is your favorite fruit?" and "Are you a disciple of anyone?" "Who is the nephew of Tsong Kha Pa?" and "How many years did Gandhi spend in prison?" And, in what comes to seem the inimitable lingo of McLeod Ganj, itself a hybrid name bringing together one nineteenth-century lieutenant-governor of the Punjab, David McLeod, with the Hindi word for neighborhood, "When we are mindful, deeply in touch with the merest moment, our understanding of what is going on deepens, and we begin to be flooded with joy, peace, and love."

One bright spring day, the slopes around Dharamsala beginning to light up with flowers of red and foaming pink, marigolds around the temples, primroses and buttercups, I meet a young Tibetan man whose dream is to become a writer. He was born in Amdo, in eastern Tibet, he tells me, but his father took him to Lhasa as a boy, and there he did what most twelve-year-old Tibetans in Lhasa do. "Lots of alcohol, play snooker, going to prostitutes. I never went to school or did job. The Chinese make it very cheap to buy beer, whiskey. Everything is cheap. So we do not like to go to school. We ask our parents for money and if they do not give, we steal from their pockets." Illiteracy in Tibet, he says, is running at 80 percent.

When he was fourteen, he tells me—and I wonder how many foreigners he has told the story to before, in his good English, knowing what it is worth, perhaps polishing its details—his father suddenly decided (because of those twelve-year-old's temptations, I surmise) that his son should go to Dharamsala. The boy joined a party of fifteen, as the youngest in the group, and, he says, "after seven days, people forgot they were from different places, different provinces, different worlds. It became really like a big family." As in a dream of exile. But after they got to India and freedom, the twenty-five-day ordeal behind them, the dream began to shiver. He became a nomad in a different key—Dalhousie, Mussoorie, southern India, Delhi. He didn't have credentials, English. He went to Tibetan schools, learned something, but still he didn't have what the world accepts as qualifications or a diploma.

"My dream is to be translator and guide," he goes on, "to work with foreign people" (to become a foreigner himself, I imagine).

"While I was running from Tibet," Tsering continues, with his engaging, unpracticed smile, "I got to know a girl. We were quite close. It often happens like that on these trips. Even we left the party behind for a while, were separate. But when we got to India, we were separated. I was going to one school, a middle school; she was two years bigger, she was sent to senior school. Two years after, I went to her. Someone I remembered, I never forget. But I was told, 'She has gone back Tibet.' So now I don't know what has happened. Only, she is gone."

It seems to speak for so many of the separations of exile. But going to Tibet sounds like such a strange thing to me, for a young woman who has risked her life to flee Tibet two years before (and who will face recriminations, perhaps, and a penalized family when she goes back).

It does not sound strange to Tsering: his own brother, having completed the treacherous flight, went back to Tibet after a year and a half. Life is easier there, he explains; there's less hustle, less need to work. You can get that cheap beer, loaf around; credentials aren't important.

"Are the Tibetans different in Tibet and in exile?"

"Tibetan people in Tibet are more honest."

"Really?" This is not what you'd expect of people living under a dictatorship, who have to work around the system or under it for every small thing.

"Sure. They believe in Buddhism, very devout, have much, much faith. They believe Buddha can help everything. Here it is more complicated. We need many books, we are thinking. We are more modernized."

"You dream of going to other countries."

"Yes." The bashful smile; our chocolate cake and Earl Grey tea are finished now. He fingers the loose spot in his mouth where he's got a sore wisdom tooth. "I want to go to native English-speaking country."

But he's been in exile long enough to know that it's a competitive business; most young Tibetans are clamoring for the few scholarships, interested girls, philanthropic sponsors who offer a way out and into the West.

"Even now," he tells me (there's folk music on the sound system of the Moonpeak Café; in the mornings it's Handel and Dylan), "four months ago, I was confused, I had two minds. One, I wanted to stay here, but also I was thinking go back Tibet. Then I thinking, if I go back, my life very easy. I have house, car; but I only help myself. If I stay here, and become a writer, maybe I can do some small thing for other people." The sweet smile that follows tells me that he knows that this good intention, like most others, is not much stronger than a prayer flag in a stiff wind.

Every year, just after the great celebration of the Tibetan New Year (which, because of the lunar calendar, generally falls in February or March), the Dalai Lama offers a set of spring teachings to reproduce Monlam, or the Great Prayer Festival, the highlight of the Tibetan calendar, which used to sweep across Lhasa in the old days. Great *thangka*s would be unscrolled across the massive white face of the Potala Palace, as many as ten thousand people would assemble to hear the Dalai Lama speak, and for sixteen days law and order would be placed in the uncertain hands of the *dob-dob*s, or soldier-monks of Drepung Monastery, five miles to the west. In Dharamsala, the teachings are the great event of the year; monks come from Bhutan and Nepal and Mongolia, from Korea and Taiwan and Italy and Tibet itself, to attend them, and laypeople from all the continents make a special effort to savor this great, almost unparalleled dose of the Tibetan leader. The rooms in many guesthouses are reserved more than a year in advance, e-mails fly across California asking for shared taxi rides from Delhi, movie stars wiggle out of important-seeming commitments to pursue what they regard as more pressing.

Every morning, the Dalai Lama comes out of his residence, surrounded by perhaps twenty or so others—senior monks, bodyguards, attendants, the spiritual head of the Mongolians (an ethnic Tibetan, as it happens), men carrying ceremonial scrolls and other objects—and takes a seat in front of his temple. As many as six thousand monks gather around him, many of them seated in a room on the second floor of the temple, able to follow him directly only by turning their backs to him and watching him speak on a TV screen. Hundreds of Tibetans sit on the ground, delighted just to be able to spend a fortnight within sight of their culture's incarnation. At least two thousand other foreigners also push into the little space, and often the crowds are so intense that they spill out onto lower terraces and rooftops where the Dalai Lama is completely out of view, but his voice, carried on transistors and large radios, booms across the valley.

It's quite a scene. Little girls in pink T-shirts—one says "Hello Kitty," one says "Om"—cavort around one year, while the Dalai Lama speaks on "Stages of the Path" once more, and Tibetan or Mongolian families pass their thermoses around, cheerfully sharing their salted yak-butter tea with everyone nearby in the audience. A foreigner with Jesus locks falling down to his shoulders sits stock-still, eyes closed, hands extended before him in the lotus position. Since most foreigners follow the rarefied philosophical explanations in translation on little six-dollar radios equipped with earphones, a crackle of English and Russian and even Chinese sounds differently in every ear. The people who cannot find room inside the main courtyard sit somewhere else out in the sun, boom boxes blasting the teachings beside them.

Foreigners keep their places in the courtyard with little handwritten signs and sleeping bags, marking them out days before the teaching begins; male and female Indian and Tibetan security officers with rusted machines laboriously check every person each time he or she comes in after breakfast or after the lunch break.

When the teachings adjourn, every afternoon around four-thirty, the paths and gulleys and slopes of Dharamsala run red with surging monks again; they stream between the flowering apple blossoms and mistletoe, and some of them head straight for the basketball court across from the Japanese, Thai, and Korean restaurants, for hard, slashing games in front of a graffiti-scribbled wall that could make anyone nostalgic for the Bronx (except that this wall says, "May Peace Prevail on Earth" and "Think Globally, Act Locally," next to some mock–Keith Haring drawings).

In a certain light, the odd contradictions of the place, and our global order, become apparent. Tibetan monks do a lot of things that look strange to Western or Indian observers: they pull out their cell phones on the street, they cluster around Internet parlors, and, enjoying their time in what for them is the big city, away from their remote settlements, they pour into little cafés for big dinners. Much of the time, like young boys anywhere, they seem to be talking about girls and cars. Meanwhile, many of the foreigners on the same streets—attorneys from Santa Monica, fund-raisers from Toronto, former ad-agency executives from Germany, students and activists from Argentina—are waking up before dawn to meditate, devoting all their services free of charge to the Tibetans, and living as vegetarians, even as ascetics. I climb up to a meditation center between the pines one bright morning and see that the day's schedule, neatly typed out, offers "Breakfast / Impermanence and Death / Suffering / Selflessness / Dinner / Equanimity."

One afternoon I walk out of my guesthouse, toward the center of town, and think of how the settlement around me has become an unlikely model of the recent history of the world. It was set up, after all, by the British as a summer retreat for those administrators from far-off Britain trying to rule India. It was then left to the Indians, and in turn handed over to the Tibetans. Now it looks simultaneously like a ragged version of a nonexistent Tibet, a mini-Kathmandu, and an epicenter of low-budget globalism. An Indian hotel, eager to get into the spirit of the Tibetan holiday, has strung a large banner across Temple Road to commemorate the Tibetan New Year, known as "Losar." The banner, placed just before the entrance to the Dalai Lama's temple and compound, says, cheerfully and unfortunately, "Happy Loser."

When I go into the Awasthi Cyber-Café, my daily haunt (needing to keep up with bosses across the world), it is to find almost all the twenty or so terminals being used, by travelers clicking away in Russian, Hebrew, Korean, and Japanese (one of them has a prized Webcam terminal and is accessing a sleepy friend in Tel Aviv). Beautiful *thangkas* from Ali Baba's Treasures hang above the computers, and a group of friendly, sweatered Indians quietly tend to every need, bringing cups of tea to anyone who pays, expertly navigating the Web to try to get around the fact that you can't access AOL, hurrying outside to start everything up again with a private generator when the electricity goes out across the valley.

As I wait the long, long minutes, stretching into hours, for the system to boot up, I notice that the man next to me (a Buddhist monk from Taiwan?) is receiving a message addressed to "Dear Ven. Tommy." The Israeli girl on the other side of me is typing, "I am so happy we are going to be married." An Internet café, especially in so remote a place as Dharamsala, is a collection of lost lives, or lives that seem very distant now, messages sent back and forth to new friends or loves you can hardly remember who, in their new (old) lives, can hardly remember you.

"I am not mean I want your money," a Tibetan blade whose on-screen name is "smileyboy" has just typed; if the girl he's wooing reads the message too quickly, I think, or is scrolling through messages in between appointments in her office above the Thames, she may see a dot after that "mean" and the whole message will be inverted, perfectly reversed. A distraught, somewhat disturbed-seeming woman is beseeching one of the polite Indian managers to help her type a message to her bank in New Zealand to authorize a cash transfer, and someone else is shouting into the phone on the desk (since the place doubles as a public call center). The photocopying machine is rolling off dozens of pages of sutras. Nearly all the messages I notice as people come and go around me—musical chairs—have to do with love or money, perhaps with the confusion between the two.

"I don't feel comfortable with you," a woman has written to the Indian who is now beside me. "Why did you fall in love with me so quickly? You must meet lots of foreign tourists. We are so different. I had a dream about you last night."

Is he used to such challenges? Is this the first? Do his words come out so fluently because he means them or because he doesn't and he's used them all before? "Yes, darling, we are so different levels as you say. You are high-class, I am only high-school. But our lives are not all so different. Today there is sun on mountain and I think of you. Rododendron everywhere, blessings are there. When I look at the mountains I think of you, darling."

Down the road, undisturbed by such age-old, universal exchanges, the center of the community sits, a little like a stupa on whom those walking around have stuck their plans, their hopes, their slogans or fashions of the moment. The last time I'd come here he had joked to me that Tibetans were teaching the local Indians "bad habits" by eating meat; now signs around the temple say, "To Be

Healthy, Be Vegetarian" and "Please Stop Eating Us, You (Inhuman) Human Beings!" and he is encouraging those Tibetans who can do so to try to become vegetarians (he practices vegetarianism himself every other day, true to his Middle Way philosophy, having been forbidden by his doctors from practicing it entirely). He has also recently decided that his government should make no profit from any information it dispenses, and so videos, posters, pamphlets are offered at cost price at a little store in town, and you can buy a feature-length video for less than a dollar, and a thick book for fifty cents at one of the tables outside his teachings.

Dharamsala is a global community based on ideals and the possibility of pledging oneself to something better; but—of course—lesser realities swim all around it, like sharks. In Tibet the Dalai Lama was an embodiment of an old culture that, cut off from the world, spoke for an ancient, even lost traditionalism; now, in exile, he is an avatar of the new, as if, having traveled eight centuries in just five decades, he is increasingly, with characteristic directness, leaning in, toward tomorrow.

It is the only thing we can do, Klaas, I see no alternative, each of us must turn inward and destroy in himself all that he thinks he ought to destroy in others.

—ETTY HILLESUM,
on her way to her death, at twenty-nine, in Auschwitz

THE POLITICIAN

Almost the first thing the Dalai Lama had said when he came to Nara, addressing the local experts in the small conference room right after breakfast, was "The world is getting smaller. So, closer understanding between humanity is necessary. We need attitude of oneness of humanity. All world is one body."

This had all sounded reasonable enough, though I had not been able to hold much confidence that humanity would rise to this sense of unity. "I believe," he had gone on, "basic human nature is more gentleness. Our whole life, human affection is most important factor for our survival." How better, I had thought, to approach a group of intellectuals?

And yet, fewer than nine weeks later, I was walking the streets of Beirut and taking in one of the most sophisticated and advanced communities the human mind has ever devised. Egyptians and Assyrians and Phoenicians and Greeks, Romans and Ottomans and French and British had been here, and after ten millennia of visitations, the city glittered with more urbanity than I had seen in Paris or New York, its people discussing the issues of the day—and philosophy, culture, history—in English and Arabic and French, with an intensity and charm I had seldom seen on any of my travels.

The result of all this history, though, was that 150,000 Beirutis had been killed in fifteen years of unrelenting civil war not very long before. Forty competing militia had run wild across a country half the size of Wales; Muslims had avenged themselves on other Muslims by attacking Christians, Syrians had joined Christians in fighting Palestinians and then joined Palestinians in fighting Christians. The governing logic of Beirut was, famously, the belief that "My enemy's enemy is my friend," not so very different from the complications of factionalism in old Tibet, where, favoring China over Britain, some people used to say, "Better an old adversary nearby than a new friend far away."

"Now," the Dalai Lama had gone on in the dusty old hotel, autumn sunshine flooding in through the wood-framed windows, "humanity is becoming more mature. We notice a larger number of humanity really showing a desire for peace. Many people are fed up with bloodshed and violence. Now we need more effort to nurture that kind of trend."

Yet who, I thought, a few weeks later, could be more fed up with violence than Beirutis, their churches pockmarked with bullet holes, their minarets having been used as snipers' nests? Who could more passionately support the peace effort? And yet mothers had seen their sons killed by neighbors, children had watched old people cut down for no reason at all. Something in us suggests that forgiveness is a betrayal of natural justice, and even if you believe in karma, or any other unbending process of cause and effect, that cannot always fill the hole in every heart.

The Dalai Lama, as it happens, knows more about Beirut than I and many of my journalist friends do; in Taiwan in 2001, he actually cited it as an example of the world's convolutions, having been told by a French writer how innocents were dying in one part of the city while arms dealers were making profits in another. Besides, growing up in Tibet, where a local warlord had to be paid off the equivalent of $2.5 million in today's terms just to let the four-year-old Dalai Lama leave his home and travel to Lhasa, coming of age as his country was swept up into decades of violent warfare, he does not need to be told about what human greed and savagery can do. He always used to change the channel, he once told an interviewer, when there was a scene on TV of an animal being slaughtered. But then he resolved that he had to watch it, since at least then something good might come out of the often needless slaughter.

Whenever I saw the Dalai Lama, often just after he had returned from Belfast or Jerusalem or Berlin, I heard him deliver his arguments for peace and understanding with a logician's suppleness and command. "It's not sufficient to say we want peace, are against violence," he had said in Nara. "Just saying this is not sufficient. Violence comes because there is some problem. So we must solve the problem. The best way is dialogue. The other's interest, our interests, are very much mixed. No independence." If one person in a neighborhood is happy and the others are suffering, he often said, no one can feel truly secure.

But then I went out into the world and saw what people who acted in the name of interdependence or of a new society had wrought. Five months before taking Hiroko to meet the Dalai Lama in Dharamsala, I was inspecting killing fields and skulls in Cambodia, where a leader who had studied under both Buddhist priests and Catholic fathers had orchestrated the elimination of 20 percent of his countrymen, 1.7 million in all. Nine weeks after I left him another year, I was in Haiti, where I was told not to go out at night "because of democracy," and signs in French and English asked citizens not to bring their guns into a hospital. The horror of Beirut was, in many ways, the very cosmopolitanism and elegance of Beirut: here was one of the most intelligent and engaged places anyone could hope to see, and it was precisely that untransformed intelligence that led to such ingenuities as suicide bombing and hostage taking, a terrorist group with its own satellite TV station and advertising agents, precisely that engagement that led to the refusal to let crimes go unanswered.

A few months after the Dalai Lama received the Nobel Prize, I was in Tibet and North Korea, and nothing I saw in either place told me that the world was more concerned than before, that human nature was moving toward "more gentleness" or that "humanity is becoming more mature."

Such challenges are posed all the time to the Dalai Lama, of course, though my talks with him had suggested that he posed them to himself even more often. What would you do if someone threatened to rape a group of Tibetan nuns? people asked. How would you respond if a man came into the room right now, wildly waving a gun? In response, he usually cited one of the Buddha's own classic teachings, about how a man may be justified in killing another if that other is about to kill five hundred people. Everything, again, depends on motivation, and at his evening talk in Nara he had remarked that though the upshot is the same, "friendly fire" is profoundly different from an act of aggression, if only because it arises from different impulses.

Even as he said all this, though, these questions were far from abstract for his people: their country really was being destroyed, their heritage raped and their community tortured. Many of them clearly felt that they had spent their entire lives in a waiting room, exercising preternatural patience, as their leader counseled, even as foreigners told them how Tibetans in Tibet could barely speak Tibetan now, that a Tibetan had been imprisoned for six years just for privately screening a video of her exiled leader, that the Potala Palace was mockingly surrounded by swan boats and the trappings of an amusement park. How can one stand by and practice "inner disarmament," I could imagine them saying, when one's own home and all its residents are going up in flames?

One warm spring afternoon I sat in one of the oldest little coffee-houses in Dharamsala, the Chocolate Log, its red-and-white-checkered tables neatly set out on a terrace so you can watch the sun casting large shadows across the mountains, the snowcaps so sharp above the settlement that you can start to believe (as in Tibet) in heavenly protection, and heard one of the settlement's most forceful and impassioned speakers, Lhasang Tsering, brief a group of American college students on Tibet and its situation.

I knew Lhasang well because he ran the area's most literate and spirited bookshop, sitting behind his desk in the mornings—his sad, burning eyes, his lean face, and his white wisp of a beard giving him the air of an exiled East Asian sage—talking about litera-ture, the latest political testaments, and, without much prompting, everything that was wrong with the Tibetan government in exile (in particular its readiness, since 1987, to concede that China could continue to control Tibet's external affairs so long as Tibetans could control their internal ones). Lhasang had once worked in the government itself, for the Department of Information; he had taught at the Tibetan Children's Village, with the Dalai Lama's younger sister; he had stolen back into Tibet, in 1980, and been instrumental, along with those now closest to the Dalai Lama, in setting up the Tibetan Youth Congress, the main activist voice of exiled Tibet, always eager to do something for stranded cousins and former neighbors under Chinese rule. Dharamsala is a small town, in every sense, and Lhasang (along with Jamyang Norbu, first cousin of the Dalai Lama's longtime private secretary) was clearly one of its brightest minds and most eloquent debaters, though now, as in some Shakespearean court, he had become the voice of indignant opposition.

"The first thing I must tell you," he told the students, in what I took to be his standard address, his gaze as mournful as it was commanding, "is that I am not from Shangri-La. In fact, I don't know where that place is. And, frankly, I do not have the time or inclination to look for it." What he was really saying, I thought, was that he was not ready, as he put it bluntly, "to stand by and watch people suffer." To talk about peace while Tibetans were dying was, he suggested, tantamount to manslaughter.

How could one take the moral high road, he went on, how could one speak of long-term consequences and universal principles when the short-term consequences—being tortured and beaten and inwardly corrupted—were being felt by others? "I don't think it is fair for us to ignore Tibetans who are suffering in Tibet," he said with rhetorical cunning, as if the Dalai Lama were practicing a kind of willful cruelty. "We are praying for world peace, and not even doing very much for world peace."

The young Americans sat around the simple table looking stunned, as if someone had hit them on the head with a hammer. Lhasang, though, his eyes flaring with soft fire, his quiet voice compelling, was speaking for a very different response to suffering than the Dalai Lama was outlining, down the road, in his annual New Year's teachings. He and his leader might almost have been monks in a classic debate, one of them (the former guerrilla in the café) lunging forward with slashing argument after argument in favor of action, the other (the Tibetan leader across the hill) sitting unmoved, and saying that tolerance, patience, forgiveness, too, are a form of action, the very opposite of passivity.

In the mornings, Lhasang sat in his shop, the Bookworm, and spoke of what he had learned working for the Department of Information (and of what he hadn't learned—he knew much more, he said, from working outside government), what he had seen being trained by the CIA, how his own brother had been wounded while fighting for the Indian army in Bangladesh. Around him the orange and gray volumes of Steinbeck and Gordimer and Camus spoke of the virtue of action, positive involvement in the fight against injustice. One morning he pressed a button on his tape player, and a scratchy sound emerged that I recognized in time as a rendition of "This Land Is Your Land," the death-less Woody Guthrie anthem reclaiming America for its oppressed peoples. But the lyrics in this version, I heard as I listened more closely, spoke of traveling from holy Kailas to the plains of Amdo. It was a new rendition of the song that he had written himself, the bookstore owner said with his melancholy gaze, after stealing into his country to see what it was like, more than twenty years before.

"Why is he thinking of the future?" Lhasang went on now, in the open-air café, of the Dalai Lama. "And not the present, the past? If you want freedom from this world, there's a lot of space still free in the mountains." He gestured toward the slopes all around, where hermits sat in caves for years, sometimes monitored and measured by researchers from America. "I want freedom in this world, not from this world.

"If a mouse is cornered by a cat, he has to make a run for it." (No, I thought, as if I were on the other side of the hill: the cat may get distracted, he may get picked up and taken away, he might spot a more tempting target—there are many reasons why the mouse might be well advised to bide his time.) The Middle Way policy of the Dalai Lama's government in exile, Lhasang implied, was just a way of shaking hands with the devil. ("In politics," he might have cited President John Adams as saying, "the middle way is none at all.")

"So you are in favor of terrorism?" a young male student asked at last when Lhasang seemed to have subsided.

"I am in favor of action. As I always say, nonviolence is not non-action. Unless we act, how can the world support us? As I keep saying, you can't sponsor a child who won't go to school."

"But what form would this action take?"

"One determined Tibetan could throw out a Chinese city's power station. Could block a road."

"In Tibet?"

"No. Only in China."

"And you think the Dalai Lama should act on this?"

"Of course. He not only can implement the policy of defending Tibet, he must do so."

"Do you favor suicide bombings?"

Lhasang said nothing, but the implication was obvious. As long as the Dalai Lama practiced tolerance, waiting for the Chinese leadership to change (as, it must be said, it had done, unexpectedly and all at once, when Mao Zedong, Zhou Enlai, and Chu Teh died in 1976), the whole world could continue feting and admiring him, but doing nothing much to help him.

"Politics," Lhasang concluded, "is just a matter of self-interest. It's not about helping others, it's about helping yourself." He could hardly have more explicitly inverted the Dalai Lama's teaching—that it is, in fact, only by helping others that you truly help yourself. One day, with no prompting, the leader's younger brother, Ngari Rinpoche, had said to me, as if it were the most obvious thing in the world, "Politics is about knowing how to serve. It's about learning how to be of benefit to other people."

The larger good and the smaller, the longer term and right now: a monk's vision and a guerrilla's. All across Dharamsala, and the Tibetan diaspora community generally, you could hear the debate going on, in tea shops, in homes, wherever members of the older generation (who had seen Tibet) and the younger (who had only dreamed of it) got together. In its way, curiously, it mirrored the very dialogue you saw in Tibet itself, where one group spoke of "liberation" (from backwardness, from poverty and filth, from feudalism, as the Chinese called it) and another, in the monasteries, saw "liberation" as referring to freedom from ignorance, from attachment, from the delusion that brings on suffering. It echoed the archetypal discussion that had separated Martin Luther King from Malcolm X, Gandhi from Nehru, and still divides one group in Israel from the other. "I purify my thoughts and devote myself to compassion," a citizen of Beirut says. "But how does that help when around me four million others are acting as before, slaughtering my loved ones, sending a shell into my home to kill my daughter?"

"It takes time," the Dalai Lama replies. "If you don't believe you can do better, you never will."

You must fight fire with fire, the Beiruti responds; extend your hand to a snake and you get bitten.

"What is burned by the fire should be healed by using fire," the Dalai Lama has calmly said, as if in reply. An eye for an eye, as Gandhi pointed out, makes the whole world blind.

Within the Tibetan community, however, the debate was growing ever more intense, more vocal, because Tibet itself was being fast erased from existence; if something is not done in the next few years, the Dalai Lama has been saying for years, Tibet as we know it will be gone forever. The first thing I saw, often, on entering the Namgyal Monastery, next to the Dalai Lama's house, was a tire cover on a jeep that said, TIME IS RUNNING OUTTTTT . . . and printed nineteen "T's" as a row of gravestones.

I knew the truth of this from my own experience. In 1985, opened for the first time to the world, Tibet had been a torrent of warmth and color, local people streaming out of their homes to greet the foreigners they had never seen before, monks chanting in the chapels to which they were in places allowed to return, a sense of possibility breaking out after decades of oppression and destruction. But almost inevitably the very presence of foreigners, the eyes and ears of the world, served to encourage Tibetans to speak out against their occupiers, and to raise in Chinese minds the specter of a popular uprising. By the time I returned to Lhasa in 1990, tanks were stationed outside the Tibetan capital and armed soldiers patrolled the rooftops of all the houses around the central Jokhang Temple. Tibet was effectively still under martial law, and tourists were allowed to visit only if they paid a fortune and traveled in a group (I went as a group of one).

In five years much of the town that had so transported me had been erased. Tibetans were not allowed into the Potala Palace, the centuries-old symbol of their culture and tradition, and stood at its gates, looking wistfully at the few tourists who were led through it backward, in the counterauspicious direction. Most of the rooms in the palace were padlocked, and the lighting sometimes went off as we wandered through it; the Chinese-trained Tibetan guide appointed to show me the sights painstakingly explained that it was a purely secular residence, the home of a king, until two nearby tourists from England pointed out that that king happened to be a monk—it was at least as much temple as palace.

By the time I made my third trip to Tibet, at the beginning of the twenty-first century, I could not even recognize the country I had visited twice before. The Potala Palace was not visible from most parts of the capital, and broad, spotless boulevards traveled between blue-glassed shopping centers and gleaming high-rises. The small Tibetan area still remaining, with its swarm of dusty lanes and little houses, was now called "Old Town," as if it were already a historic area commemorating the curiosities of an indigenous population long gone. The signs along Beijing Lu, as the main drag is called, were for Giordano and gelato.

The students who listened to Lhasang give his powerful appeal for action probably did not know that his shop, like every other shop in Dharamsala, featured a large framed picture of the Dalai Lama at its center, draped in ceremonial white scarves, and next to it, similarly adorned, a picture of Mahatma Gandhi. Large sections of the store were devoted to books by or about the Dalai Lama, and about Tibetan Buddhism as a whole. This was in part, no doubt, because any shrewd businessperson knows that these are the kinds of books a foreign visitor to Dharamsala most wants to buy; but it was also because, even for so outspoken and uncompromising a prosecutor as Tsering, his leader, the object of his devotion, and the center of his Buddhist life was the Fourteenth Dalai Lama.

In thirty years of traveling around Dharamsala and Tibet I could not remember hearing a single Tibetan say a word against the Fourteenth Dalai Lama. Over and above the ritual authority that his institution carries, Tibetans inside Tibet and outside know that he is their one hope, the living symbol of their culture, and both their future and their past; they hold on to him, in their heads, as if on to life itself. And they cannot fail to see that he is working, to the point of exhaustion, to try to protect their welfare. Yet for more and more of them, especially the young but even many of those who had worked inside his government and can no longer contain their restlessness, there is less and less hesitation about criticizing his Middle Way policy and the government deputed to implement it.

I thought back to the book of English-language poems I had been given and recalled that, even in its introduction, its editor had written, "The collective conscience expressed by [exile youth] has a root of deep resentment directed towards the U.N. and the exile government for their failure to find a workable political solution to the dilemma of Tibet's occupation." And even before that, in words that would shake the Dalai Lama's heart—referring to the classic Tibetan Buddhist notion of a limbo between life and death—the editor had written, simply, "We float in a *bardo* of statelessness."

When I walked around the Lingkhor, or ceremonial path around the Dalai Lama's home, each morning, hearing the mostly elderly petitioners stop to sing their national anthem and throw barley flour up toward the blue heavens and their leader's house at the top of the hill, I could not fail to see a bust of Pawo Thupten Ngodup, a fifty-year-old Tibetan who in 1998 had set fire to himself, fatally, in the streets of Delhi after a long hunger strike, protesting the Chinese occupation of Tibet. The Dalai Lama opposed such acts as acts of violence and squanderings of the special opportunity that human life is thought by Tibetan Buddhists to be. But near the bust were written the words VICTORY TO TIBET, and on the mani stones I saw nearby one day, someone had painted, ambiguously, TIBET NEEDS YOU. One of the prayer flags along the same path consisted of a citation, in English, of United Nations Resolution No. 1723 (XVI) (on Tibet), from 1961.

The Dalai Lama had been practicing nonviolence and moving the world with his example for almost half a century, the messages might have been saying; but he had moved China not at all, and Tibet now was almost gone.

One bright March afternoon I made my way through the muddy streets of central McLeod Ganj and climbed up toward the pine-covered slopes to visit the Tibetan Youth Congress, the official voice of unofficial Tibet in exile. The organization is centered in a slightly broken building that looks like where you might put together an alternative newspaper, but in reality the TYC is exiled Tibet's largest organization, linking thirty thousand people in eighty-three chapters across eleven nations, a framework for offering an alternative, highly engaged response to the Tibetan situation different from that of the government in exile. In fact, however, the Congress was partly founded by the man who has served as the Dalai Lama's private secretary for more than forty years, and its former members now constitute 90 percent of the official leadership, including a recent prime minister. In the tiny world of Tibet in exile—smaller in population than Newport News, Virginia—the parallel world to the government in exile and the government itself overlap at every other point, so that the debate across the community begins to sound like an internal dialogue.

"The TYC is not supposed to be an NGO," Lobsang Yeshi, its then vice president, said as he ushered me into a conference room around a long table, the sun streaming in through windows on every side of the slightly rickety construction. "We're supposed to be a national organization. TYC is said to be very militant, separatist, whatever. But His Holiness is our strength, our power, our ground, everything. We cannot think of anything without His Holiness." Without perhaps intending to, Yeshi had put his finger on the core of the Tibetan predicament, which everyone (not least the Dalai Lama himself) has to work around: those calling for independence are themselves dependent on a man who counsels against such an external dependence (and calls, rather, for a deeper independence within). Even those not completely convinced of the wisdom of the Dalai Lama's political policy defer to him as their leader, their hero, and the incarnation of a god it would be near sacrilege to go against.

"The Dalai Lama is the most democratic of democrats," Yeshi volunteered, in words that no one outside of Beijing would challenge. "No one has ever objected to his rule, to his advice. He is the only one to object to his rule. He frankly likes people to challenge him, to criticize, to give another side. He doesn't like those who just kowtow." Thus, again, the second distinctive conundrum of the Tibetan situation: the Dalai Lama constantly tells his people to look to themselves, not to him, for their strength, to lay claim to the possibilities of democracy, to let him, in effect, depose himself, and they say that they'd much rather leave all the decision making to him. As a result, he has been forced to attempt a sustained and systematic revolution to topple himself and to "impose" (as his current prime minister put it to me) democracy on his people.

"When we arrived here," the TYC vice president told me, with a lawyer's articulate ease, "our aim was to settle down, to settle down the refugees. Now, after forty-five years, we have settled down. Now is the time to act!" Almost everything in Tibet in exile had been a step forward, in ways people could hardly have dared expect; in a climate, terrain, and nation very foreign to their own the Tibetans had not just re-created and reinvigorated their old institutions and principles—reforming them in the process—they had also prospered and kept up their ties worldwide, to the point where the *Economist,* never fulsome in its praise, had called theirs "by far the most serious" government in exile in the world. Yet in the same forty years, everything in Tibet itself had been dismantled and suppressed in ways beyond most people's imaginings. And the relatively successful exile community had been unable to do very much at all for its imprisoned cousins back home.

In some ways, the sense of hopelessness and powerlessness that resulted could almost have paralleled or been quickened by the way that all the world raced to offer the Dalai Lama its respect and affection, its open ears, but very few in power did much to help him. "Here we are," Yeshi said, "the TYC was organized thirty-five years ago, but we still haven't achieved what we're looking for. We haven't achieved even one government recognizing us. So frustration is there, anger is there." And beyond even that, a cutting sense of displacement conveyed by the fact that he was saying all this in English, and in cadences that were distinctly Indian.

"Everyone always says China is trying to Sinicize us," he went on. "But, in fact, we are ourselves being Indianized. We speak Hindi, we eat Indian food, we watch Indian movies. We are like Indians with Tibetan faces." Since Washington had opened the door to a thousand Tibetan refugees in 1991, more and more young Tibetans were setting their sights on the New World. They told their friends (perhaps they told themselves) that they could do more for Tibet by going to America, the center of power, by getting rich and telling the world about the situation in their homeland; but the suspicion lingered that, in reality, the very process of getting rich would prevent them from thinking about their homeland,

and soon they would become just Tibetan-Americans, and then maybe even Americans.

"We've achieved something here," Yeshi said as we sipped from two silver tumblers of tea, "but it's mostly because of the hard work our parents have done. They have done everything. They have set up schools, they have educated us. Most of the Tibetans are well-off, comfortably settled, sometimes too comfortable." In some ways, the implication went, the very success of the Tibetan exile enterprise had made Tibetans in places like Dharamsala too prosperous, too distracted by the opportunities of the wider world, too ready to forget those suffering in Tibet itself. They needed, Yeshi told me (echoing in more forceful terms what the Dalai Lama always said), to take more responsibility, to rise to the opportunities of democracy, and to show their devotion to their leader by actually sharing some of the load with him.

And the more Yeshi spoke, the more I could see what lay beneath all the reasoning and the careful dialectics, and what only increased as the years went on. "We're human beings," he said. "We have lost our homeland; we have seen our forefathers killed. Even if you find us smiling, laughing along, deep down the frustration is there. We're not carrying our political life. China should be grateful to the Dalai Lama." His eyes began to flash, a little as Lhasang Tsering's had done. "They call him a separatist, a splittist, but if the Dalai Lama weren't there, the Tibetan struggle would have taken a different turn." (The vehemence in his voice left me in no doubt as to what kind of turn that would have been.)

"The Chinese say we're savages," he said, "we're nothing, we aren't a civilization. They say we badly need them. But in the last forty-five years we have shown we can really come up, and build a civilization. Even in exile." It was a variation, beneath the words, on what I heard so often in Dharamsala, a variation on the human,

Beiruti response: His Holiness asks us to extend forgiveness and tolerance, but how can we forgive those who have slaughtered our families? We are not monks or saints.

Yeshi himself, like the other three top executives of the Youth Congress, lived on the far side of the country from his wife and children, to bring his eloquence and persuasiveness to the Tibetan cause; his father and two brothers were among the five thousand or so Tibetans fighting for the Indian army, risking their lives to repay their debt to their hosts. But all these sacrifices had not borne visible fruit.

"Today," he said, and this was the closest he came, really, to criticizing his leaders' assumptions, "the world has taken Tibet as a bargaining chip, a guinea pig. To try an experiment, to try out a new notion of world peace." But the part that was sacrificed to make this gamble possible was Tibet itself. "If I tell you you are a very good human being—kind, philanthropic," Yeshi said (and I heard in his voice the echo of all that the rest of the world says to Tibet, as to Shangri-La), "it may hurt you; it may damage your cause. It's a good experiment, but not for us."

This could never be a purely theoretical issue for the Dalai Lama. Every month brought new refugees out of Tibet and into Dharamsala, and when they saw him, as I had witnessed, the very tears in their eyes, the hopes they placed on him, not only reminded him of his responsibilities but also asked a silent question: how can you continue exercising patience and extending trust when we are seeing everything torn apart around us? In this way, too, the small town looked like a Buddhist parable, the kind of story a grandfather might tell the children at his knee: a monk sits in his small house, devoting hours a day to thinking about peace, understanding, kindness, and the other hours to trying to make these workable within the unforgiving context of Realpolitik. And every day at his gates people gather—the very people it is his first priority to serve—asking him, in effect, to forswear his first monastic vows (which call for nonviolence, honesty, and celibacy), to give up his devotion to the Buddha's example, to act not in the there and then but in the here and now. Tibet, Yeshi had implied, was giving the entire world a shining example of forgiveness, while the people who were most intimately affected by it were raging, often, at the inaction.

As a Buddhist, the Dalai Lama, I knew, could never step down from his root principles; but as a Tibetan, surely, it could not be easy for him to look at the short-term consequences of what his policy was doing.

The heart of the conundrum, again, seemed to lie in the fact that the Dalai Lama served two constituencies—his own people and the world—and the smaller group and the larger often pulled him in opposite directions. The more he gave himself to the world, sometimes, the more his own people felt, as Yeshi had implied, like natural children bewildered by the fact that their father has adopted three others. The old among the exiled Tibetans clung to the Dalai Lama, to the temple, to the rites they had grown up with, as if to magic their old country into reexistence, but the young, taking the Dalai Lama at his word—that Tibetans should learn to be more modern, more practical, more concerned—came to him with the cries of Beirut. Even in old Tibet, some had been heard to mutter, "Too much religion, too little politics," in claiming that the huge monasteries, by hanging on to the old ways and refusing to adapt to the modern world, as the Thirteenth Dalai Lama had urged, had lost their country.

The larger world wanted the Dalai Lama to be something more than a politician—to be, in effect, a wise man, sitting above all nation-states and offering global counsel. At the annual teachings in Dharamsala, foreigners from every continent gathered for day after long day, fending off germs and rainstorms and surging crowds to hear him explain a complex text on the nature of suffering. But one year, the day after the teachings concluded, the Dalai Lama came out at the same time to the same courtyard to deliver his annual state-of-the-nation address, on Tibetan Uprising Day, March 10, and nearly all the foreigners of the day before were gone. It was mostly Tibetans who were standing in the rain as a small marching band from the Tibetan Children's Village banged drums and unfurled the snow lion and the mountains of the outlawed Tibetan flag, while their leader offered his political assessment of their situation.

How to be global and local at once? Both Martin Luther King and Mohandas Gandhi had in some ways concentrated on helping, even saving, their people as a way to inspire—and perhaps save—the world; but in the Tibetan situation, again, the clock was less indulgent. If the Dalai Lama offered a new vision for the global century just dawning, he was essentially addressing a century in which Tibet as we knew it no longer existed.

All of us live in two worlds at once, the Dalai Lama writes in his book on Buddhism and its correspondences with science, *The Universe in a Single Atom.* There is the world of "conventional reality," in which each of us scuttles along with his own particular direction and character and destiny, and, beneath all that, there is the realm of "ultimate reality," in which the chaos of human affairs is seen from a different perspective, behind the surface, and all the individual lives and movements become nothing more than nodes within an all-encompassing network. The conventional eye accepts the reality that China and Tibet do indeed have different traditions, customs, and languages, and that each has a very different destiny; the ultimate eye sees that Chinese and Tibetans are not so different in their basic human instincts, their longing to be happy, their eagerness to avoid pain.

The Dalai Lama's hope was to bring some of the light and clarity of the monk's domain, "ultimate reality," into the politician's world of conventional reality; to be able, in effect, to stage a kind of Copernican revolution by getting us to see that the world does not revolve around the self, but the other way round. It was as if, seeing the forest through the trees, seeing the pattern and order, the possibility within the seeming chaos, he was arguing for a complete reorientation of the center of gravity in politics; while politicians squabbled about whether to paint the vehicle of society red or blue, he was calling for a rewiring of the engine.

Of course we could win small victories against the Chinese, he was essentially saying to young Tibetans, as guerrillas do in Northern Ireland and Spain and Peru; but in the long term we would be losers, by squandering the respect of the world and sparking the rage of a nation two hundred times more populous than our own. Of course we can see the Chinese as enemies, but if we do so, we are saying, in effect, that we are going to spend all our lives in the midst of enemy forces; the better solution is to change how we think of the situation, perhaps by seeing that our real enemies are our own habitual tendencies toward thinking in terms of enemies. We can always see the decisive effects of action; but what underlies action, in the way of viewpoint and motivation and feeling, is where the real change has to come.

It was, again, an idea that was often voiced by others, and it is perhaps no surprise that the first head of state officially to recognize the Dalai Lama—only thirteen hours after coming to power—was a man who likewise spoke for what could be called "transpolitical politics" and what he once called "transcendental responsibility." Like the Dalai Lama, Václav Havel had never campaigned for office, had never obviously sought power; he gained such respect as he had just from being a man of conscience, an everyday citizen who had spoken out for justice when it was a crime to do so. Like the Dalai Lama, too, the celebrated playwright had lost no time, when finding himself in power, in arguing for Henry Adams's idea that "knowledge of human nature is the beginning and end of political education," in stressing that a change in any one place would, these days, have consequences in every other place.

His power, Havel always said, came not from his public position but from whatever positions he held internally. Over and over, in his talks before other leaders, he referred to "Being" and the soul and other unquantifiable forces, as if to stress that a man who rules others must first rule himself, and be aware that he is not an end in itself so much as a beginning. Indeed, as he constantly spoke for an affiliation larger and more enduring than "my family, my country, my firm, my success," he might have been saying that we remake our world not just by rethinking what "the state" means but by rethinking the "we."

The Dalai Lama clearly echoed his friend and champion even as, in both cases, the leaders set up hopes so exalted that many came away disappointed, muttering that good intentions alone could never defeat the internal combustion engine. And as the years went on, the Tibetan leader came more and more to define himself as "an internationalist," as he put it in a 2005 book, and to invoke the specific word "global." The "best solution to terrorism," I heard him say in Switzerland that same year, "is to see the whole world as a single unit, taking everything as your own." Certainly this would require lifetimes and might even then never bear fruit, but, as he said, not plaintively, "what other option do we have?"

It was little solace or instruction, often, to the Tibetans who called for action now, and an action that the whole world could witness, but for me what was exciting about seeing the Dalai Lama and others like Havel pressing forward was, in part, their sense that they could seize those new opportunities that he had discussed forty-five years ago with my father. Planes, phones, broadband hookups all linked us now, and what we could make of these links was not just a metaphor for the net of interdependence but a sense that any individual was operating in a sphere much wider than his immediate physical neighborhood and country, where the stakes were universal.

"Our worst mistake, our greatest mistake," the Dalai Lama told me once of the Tibetan situation, was being isolated from the world, and now, with assistance from circumstances, he was doing what he could to redress that problem; in a narrow, secular sense, conversations between scientists and monks, between Westerners and Asians, between Tibetans and Chinese were at least a beginning in making and seeing new openings. If Tibet in the past had stood for the farthest extremes of self-containment and remoteness, now he would make it one of the central players in a global vision that showed that Tibetans could, for example, help the Indians they lived among, and foreigners could help Tibet. In earlier generations, the main relationships between countries had seemed to be political and economic ones, alliances and deals; now, he was suggesting, there was a deeper and perhaps even more valuable kind of connection—an inner and human one that could be made in terms that were not inherently divisive.

In a curious way, therefore, without even necessarily intending to, the Tibetans had begun acting on the clairvoyant idea of Gore Vidal, decades ago, that in a global world, the center of power might be not just Washington but Hollywood. Having found that most politicians clamored to see him but were reluctant, practically speaking, to do much to help him, the Dalai Lama had, almost literally, allowed his cause to be taken to the streets, permitting movie stars and rock musicians and artists to reach a greater global audience than any national politician could. Through a typical process of pragmatic experimentation, he had perhaps noticed that Richard Gere, who had worked so selflessly for the Tibetan cause for more than a quarter of a century (even the toilets outside the Dalai Lama's main temple were funded by him), could in some ways reach people and speak out for conscience in ways that a typical traditional politician, hemmed in by interests and obligations, could not. Philosophers, scientists, men of the cloth—he was both finding and bearing out—could talk to people in the far corners of the planet and enjoy real dialogues and exchanges, even as governments were constrained by their wish not to antagonize the largest market in the world, or to imperil some other alliance.

Thus even politics, which people like myself were tempted to see as the realm of the fallen and the corrupt, were no more tarnished than the minds and expectations we brought to them. "We say, 'Dirty politics,' " he had said in Constitution Hall, on one of his earliest trips to the United States, "but this is not right. Politics is necessary as an instrument to solve human problems, the problems of human society. It itself is not bad; it is necessary."

The problem in politics had always been that whoever sought office almost by definition was someone many of us would not trust with it; by the very act of entering politics, he seemed to suggest (to our jaded way of thinking) that he was more committed to his needs and hopes than to our own. Yet a politics without politicians had never been easy. The Tibetan system dared to place a monk at the head of the state, in the hope that he could transform the political process from within. In practice, though, the Dalai Lama was often as much a victim as a maker of the system— in the entire nineteenth century not a single new Dalai Lama reached the age of twenty, and their deaths were seldom presumed to have come from natural causes.

It seemed clear that the Tibetans had paid a high price at times for being associated with movie stars and for seeing their predicament taken up as the fashion of the moment, sometimes among people so smitten with the idea of Shangri-La that they barely seemed to notice the six million individuals suffering in Tibet. Yet part of the unusual fascination of Dharamsala was that Lebanese TV cameras, Mexican Catholics, Chinese scientists from the mainland all assembled here to find answers from the other groups for their local problems. Buddhism, in fact, had come back to India, its homeland, with new vitality, thanks to the exiled Tibetans.

And in Tibet itself, such few gains as had been made had often come from foreigners, like the forty or so who had witnessed and recorded the first demonstrations in Lhasa, in late 1987. Many had risked their lives to collect information, to bring supplies, to speak out against an oppressive government; the streets of Dharamsala were still full of foreign lawyers, doctors, architects who were turning away from lucrative jobs to devote their services to Tibet. Among the handful of hopeful developments in Tibet's recent history was the simple fact that it had become a global concern among those who saw it not as a matter of China and Tibet but as one of right and wrong. When the Nobel committee rewarded the Dalai Lama for his efforts for peace, offering up the prize "in tribute to the memory of Mahatma Gandhi," the Tibetan spoke again for this larger sense of community by giving some of his prize money to Mother Teresa, to help the poor in India; some to Africa, to feed the hungry; and some to Costa Rica, to help set up a university for peace.

The deepest of all the conundrums the Dalai Lama sat upon, though, was, simply, the fact that he was both spiritual and temporal leader of his people, and whatever he did to serve one aspect of his mandate could seem to go against the other. When he spoke from the heart, extending trust, as his monastic vocation urged, he could be accused of being too innocent or unworldly; when he operated with canniness or pragmatism, as he often did, he could be seen as forfeiting his spiritual authority. Often, as when he said in 1987 that he was seeking not full independence from China but only autonomy—a Buddhist notion, if one stopped to think about it—he got assailed from one side for being too expedient, and on the other for being too idealistic.

"My own understanding," said the Dalai Lama's first elected prime minister, Samdhong Rinpoche, when I went to see him in 2005, "is that spirituality cannot be separated from any life. It may be family, it may be society, it may be nation or state. You need a little bit of spiritual background—not a little, but quite strong spiritual background—without which I don't think order can be maintained. That order should come from within. It cannot be imposed. The Communist system, the imposition of everything from the top, has totally failed."

Yet Samdhong Rinpoche was also a Tibetan monk, which meant that he was a dialectician; indeed, he had served for many years as head of the Central Institute of Higher Tibetan Studies in Sarnath, the first official university for Tibet in exile. "Organized religion should not interfere in state affairs," he went on, quoting his leader directly. The government in exile had taken pains to include the word "secular" in the charter it drew up for the Tibetan parliament in 1991—only to be overruled by a few votes, from people who thought it meant not just an absence of religion but an active avoidance of it. Indeed, when, in 2001, Tibetans in exile had been invited, for the first time in Tibetan history, to vote for their own prime minister (previously, he had been appointed by the Dalai Lama or, more recently, his Cabinet), they had selected this celebrated monk and scholar. "His Holiness sometimes jokes," Samdhong Rinpoche told me, in his gentle, Indian-inflected English, " 'I ask people to choose their own political leadership and again they have chosen an old monk, instead of young, energetic, educated, secular people!' "

Yet it was clear, even to the man I was talking to, that few Tibetans would listen to him as they listened to the man they regard as a god, with hundreds of years of the Dalai Lama lineage behind him. I remembered the Dalai Lama once telling me that he constantly urged his people, in an informal way, to practice democracy—"You should carry your work as if I didn't exist," he told them, because "that day will come, definitely." And he frequently urged members of his immediate staff to take on many of the jobs—speaking to foreign politicians, addressing international support groups, explaining the situation in Tibet—that they could do, he felt, at least as well as he could. Meetings with scientists, with certain religious practitioners, and public teachings, he knew, he'd have to continue taking on himself. Because "even if some of our Cabinet members wanted to give these talks, nobody would come!"

For the Dalai Lama, democracy was the rare, happy place where Buddhist principles and real-world political systems converged. Nothing could better speak to his sense that each of us has a power in ourselves and an equal right to put forward his opinion and then be challenged in turn. Nothing could better represent his idea of independent choices within an interdependent network, each person thinking of his role in the larger whole, and debating giving everyone a say. For many Tibetans, though, especially in exile, what democracy really meant was giving up the very system and line of power that had held them up in Tibet and was all they had to cling to now.

During only his fourth year in exile, the Dalai Lama had drawn up a new constitution, both for exiled Tibet and for Tibet once it was free, taking care to write in a clause that allowed for his own impeachment. His Cabinet—almost inevitably—had taken it out, and he, in a rare exercise of executive power, had put it in again.

More recently, in 1996, he had held a referendum, so that his exiled people could choose what form of government they would like to see. No doubt reluctantly, and perhaps in deference to others' wishes, he had added one final option—that power be left in the hands of the Dalai Lama. Almost inevitably again, the majority of Tibetans chose that the Dalai Lama be in charge of everything and, in honoring the principle of democracy, he was obliged to accept a nondemocratic system.

A few days after his talk to the students, and just before I left Dharamsala, I asked Lhasang Tsering if he would join me for a final cup of tea. Urbane and obliging as ever, he instantly agreed and led me to a lawn outside an Indian government hotel, where we sat at a small table and sipped the strong Indian chai he ordered, in fluent Hindi. Journalists love to talk to Lhasang, the most quotable naysayer in Dharamsala, and he seems to love to talk to them. "Freedom will not come from waiting," he declared, in what I took to be one of his many carefully polished epigrams. "We have lost a clarity of purpose." For a practicing Buddhist, I thought, freedom did in fact come from just sitting, as the Buddha had done, and patiently seeing through all the dust and obscurations in the mind, precisely in order to find the clarity of purpose for which the Dalai Lama and other monks were famous. It just happened to be a purpose (universal and far-reaching) that did not answer the impatience of many Tibetans right now.

I kept my peace, though (Lhasang, after all, was a Buddhist by birth, as I was not), and he went on, with typical passion: "I'm afraid our leaders are acting more like a welfare organization than a real government" (thus suggesting, in effect, that compassion ranked lower than politicking, and could not be a part of it). "His Holiness, as everyone knows and accepts, is our greatest strength," he had said to the American students. "But therefore he is our greatest weakness. We have forgotten the ability to think for ourselves, the ability to do things for ourselves, to stand on our own feet. And yet there was a Tibet before the Dalai Lama. It was only in the sixteenth century that a Dalai Lama took over Tibet. Our history goes back two and a half thousand years."

Often, listening to him speak, I had the uncanny sense of hearing the very words the Dalai Lama used and insistently stressed—"realism," "impermanence," "suffering"—but turned in the opposite direction. One of them was speaking the language of the spirit, it seemed, of "ultimate reality" and what was good for everybody; the other much more the language of the mind, which insists on its divisions and distinctions and asserts that we cannot abandon or be free of the realm of "conventional reality." Hearing the Dalai Lama speak of "reality" (in a way that suggested we need a microscope in order to see everything that this entails) and then hearing the voice of Beirut speak of it, often with striking and enviable fluency, seemed to me to mark all the difference between wisdom and great cleverness.

I was most interested, though, in hearing Lhasang's own story. He had been a boy of six, he told me, when his family came to India, in 1958, on a pilgrimage (his father, a renowned Tantric master, had seen trouble coming to Tibet), and while traveling in India, his father had suddenly died, leaving a widow and three children somehow to find a way to survive in the foreign country. They set about working on roads, as a few years later many Tibetans would do, taking on the jobs that no Indians were eager to assume. Like many Tibetans in these inhospitable circumstances, they flourished. Lhasang, in fact, soon proved himself an excellent student, and one, therefore, faced with the same choice that confronts the best in the exile Tibetan community even today: would he serve his country or just his family? In financial and practical terms, it was hard for the Tibetan exile to serve both: Lhasang wanted to put his intelligence to the use of the greater good, he said, but he could not soon forget the Tibet he had grown up in—or the sight of his father's pyre by a river in India.

He went on to tell me about the scholarship he had been offered to study medicine at Johns Hopkins, and his confrontation with the Dalai Lama, his telling his leader that he had to see Tibet and the people he was working for to serve them best. It wasn't hard, as he spoke, to imagine that Lhasang had inherited the firelit power of his father; he spoke with a rare intensity and eloquence, his voice now soft, now rising to a roar, and I remembered the time when, suddenly, in his bookshop, he had launched into Brutus's funeral speech for Caesar, in which the Roman explains why he has betrayed his longtime friend and leader, even as—or maybe because—signs around town had taken to calling him "the Invincible God."

"His Holiness congratulates the Tibetans who fight for India in the Indian army," Lhasang now said, calling on an example he often used. "He congratulates the Tibetans who give their lives to the war in Bangladesh. But a poor young boy in Lhasa, without any hope, picks up a stone and throws it at a Chinese tank, and His Holiness condemns it as violence? It is okay for us to fight for India in Bangladesh, but not for Tibetans in Tibet?" (Yes, I thought, you could make a case for doing your duty to a host as being more important than fighting for yourself.) I remembered how the Dalai Lama, nine years before, had said to me calmly, in counseling patience among young Tibetans, "And one way, yes, my position has become weaker, because no development, no progress. In spite of my open approach, with maximum concessions, Chinese position becomes even harder and harder."

But there was something else about Lhasang that affected me even more (and might, I thought, have moved the Dalai Lama more than could any of his words or ideas, which sometimes had the sound of thrice-told arguments delivered to a partner, in a relationship conducted for too many years in much too small a space). What books do you recommend reading, I asked him, to try to bring us onto less painful topics, and he said that somehow he hadn't found the energy to read in recent times. He'd lost all stomach for it, he said sorrowfully. And writing? The poems he had written he sometimes gave out as bookmarks in his shop, reminding customers, for example, of the great debt that Tibetans owed their host, India. No, he said; somehow all the life had gone out of him. When he'd worked in the government, what he'd seen had so shocked him that he'd had a mild stroke, while only thirty-three. Nowadays he still suffered blackouts and, as his wife vigorously attested, was constantly haunted by the moment when "I even forgot who I was."

A debate like Dharamsala's will never end, perhaps, as we never manage to live entirely in the world we hope for, even though we accept that to give up hope entirely is to give up a reason for living. And even within the Dalai Lama's own family, the debate raged on without end. One of the strongest voices for full independence—and the man who had written the foreword to a book featuring pieces by Lhasang Tsering and Jamyang Norbu, arguing that the Dalai Lama's position was, in Norbu's phrase, "a pathetically watered-down compromise" sponsored by "pocket Kissingers, 'friends' of Chinese leaders, even well-meaning imbeciles"—was, in fact, the Dalai Lama's eldest brother, himself an incarnate lama, and resident for many decades in Indiana. Yet the most visible spokesman for conciliation, constantly going back and forth to Beijing, based in Hong Kong, fluent in Chinese, and long married (until her death) to a Chinese woman, was the Dalai Lama's other older brother, Gyalo Thondup. The positions seemed as inseparable as the monks in the courtyard, one standing up and lunging forward, the other sitting unmoved before him.

The Buddha himself had once faced just such a situation, when a mass murderer called Angulimala slaughtered people all across the Gangetic plain. The Buddha worked with this terrorist—the spokesman for Beiruti justice, you could say—just by talking to him patiently and showing him the self-destructiveness of his actions. Yet those who had lost their husbands and daughters could not give up their sorrows so easily. They came to the Buddha and said, "How can you ask us to forgive a man who has all but destroyed our lives?" The Buddha's answer, like that of a doctor in a refugee camp, was simply to speak to each victim individually, explaining that if suffering lay inside them, so, too, did the means for overcoming suffering.

I remembered attending an event once in which, as the Dalai Lama walked into a temple, suddenly a raging young woman stepped forward and shouted out, "Lama! Dalai Lama! I need to talk to you. I am divine." She was pulled away by security guards, her screams and indignant shouts reaching even the small chapel in which the Dalai Lama sat. To my surprise, though, when he emerged from the temple a few minutes later, the Tibetan leader had his assistants bring her to him and stood before her, blessing her and cupping her face affectionately in his hand. You do not heal problems just by shouting at them, he might have been saying. You look at them and offer what you can.

On my last night in Dharamsala, a group of Tibetans invited me to dinner at the Hotel Tibet. There were six of them, all male, quick-witted, eager to talk, the bright young prospects of the Tibetan diaspora. And almost as soon as we sat down, one of them, the sweetest and most optimistic, a student of law, said, "Democracy is going to take time. Look at the U.S. It took two hundred years for democracy to settle down there."

"We don't have two hundred years," another replied.

"But we've got to be practical," the first went on. "We're new to this."

What do we do when the Dalai Lama is no longer around? Though nobody said it, that was the real topic of the discussion, as of so many discussions around Dharamsala. It was the shadow question that haunted almost every home and silence here. One of the young men present, working for the government in exile, had told me that he foresaw civil war and terrorist action in Tibet once the Fourteenth Dalai Lama was no more; the more hopeful law student had answered that Tibetans could flourish in the democratic patterns laid down by the Dalai Lama. Around us foreign scholars, wealthy Tibetans, high-up monks in the Dalai Lama's administration, and noisy backpackers tucked into Tibetan, Chinese, Indian, and Continental food while "Hotel California" reminded us that you can check out anytime you like, but you can never leave.

"We in Tibet always have this discussion," one of the boys explained to me, almost by way of apology. "Because on the one hand we're taught to be nationalist. To be proud of Tibet and work on behalf of Tibet, to protect our country. But on the other we're always getting the spiritual lesson, to be patient, forbearing, nonviolent. So, really, we don't know what to do!"

His own hope, the law student said, lay in a country like Sikkim, which was to some degree its own world, even as it was part of India. Earlier in the evening, when the boys had asked me to say a few words about Tibet from a foreign perspective, we had heard Lhasang say, with characteristic fury, "If a man is raping a girl and she cries out for help, you don't wait and pray for peace."

"The Chinese are playing for time," he had also said, in what was his favorite aphorism, "and we are playing into their hands. What is the good of extending a hand if the other person does not? Nothing. It takes two to shake hands."

"But if you extend no hand at all," I'd said, "you've given up. Nothing can be achieved."

"You can use that hand as a fist!" His eyes, as so often, had been on fire.

Now we shifted the conversation in the restaurant a little, to what foreigners could do or had done for Tibet.

"Yesterday," said one of the boys, "an American man said to me, 'Do you meditate?' And I couldn't tell him that very few Tibetans meditate. It's really not a part of our culture."

"And," a more innocent boy piped up, "this Frenchman was saying to me—I get it all the time from Westerners—'If Buddhism is about nonattachment, why are you attached to Tibet?'"

"What do you say?"

"I say that Tibetan religion and culture help everyone. So naturally I want them to continue. We sometimes say that people want to enjoy the food of Tibetan culture and religion but don't care what's going on in the kitchen."

"We say in Tibet sometimes," put in another, who had not spoken all evening, "that spirituality is the means, but the end is political. Please could you tell Westerners that we are proud if they enjoy our spiritual life, but what we care about right now is politics?"

Nine months later, in a move that shocked the world, the king of Bhutan, an Oxford-educated Buddhist who had been taught by one of the same rinpoches who'd taught the Dalai Lama, announced that, though only fifty, he would voluntarily step down from his throne two years later, to bring democratic elections to his country. His people were distressed—they had known only hereditary monarchy for the past ninety-eight years and wanted him always to be in charge of them—but he felt that his kingdom had to change with the times. The chain of cause and effect in a web, a Buddhist might have told me, is not always linear or easy to predict. The "butterfly effect"—so often spoken of by leaders like Havel—whereby an insect shaking its wings leads to a tornado many continents away took many forms, it seemed. An idea over here, and a sudden effect over there. Every word and tiny act has consequences, the Dalai Lama might have been reminding us, though often they are consequences we cannot and will not ever see.

For in this world of ours where everything withers, everything perishes, there is a thing that decays, that crumbles into dust even more completely, leaving behind still fewer traces of itself, than beauty: namely, grief.

—MARCEL PROUST

THE FUTURE

O
ne day in Dharamsala, an autumn day, the light golden and sharp outside his *thangka*-filled room, though it was cold not far away and snow was gathering on the mountains above, the Dalai Lama suddenly leaned across to me, as he often does (leaning into the world has become his characteristic position, as much as sitting stock-still in meditation), eyes alight, and, though nothing in our conversation had led to this, went off on a sudden tangent. He'd been talking about his love of informality, the way that sometimes it seemed to relax people and open them up, and then he remembered how, on his first trip to England, in 1973, after his talk "one old English gentleman—very gentlemanly—one old one come to me, and he expressed he very much appreciated that the Dalai Lama said, 'I don't know.'"

In Tibet, he went on, this would sound strange. Tibetans appreciate humility and laugh at one who claims to know it all, but still they would never think of congratulating someone on saying "I don't know." He was so taken aback by the old man's comment that he was moved to reflect on it twenty-three years later. Maybe, he speculated, "it's becoming rare—to admit you don't know. And once rare things happen, that becomes a surprise. I don't know. What do you feel?"

I fumbled for an answer—the question was so genuine—and I could see that the Tibetan was probing a serious aspect of cultural misunderstanding. He's always eager to offer assistance where it's required, and yet he is in no hurry to speak on things he knows nothing about. But when I went back to my room, crossing the flower-bordered driveway outside his house, walking between the gates into the shady courtyard filled with monks in their red robes, and Tibetans in prayer and the odd foreigner come to inspect the sense of devotion and ritual debating, as I went down the slope and along the road crowded with dogs and refuse and beggars, Tibetans setting up stalls to sell Dalai Lama posters, photographs, tapes to sightseers, and I climbed the steep, unpaved hill back to my guesthouse and my simple, sunlit room, I thought that saying "I don't know" was actually one of the better lessons he had taught us. He traveled everywhere in part to transmit what he did know, through his training, his meditation, his experience: about hard work in the face of suffering, about kindness and the way it makes everyone feel better, about interconnectedness and the logical basis for thinking of others (if they are a part of ourselves). People flew across the world and lined up for hours to hear him give all the answers. A monk is a walking answer, in the commitment that is the basis of his life. But he is also a man whose duty it is (and whose nature it surely is, too) to have questions. He is one who lives daily in the presence of something he can't put a finger on.

The Dalai Lama's whole life sometimes seems to be a lesson on how little we really know. Who could have guessed that the little boy clambering around in a tiny village in eastern Tibet would be pronounced the ruler of his people and brought to the Potala Palace at the age of four? Who could have expected that, while not yet ten, he would have to be the figurehead of his people during the tumult of World War II? And who could have known that just as the war ended, his own problems would begin? He didn't see the Chinese occupation coming, it seems fair to say—his Cabinet was still taking picnics as Chinese troops crossed into eastern Tibet—and he could never have known that he would be spending nearly all his adult life far from home, in India. People credit the Dalai Lama with great intuition and prescience, and these he might have, but he also has, surely, a human capacity for being surprised, and sometimes mortified.

He has made of "I don't know" one of the great cornerstones of his optimism. There are no grounds for hope regarding Tibet as we know it: things just keep getting worse and worse, to the point where Tibet is almost a place of memory now. China has no real reason for wishing to give up an area it knows as the "Western Treasure House," at the very center of Asia; the moral pressure of other governments has achieved nothing. Tibetans are in no position to resist a force that sees itself as the center of the earth and everywhere else as its mere satellite. There is simply no reason to imagine that an old Tibet could magically return.

And yet, overnight as it could seem, the Berlin Wall came down, and eight weeks after his most recent stay in prison, Václav Havel was unanimously selected as president of his country. Suddenly, through the moral efforts of Desmond Tutu and Nelson Mandela, among many others, decades of apartheid in South Africa were over. The aftermath of all those liberations has been troubled, an instant rejoinder to those who think that all will be well with the world (as Buddhists are seldom inclined to think). But no one at the beginning of 1989 expected that, by year's end, the Cold War would be effectively over, and no one imagined, when Mandela emerged from prison, that apartheid would soon be driven out of his country. The Dalai Lama reposes his confidence on such surprises—the sudden result of what has been building invisibly for years—as if to say, as he put it once, "Until the last moment, anything is possible." Maybe a new leader will come to Beijing who cares deeply about Tibetan autonomy. Maybe an American president will demand concessions that China will have to make to appease its main rival. Maybe the Chinese in Tibet will have a change of heart. All we can do is remain ready to make the most of every eventuality.

A monk, in any case, is one who sees things in the largest light possible, who sees, that is, how much we can't see, with our limited, partial view, our perspective from our spot in the middle of the flux and chaos. His job, in some respects, is to mix agnosticism with faith: to recall that he knows nothing of what will come tomorrow, and yet to remain confident that it will have meaning and will fit into a larger logic. Hope, as Václav Havel has said, is not the belief that everything will end happily ever after; it probably won't. It is simply the belief that something makes sense, regardless of how things turn out, and even if that sense is not apprehensible to us.

The central question mark hanging over Tibet and the Tibetans was, ever more, what would happen when the Fourteenth Dalai Lama was no longer. The man in question had been addressing that issue, straightforwardly and without flinching, ever since he was in his mid-thirties; as long as the Dalai Lama has some use, he always said, and can help the Tibetan people and others, he will be around, even if in some radical form. The sign of a true Dalai Lama is that he continues the work of previous Dalai Lamas. This shrewdly counteracted the very distinct possibility that, as soon as

he died, the authorities in Beijing would suddenly produce a com-
plaisant little boy under their control and present him as the Fifteenth Dalai Lama. But beyond strategies, it also spoke for a real
truth, which is that everything changes, and some roles outlast
their usefulness, but something uncreated or unconditioned, in the
Buddha's words, endures. The analogy often used for reincarnation
is that of a flame that is the same flame even as it is passed from
one very different candle to another.

"When I go," the Dalai Lama told me in the spring of 2005, "I
don't know. All depends on the respect of the Tibetan people for
their popularly elected leader. One hundred percent popular,
impossible! But sixty, seventy percent, and still thirty, forty percent
opposed: it can create some problems. We're in a foreign country;
meantime, if Indian government withdraws some formal recogni-
tion, then I don't know. Very complicated."

What he was really saying was that those restless young
Tibetans outside his door might finally try to act on their understandable frustration; that even though he had tried to lay down
the foundations of democracy, he was aware that Tibetans had got
into the habit of listening only to those with the ritual authority of
the Dalai Lama; that all the planning in the world could not take
care of every contingency or wipe out old reflexes in an instant. It
was a sobering reminder of just how entangled his position was
that one of the first factors he mentioned when contemplating the
future was not Tibet or even China but India (which allows the
Tibetans to stay as a group of spiritual refugees but would grow
anxious if they started to assert themselves too much as a political
force).

An elected prime minister meant, he hoped, that people are "no
longer relying on Dalai Lama. So whether Dalai Lama is alive or
not, we have already leadership. And in terms of religious matters,

we have younger generation of lamas from various traditions. So, theoretically, we have already planned everything. But in practice, of course, it depends on many matters. So, I don't know."

His own position has always been that, in the deepest sense, if we can live free of ceremony and superficial tradition, the Dalai Lama, Tibet, Buddhist temples won't have to exist at all, so long as we keep the principles they represent alive inside us. People and cultures and buildings are perishable, changeable things, he keeps on saying—himself as much as any; but truth, possibility, fairness, kindness are not. The open road is always leading around the next corner, calling for further investigation, even if no final destination is assured.

"Change is part of the world" is how he once distilled Buddhism into six words. When he was growing up, Sera Monastery in Lhasa was among the largest monasteries on the planet, with ten thousand monks on its rolls. Now Beijing enforces a limit of five hundred in any monastery. Yet the new Sera Monastery that refugees from Lhasa's Sera have built in southern India is flourishing, its population having surged from five hundred to four thousand. There are now two hundred Tibetan Buddhist centers in Taiwan alone. And many, many of the Chinese who flock to Tibet (and Chinese represent 90 percent of the millions of tourists who visit every year) are making offerings at the Jokhang Temple, even taking on Tibetan names and seeking out Tibetan lamas. Even as Tibetans are sometimes denied the chance to learn Tibetan, more and more Chinese are taking up the language.

In China, the Chinese writer Ma Jian wrote after visiting Tibet, "there is a saying: that which is united will eventually separate, and that which is separated will eventually unite."

"If, thirty years from now, Tibet is six million Tibetans and ten million Chinese Buddhists," the Dalai Lama told me in 2003 (not wishfully, but because he followed events in Tibet so closely that he could reel off the names of monks and remote monasteries that were doing good work there), "then, maybe, something okay." Once upon a time, after all, Tibet had occupied much of western China and entered the great T'ang capital of Changan, installing a puppet emperor there; less than seventy years later, as the Dalai Lama had reminded my father in 1960, monastic Buddhism had been pushed out of central Tibet for more than sixty years, and not a monk or a sacred text could be seen.

The story, in other words, did not end with one particular being, the Fourteenth Dalai Lama; if anything, it began there (the story of a Tibet that is part of the wider modern world, of a modern world that is part of Tibet, and of those who see, as the Buddha had stressed, that the teacher is not important, only the teaching). Many of the ideas that this particular Dalai Lama had put into circulation enjoyed such currency now that it seemed more than possible that Americans, Germans, Indians—Chinese—might take them further. I asked his younger brother, one sunny winter day in San Francisco, how he saw the future of Buddhism, and Ngari Rinpoche answered, calmly, "In the future I think people will follow the principles laid down by a man called Gautama. But the word 'Buddhism' may disappear. Which is fine: we don't need the name."

Then came the subversive laugh, and the kind gaze behind the glasses—he was about to say something about my hair—and I saw one form in which the ideas were already finding a new voice and vessel.

Three years to the day after the trip to Nara that began this book, the Dalai Lama was back in Japan, walking through a park again in the brilliant autumn sunshine, one hand holding that of his old friend Desmond Tutu, the other linked to that of their fellow Nobel peace laureate Betty Williams, from Northern Ireland. They were striding through the November day along a broad avenue that leads to the peace memorial in Hiroshima, the sun glinting off the high-rises in the reborn city all around; they had spent the previous two days addressing a mostly young and international audience on what hopes for peace were still feasible in a city whose name had become a byword for destruction.

Japan is the strongest Buddhist nation in the world, the Dalai Lama often noted (upending the everyday assumptions of those of us who see only its modernist forms), and insofar as it felt an emptiness in its heart, it ought to bring its special skills and training to Latin America, Africa, other places where they could be of use. You make yourself feel better, richer, by giving what you have to others. Meanwhile, the rest of the world was flowing into Japan: one day before, I had followed him up through the sunlight to a steep hill in Hiroshima where a Tibetan lama had been teaching for twenty years, filling the bare serenity of a Japanese temple with vibrant Tibetan colors. The very next day, the Dalai Lama would go to the sacred island of Miyajima and offer teachings at a temple founded by the Japanese monk Kobo Daishi after he had brought something akin to Vajrayana mandalas and mudras and principles to Japan twelve hundred years before.

So much had happened in the years since I'd last seen the Dalai Lama in the mild sunshine of an autumn in Japan, I thought: a onetime party chief of Tibet, who had gained favor in Beijing by cracking down on the Tibetans in the late 1980s, had now become the paramount leader of all China. A high-speed train linking Beijing and Lhasa had been completed, ahead of schedule, ensuring that more than six thousand Han Chinese could now pour into the Tibetan capital every day, doubling its population again. War had broken out, once more, in Beirut, and the Dalai Lama had gone through severe challenges to his health that had brought all of Tibet up against the real truth of mortality. As for my own life, I was just back from a trip to Sri Lanka, where I'd seen Buddhist monks urging the hard-line government of the day toward war against the Hindu Tamil insurgents in the north; my own people, the Tamils, were busy picking off civilians, children, innocent sightseers, using even pregnant women to carry suicide bombs; and the great Buddhist temples were more full of soldiers than of monks.

And yet in other ways, much was as it had always been. The same attendant was tending to the Dalai Lama's robes, as he had been doing almost since they were both in the Potala Palace, fifty years before. The Dalai Lama's nephew was running his office in Dharamsala during his absence (and another nephew was organizing his Web site). When Hiroko and I went to his hotel room in Hiroshima—sunlight flooding through the windows, and a newspaper lying half-open on a long table—one of the first things he told us was that "doubt is very important. Without skeptical attitude ('skeptical' not in a negative sense) or doubt, there is no possibility to bring investigation. Without investigation, you cannot see the reality." He even cited some contradictions or exaggerated statements of the Buddha's to show that—because the Buddha adjusted his teaching according to his audience—even his words could be taken in the wrong way.

Yet in the long run, he stressed, as he had said to my father forty-six years before, a valid view would always triumph over a distorted one. And even out of chaos, he somehow seemed to conjure hope. The current war in Iraq, he said, was "the symptom of some great mistake, some negligence, in the past, even from as far back as the nineteenth century. Similarly, on the other side, if we start some effort with vision now, then some positive result may happen end of this century, beginning of next one." Some of our dreams, he told the audience in Hiroshima, "we may not achieve in our own lifetime. Maybe no sign of achievement even within this twenty-first century. But you must make effort."

When I followed him to Miyajima, the island not far from Hiroshima that is sometimes called the holiest place in Japan—two thousand deer grazing among its many temples, and a one-story orange shrine now in its seventh incarnation sitting on the water like a vision—I felt more than ever as if Tibet, or Dharamsala at least, had come to the country where I lived.

Day after day, great flocks of people climbed up the steep, narrow steps to Daisho-in, the temple in the hills that Kobo Daishi had set up, its gray roofs hovering above the turning maples like mist in the bright sunshine. As the Dalai Lama consecrated the new chapel, twelve of his monks from southern India sat next to the Japanese monks from the temple, red and yellow mingling with lustrous purple, one group of chants following another. When he began his two days of teachings—before days of empowerments and initiations—one young Taiwanese student from California offered a simultaneous translation to an excited group of pilgrims from Beijing, someone else delivered them in Korean to a small group on the other side of the golden Buddha, and a doctor of metaphysics from the Institute of Buddhist Dialectics in Dharamsala delivered the words in English (89 on the FM dial).

All the while he was speaking—the elegiac sunshine outside offering its own vision of mortality and radiance—the Dalai Lama looked as alert as ever. In the moments when he was waiting for his Japanese translator from Dharamsala to render his words into

Japanese, he looked around the individual faces seated before him, beaming, bursting into his spontaneous laughter, at one point motioning for his monks to make way and offer their seats to some Japanese monks, at another point asking an individual in the audience if he was sure he could follow without a translator. Sometimes he turned to a rinpoche in the front row to ask his scholarly advice; sometimes he turned to his hosts to ask them to make sure that those in the courtyard outside could hear and feel a part of things. Sitting only a few yards away from him, for day after day, I thought he seemed the very picture of vigorous attentiveness. When I went in to see him at the end of one day's teachings, though, I noticed that his eyes were red and smarting, visibly tearing from the effort of talking for five hours. The teachings were taking a real toll on him.

It seemed less and less relevant, at least in this context, to put boxes around any of what he was talking about, whether those boxes said "twenty-first century" or "radical" or even "Dalai Lama." If an aspirin works, you don't care where it comes from. If lightning sets off fires, you don't quibble about religions. If a "new reality" is around us—he had sounded that theme again in Hiroshima—then you look at it, as at the hand you've just been dealt. There was a candle in this temple, set up by the Japanese monk who had traveled to China to bring back a system very similar to the Tibetan (originally from India), that had been burning continuously, so it was said, for more than a thousand years.

I happened, as I began this book by saying, to travel down to see the Dalai Lama the very day after he had been awarded the Nobel Prize in 1989. He was attending a meeting with scientists south of Los Angeles at the time, and, after hearing news of the prize on the radio while drifting around Santa Barbara, I had decided to drive down to intrude on him with my congratulations and some questions for an interview. He was characteristically open when I arrived at the house where he was staying, welcoming me in as if this were just another day (as I suppose it was), leading me by the hand into a side room as if he had all the time in the world, and taking care to look around, it seemed reflexively, for a chair in which I would be comfortable, as if I were the one who was being feted. He asked me how he should use the money and looked at me piercingly, clearly waiting for an answer. He told me that sometimes he felt that he could never do enough, and that nothing he did could ever really affect things (a prescient and far-sighted concern, in some ways, as, after the excitement and sense of possibility the Nobel awakened had subsided, Tibet was only ten years closer to destruction). He told me that it was "up to us poor humans to make the effort," one step at a time, and again, as if invoking the final words of the Buddha, he spoke of "constant effort, tireless effort, pursuing clear goals with sincere effort."

Then, as we were walking out of the room, he went back and turned off the light. It's such a small thing, he said, it hardly makes a difference at all. And yet nothing is lost in the doing of it, and maybe a little good can come of it, if more and more people remember this small gesture in more and more rooms.

I drove back to Los Angeles and filed my article (for an editor who wasn't especially interested in the thoughts of a Tibetan monk and all but deleted it). I went back to my life, seeing the Dalai Lama next a few months later, when he came to Santa Barbara just after my house had burned down and I had lost everything I owned.

Six thousand days or so after that morning, when he came back to Japan, I thought about that simple gesture of turning off the light. Every one of those six thousand days, it seemed to me, I had

had some revelation, encountered some wisdom, scribbled down sentences I'd read or come up with myself about the meaning of the universe, the way to lead a better life, the essence of the soul, the unreality of the soul. I had had more lightning flashes and moments of illumination than I could count in the next six thousand years. And yet now, on this bright autumn morning, I could remember not a one of them, except the simple, practical task of turning off the light. Not enlightenment, not universal charity, not the Golden Rule or the wisdom of the ages: just something I could do several times a day.

I went home after hearing the Dalai Lama on the sunlit island, and then went out for a walk. I closed the door behind me and was about to turn the key in the lock when I remembered the long-ago day. I opened the door again, and turned off the light.

Nothing is secure but life, transition, the energizing spirit . . .
No truth so sublime but it may be trivial tomorrow in the light
of new thoughts.

—RALPH WALDO EMERSON

READING

The starting point of any book, at least for me, is an exhaustive reading of as many of the other books in the field as possible, to see what has been done already and what does not need to be done again. In the case of the Fourteenth Dalai Lama, this is a task as formidable as it is rewarding, and very quickly even a newcomer realizes that the basic biographical details of the Dalai Lama's life have been covered wonderfully, in films and biographies and autobiographies, and nothing more needs to be said. As for the intricacies of his practice and his philosophy, the steady stream of books coming out under the Dalai Lama's own name—of lectures, of interviews, of official teachings, and even just of aphorisms—share a complexity and sophistication that few of the rest of us could hope to reproduce. On Tibet and Buddhism as a whole, the library is enormous, and many of its items are quite exceptional, the kind of works that can change your life and make you see everything anew.

I sometimes feel, in fact, that the very high air, intensity, and power of Tibet have a transformative effect on many of those who visit it even on the page (or in the mind). I have tried in this book to be a general reader speaking to other general readers, and bringing little more than the curiosity and interest of a journalist who has never practiced Buddhism and knows little about it but is intrigued to see how it might expand the thinking of anyone, Buddhist and non-Buddhist alike. For those who wish to turn to books of real authority and wisdom on the subject, though, I would like to salute, and to direct readers toward, some of the works that have most deeply instructed me and brightened my life.

In relation to the life and lives of the Fourteenth Dalai Lama, the place to start is surely his second autobiography, *Freedom in Exile,* a vivid and characteristic blend of human reminiscence and sharp-eyed philosophy and politics, and *In Exile from the Land of Snows* by John Avedon, which, after twenty-five years, remains unsurpassed in its account of both Tibetan culture and its recent history. At a time when not many people had even heard of the Fourteenth Dalai Lama or were concerned about Tibet, Avedon gave himself so fully to these worlds that he discovered more, perhaps, than anyone had a chance to do thereafter.

Martin Scorsese's film *Kundun* offers a mesmerizing evocation of the Dalai Lama's years in Tibet (closely monitored by the man himself) and a searching view of how to hold to something worthwhile in the middle of the world's challenges and confusions. Other warm and humane perspectives are offered by the Dalai Lama's mother, Diki Tsering, in her book *Dalai Lama, My Son;* by his eldest brother, Thubten Jigme Norbu, in the book he cowrote with Heinrich Harrer, *Tibet Is My Country;* and by his younger sister, Jetsun Pema, in *Tibet: My Story.* The Dalai Lama's first autobiography, written in 1962, *My Land and My People,* offers an invaluable look at how he thought and saw his life soon after he came into exile, and Michael Goodman's *The Last Dalai Lama,* though less reliable in terms of details and nuances than much that has come out since, remains a vibrant and thoughtful account that feels right in both tone and proportions.

For a fine and sympathetic description of the whole of the Dalai Lama's family and the continuing and spirited debates between its members, Mary Craig's *Kundun* is hard to beat.

When I am trying to get a general, nontechnical feel for what the Dalai Lama is striving to share with the wider world, the first books of his I turn to are *Ethics for the New Millennium* and *The Universe in a Single Atom,* which, respectively, show clearly and fully the moral vision he is trying to take around the world and the scientific explorations that most excite him. He devoted a great deal of time and attention to both works, and it seems safe to assume that both offer a highly accurate record of what he really wishes to communicate. An early collection of his, *Kindness, Clarity, and Insight,* compiled after his first travels to the United States, remains invaluable, and among the many remarkable books that have arisen out of particular teachings, the ones I have heard those close to the Dalai Lama most recommend include *The Four Noble Truths* (a general introduction to Buddhism), *The Good Heart* (in which the Dalai Lama addresses Christians on the Gospels), and *Destructive Emotions* (recording a seminal Mind and Life Institute meeting in which scientists and philosophers came together to see what reflexes and impulses tear us apart).

Other books that have helped me understand both Tibetan Buddhism and the Fourteenth Dalai Lama's particular vision of transformation include Robert Thurman's characteristically inspiring *Infinite Life* and Matthieu Ricard's *Happiness,* a clear and serene handbook to thinking differently about your life and embarking on the business of transformation, which offers some of the spaciousness of its author's retreat in the Himalayas. Howard C. Cutler's *The Art of Happiness* is rightly renowned for giving the Dalai Lama a chance to address specific case studies brought to him by a Western psychiatrist, and Victor Chan's *The Wisdom of Forgiveness* gives us an intimate and completely convincing view of the man by whom so much of the world is fascinated.

As a glimpse into the Dalai Lama's day-to-day life—and, more mysteriously, into the person who moves through it—Manuel Bauer's book of documentary photographs, *A Journey for Peace,* is impossible to better.

The history of Tibet is a field that has drawn more and more arresting minds to it in recent years, to supplement some of the formative early work of scholars such as Giuseppe Tucci, Hugh Richardson, and David Snellgrove. Tsering Shakya's *The Dragon in the Land of Snows* is an extremely solid and balanced account of Tibet's history since 1947; Melvyn C. Goldstein's *The Snow Lion and the Dragon* is both unsentimental and rigorous; Donald S. Lopez Jr.'s *Prisoners of Shangri-La* is a questioning look at the myths that surround Tibet, by a scholar who has long shown himself to be deeply sympathetic to Tibetans.

Some of the classic old books to read on Tibet before the Chinese occupation are Sir Charles Bell's work on the Thirteenth Dalai Lama and his country; Peter Hopkirk's entertaining popular history of early Tibetan exploration, *Trespassers on the Roof of the World;* Alexandra David-Neel's richly colored accounts of her trips; and, of course, Heinrich Harrer's immortal *Seven Years in Tibet.* Scott Berry's *A Stranger in Tibet,* on the eccentric Zen monk Ekai Kawaguchi and his early ramblings around the country, has long been a personal favorite of mine, and in the early years of this century two excellent books have helped us to see and feel what Tibet is really like under Chinese rule: Patrick French's agonized but deeply scrupulous *Tibet, Tibet* and Robert Barnett's careful and fair-minded *Lhasa: Streets with Memories.* I have enjoyed, too, reading about modern Tibet as it strikes such contemporary Chinese visitors as Ma Jian, in *Red Dust,* and Xinran Xue, in *Sky Burial* (as well as such early visitors as F. Spencer Chapman, Peter Fleming, and Lowell Thomas Jr.).

Isabel Hilton's *The Search for the Panchen Lama* remains the definitive work on the sudden death of the Tenth Panchen Lama and the tangled search for his successor, and Mick Brown's *Dance of 17 Lives* provides a vivid and engaging look at the Karmapa legacy and its present complications. Thomas Laird's 2006 book, *A Story of Tibet,* in which the author gets the Dalai Lama to travel through the whole of Tibetan history from his perspective, already seems to me one of the essential and irreplaceable books in the field, and allows one to hear and feel the Dalai Lama's particular voice with unique immediacy.

For an understanding of Tibetan Buddhism, I am grateful to many books, perhaps the most detailed and scholarly of which is Thupten Jinpa Langri's *Self, Reality and Reason in Tibetan Philosophy.* Karen Armstrong's *Buddha* is a no-nonsense small biography of Gautama himself, as seen by a onetime nun and scholar of many religions, while Pankaj Mishra's *An End to Suffering* is a more probing and wandering look at his life and influence today by a thoughtful traveler. Huston Smith's work on Buddhism is as lucid and inspired as his work on every other major religious tradition.

Some of the most spirited works I've read on Buddhism in the West include *The Buddha from Brooklyn,* by Martha Sherrill, *Dragon Thunder,* by Diana J. Mukpo with Carolyn Rose Gimian, *Shoes Outside the Door,* by Michael Downing, and *Crooked Cucumber,* by David Chadwick. Rick Fields told the story of Buddhism coming to the West superbly in *How the Swans Came to the Lake,* Jeffery Paine retold it entertainingly in *Re-enchantment,* and the works of Stephen Batchelor, Steve Hagen, Mark Epstein, and many others have brought complicated practices and ideas wonderfully into my reach.

Two of the most stirring and radiant works on the Buddhist path I have ever read—and reread and reread, at least five times each over the last twenty years—are Peter Matthiessen's *The Snow Leopard,* about his discovery of Buddhism and reality in the high Himalayas, and Andrew Harvey's *A Journey in Ladakh,* about his encounter with Tibetan Buddhism and some charismatic souls in northern India.

It should be obvious from the pages that precede this that one of the main things I have attempted in this book is to bring the Dalai Lama out of Tibet and Buddhism and into the larger community of ideas and thinkers, to show how much and how often his interests chime with those of other traditions and explorers. I have tried, for that reason, to include quite a bit of the warm and inimitable voice of Desmond Tutu in this book, as well as the ideas of the Fourteenth Dalai Lama's good friend and colleague Václav Havel; I also wanted to see how the Dalai Lama's words and ideas could be explained and reflected back to us in different forms by the Thirteenth Dalai Lama, by the Dalai Lama's younger brother, Ngari Rinpoche, and by the Buddha himself.

Over the years I was pursuing all these themes, I constantly read and returned to such writers as Graham Greene, Ralph Waldo Emerson, Henry David Thoreau, Thomas Merton, Leonard Cohen, Aldous Huxley, Emily Dickinson, William James, Stephen Mitchell, Somerset Maugham, Robert Stone, Annie Dillard, Etty Hillesum, and many others to try to give a larger framework for the essential—and highly universal—ideas being advanced by the Dalai Lama; and in 2005–06 I flew all over the world, while following the Dalai Lama, to see U2 give concerts in New Jersey, Copenhagen, Los Angeles, and Tokyo. In his constant work and interviews, Bono, U2's lead singer, has seemed to be laboring sincerely and tirelessly on behalf of many of the same principles that the Dalai Lama elucidates so richly, especially a sense of global community, of social justice, and of responsibility toward the poor everywhere, lit up by an infectious and alert challenging of his own assumptions (and his tendencies toward self-righteousness). Listening to the soaring anthems of U2—and seeing how thoughtfully the group advances the evergreen problems of living a life of conscience and spirit in the world—lifted my heart, sent me spinning across the room, and helped me clarify my ideas about a man who stands, I think, in a network of others, from Gandhi and King to unknown inspirations in the future, for possibilities that lie outside Tibet, beyond Buddhism, and further than the purview of any single life.

IN GRATITUDE

It must be evident that my first debt of thanks in writing a book like this belongs with His Holiness the Fourteenth Dalai Lama, who not only gave me much of his precious time over many years, allowed me to travel with him, even said (characteristically) that "it would be a privilege to help with any information," but who also—more importantly, and typically again—always gave me the sense that he didn't want a flattering or needlessly sympathetic account of him and his life (even though he did cherish precision, fairness, and a sense of responsibility). It's rare to meet someone, especially someone in so delicate a political position and so much in the public eye, who so clearly likes to be challenged, questioned, even proven wrong. And it's still rarer—and maybe this is part of the reason I wrote this book—to meet someone who holds to such high standards of rigor and analytical clarity and scientific impartiality, while also remaining such a warm and vibrant model of humanity and kindness.

In the same light and spirit, I am deeply grateful to the members of the Dalai Lama's family who gave me their time—and always their hospitality—such as his younger sister, Jetsun Pema, and many in the family circle. It will be evident to any reader of this book how much I owe his younger brother, Tendzin Choegyal—alias Ngari Rinpoche—who was always ready to answer any question, to invite me to his terrace for long talks, to tease me about my hair (or lack of it), everywhere from California to India, for several decades. Mr. Choegyal was always hardest on me (true to his brother's teaching) when he thought I was giving institutional Tibet—or himself—too easy a time and not being strict enough in my challenges of them.

It has been a huge delight and privilege, for more than a quarter of a century now, to work with those in the Dalai Lama's private office, who themselves have taught me so much about patience, kindness, and consideration, starting with the irreplaceable Tenzin Geyche Tethong. There are few jobs I can think of more difficult than trying to allocate the time of one of the most sought-after people on the planet and, more than that, working with someone who always speaks for the highest standards of openness and candor. Tenzin Geyche-la has somehow done all this, on many continents, for more than forty years, and in the process become something of a miraculous presence in my life; whatever was happening, and whatever request I threw at him, there was his steady, kind, and imperturbable voice at the other end, trying to see what he could do to make everyone happy. Anyone who has watched the Fourteenth Dalai Lama working with his longtime secretary and translator has seen what often feels like two expert musicians in perfect sync, each reading the other's cues or taking over an original melody from the other, and both knowing the other so well they seem to read each other's mind. Those of us who talk to the Dalai Lama often feel we learn something about wisdom and clarity from the people at his side.

In this context, I have been thrilled, over the past decade or so, to get to know and work with Tenzin Taklha, as elegant and sweet a presence as I have met on my travels, and someone who manages, as private secretary, somehow to be both a consummate professional and an always human, smiling face and protector; and in recent years Chhime Choekyapa has become a perfect colleague, brisk, friendly, and always ready to cut through red tape to get to the essential. Thubten Samphel, in the Department of Information and International Relations, has been a kind and loyal friend for years, tirelessly answering my every question with great efficiency and accuracy, and many others in the Tibetan world, from the Office of Tibet in New York to the entire staff of Tibet House in Tokyo, have touched me deeply by constantly asking how they could help, what I might need, what solutions they could come up with. Tempa Tsering, Geshe Thupten Jinpa Langri, Geshe Lhakdor, Geshe Dorji Damdul, Kusho Paljor-la, and too many others to name have helped round out both my understanding of Tibet and a sense of warm community, for me and many others.

One of my very first Tibetan friends and contacts, whose company I still treasure, was Tenzin N. Tethong, then the representative of the Dalai Lama in New York and later head of the government in exile's Cabinet. The current prime minister, Professor Samdhong Rinpoche, was also kind enough to talk to me during a busy time in his schedule.

Beyond all the official contacts, the entire family of Tibet in exile has taken me in, as it has thousands of others, teaching us in a living way what the Dalai Lama means in speaking of the globe as a large "human family." Rinchen Khando Choegyal and her family, Kelsang Chukie Tethong, Tsering Drolkar Taklha, Maria Rinchen and so many others have somehow made us feel that it is their joy to look after us, and asked for nothing in return.

In Dharamsala, the extraordinary staff of Chonor House, beginning with its manager, Dechen Maja, and its longtime receptionist (now our good friend) Dawa Dolma, have made Hiroko and me want to spend all our springs there, for months at a time, imagining ourselves in old Tibet; and down the road, Ashwini Bhatia and Angus and Zos and their staff (especially Lobsang) have transformed our lives, thanks to the Moonpeak Café. Lhasang Tsering, with his wonderful Bookworm shop, was always extraordinarily generous and forthright in sharing with me—and all foreigners—his powerful and eloquent opposition to his government's positions, and Lung Ta restaurant became another home away from home. Jagmohan Gupta, at Ways and Means Tours, always found a way to get us to Dharamsala (as did the great and legendary office manager of *Time*'s New Delhi bureau, Deepak Puri, who seems to hold up much of the Time-Life empire and, I sometimes suspect, most of India single-handedly); and such new friends around the Norbulingka Institute as Dolmakyap Zorgey, Kim Yeshi, Jeremy and Pippa Russell, and Thubten Tsewang have always opened their elegant doors to us. The calm and unshakable miracle workers who run the Awasthi Cyber-Café, the staffs at Pema Thang Guest-House, Kashmir Cottage, the Namgyal Café, Khana Nirvana restaurant, the Current Event, and Ashoka restaurant, as well as many other favorite haunts, surely know how much they are loved and appreciated around the world.

One of the magical things about being around the Dalai Lama and the Tibetans is that they have become a focal point and a meeting point for some of the most interesting souls I have met, and a great global community has begun to form around those interested in their ideas, which has made many of us feel at home everywhere. I consider myself lucky to have met so many talented, committed, and selfless individuals through my contact with Tibet. Some of them—Robert Thurman, Richard Gere, Martin Scorsese, Melissa Mathison, Matthieu Ricard—have become quite well known; many others are less cele-brated but no less inspiring. Every day, it seems, my in-box is filled with greetings and news from people I've met through Tibet, whether their names are Darlene Markovich or Sole da Silva or Yusuke Memoto or Vivian Kurz. I consider myself lucky to have got to spend time in Dharamsala with Brigitte Lacombe and her inimitable assistant Gus-tav Bruns, with Martine Franck and Steve Lehman and ageless Rosette Jein from Paris; and in the larger circle of those who work with the Dalai Lama, it has been great fun to get to know the superbly gifted and engaging Manuel Bauer and such good-natured and companion-able colleagues as Howard Cutler, Victor Chan, and Rajiv Mehrotra.

I owe heartfelt thanks to Justin Williams, met by chance in a Dharamsala restaurant one day, for teaching me, with great gentleness and unpretentiousness, what the meditative tradition in Tibetan Bud-dhism is all about, and to Huston Smith, for sharing with me his experiences of talking to the Dalai Lama over a period of forty years. In my own hometown, I had the good fortune to meet José Cabezon, holder of the Fourteenth Dalai Lama chair in Tibetan Studies at the University of California, Santa Barbara; José was strikingly generous in offering the fruits of his scholarship and his experience to a stranger. Keido Fukushima-roshi, in Kyoto, has offered me a cherished glimpse into the Zen tradition (as well as a lifelong partner). And Leonard Cohen, over many years, has given me a radiantly calm, eloquent, and gracious vision of what Buddhist discipline, humility, and attention are all about (in life and on the page).

Away from the Buddhist orbit, Annie Dillard and Bob Richardson spurred me on to become a bit more practical in supporting myself, and Caryl Phillips, Meredith Monk, and my incomparable editor at the *New York Review of Books,* Bob Silvers, supported me in this effort. In bringing this book into print, I owe, as ever, huge thanks to my agent, Lynn Nesbit, and my longtime friends and sponsors at the Knopf Group, Sonny Mehta, Dan Frank, Marty Asher, and Robin Desser.

Dan Frank, in fact, pushed me and pushed me toward more rigor and sharpness, with the attention and challenging kindness one can expect only from the most understanding of friends, and Fran Bigman made every step of the process painless and fun. In the production of the book I was buoyed and inspired, as many times before, by the incomparable book designer Abby Weintraub, whose art has now graced four of my covers, and by my engaging and inimitable photographer of choice, Derek Shapton in Toronto. And Pam Henstell in L.A., Cullen Stanley in New York and Sheila Kay in Toronto have worked ceaselessly for years to spread my words about.

Stephen Mitchell, astonishingly, offered to read the whole manuscript although we had met only twice (again, I got a humbled sense of what Buddhist training and meditation are in the service of), and two days after I sent it to him offered me a beautifully informed and precise list of places where I'd misinterpreted the tradition. In Kyoto, my old, great friend Michael Hofmann, who first opened the door to Buddhism for me when we met in 1987, brought to both me and my writing great kindness, clarity, and insight, always trying to keep me honest and reminding me of how much I didn't know.

It was my late father, as described in these pages, who handed down to me his acquaintance with the Fourteenth Dalai Lama and, in fact, brought Tibetan monks and symbols into our living room when I was a very small boy; as the years have passed, I have come to see that this was one of his most precious bequests. My mother, to my delight and gratitude, shares her graces and gifts with me daily. In California, my friends at the New Camaldoli Benedictine hermitage have been teaching me for seventeen years why monks do what they do, and what the fruits of their stillness, devotion, and compassion really mean; and in Japan the indomitable and cheerful members of the Shikanodai Ping-Pong Club have offered something of the same in a less formal context.

When I began writing on Tibet, half a lifetime ago, it was very much a solo endeavor; I can still remember explaining a bit about the country and its traditions to my sweet and shining companion, Hiroko Takeuchi, when we met in 1987. Since then, Hiroko has taken Tibet to her great heart, become the uncrowned princess of her second home, Dharamsala, and has tried hard to implement what she has learned from the Tibetans, often breaking the ice in conversations with the Dalai Lama while I was dancing over the surface. When he heard I was working on this book, the Dalai Lama told her to "check on him and make sure he's not going wrong," a useful reminder to us both about how universal responsibility begins at home.

Finally, as one living in a small apartment in suburban Japan, I am always much influenced and colored by such works as visit me from afar. In this case, I feel a great debt to some of the material that really moved me and gave me food for thought while I was working on this book: Julie Taymor's film *Titus*, Isabel Coixet's *My Life Without Me*, the writings of Philip Roth, Tracy Kidder's *Mountains Beyond Mountains*, the art of Bill Viola, and, as mentioned, the rigorous and self-mocking global optimism of U2, whose work for liberation and conscience soaringly chimes with much that this book is about. Insofar as this work, like all my books, is about how to find clarity and peace—a larger meaning—in the midst of our accelerating, jam-packed, exhilarating new global order, U2 clearly offer an example of how to laugh at one's own claims to goodness while still working overtime to do some good for others. I appreciate the attempt of such individuals to take on the world, with open eyes and ferocious determination, without ever giving up on a devotion to what is not so often visible in the world.